Rekindling Embers of the Soul

An Examination of Spirituality Issues Relating to Teacher Education

A Volume in Chinese American Educational Research
and Development Association Book Series

Series Editor

Guofang Wan
Loyola University Chicago

Chinese American Educational Research and Development Association Book Series

Guofang Wan, Series Editor

*Rekindling Embers of the Soul:
An Examination of Spirituality Issues Relating to Teacher Education* (2024)
edited by Miranda Lin and Thomas Lucey

Critical Issues in Early Childhood Teacher Education (2020)
edited by Miranda Lin and Ithel Jones

*Critical Issues in Early Childhood Teacher Education:
Volume 2—International Perspectives* (2020)
edited by Ithel Jones and Miranda Lin

Gifted Education in Asia: Problems and Prospects (2015)
edited by David Yun Dai and Ching Chih Kuo

*Advancing Methodologies to Support Both
Summative and Formative Assessments* (2014)
edited by Ying Cheng and Hua-Hua Chang

Teaching and Learning Chinese: Issues and Perspectives (2010)
edited by Jianguo Chen, Chuang Wang, and Jinfa Cai

*Model Minority Myth Revisited: An Interdisciplinary Approach to Demystifying
Asian American Educational Experiences* (2008)
edited by Guofang Li and Lihshing Wang

Rekindling Embers of the Soul

An Examination of Spirituality Issues Relating to Teacher Education

Editors

Miranda Lin and Thomas Lucey
Illinois State University

INFORMATION AGE PUBLISHING, INC.
Charlotte, NC • www.infoagepub.com

Library of Congress Cataloging-in-Publication Data

CIP record for this book is available from the Library of Congress
http://www.loc.gov

ISBNs: 979-8-88730-378-9 (Paperback)

979-8-88730-379-6 (Hardcover)

979-8-88730-380-2 (ebook)

Copyright © 2024 Information Age Publishing Inc.

All rights reserved. No part of this publication may be reproduced, stored in a retrieval system, or transmitted, in any form or by any means, electronic, mechanical, photocopying, microfilming, recording or otherwise, without written permission from the publisher.

Printed in the United States of America

CONTENTS

Preface
    Cheryl Torrez .... *vii*

Acknowledgments .... *ix*

Introduction
    Miranda Lin and Thomas Lucey .... *xi*

PART I

1. Compassion and Transformational Pedagogy: A Reflexive Approach
   Eilidh Lamb 3

2. The Many Ways to Talk About Spirit and Spirituality in Teacher Education: The Decolonizing Potential of Dialogues About Spirit
   Shannon Leddy 29

3. The Electricity of the Religious Education Classroom: Lessons From Buber and Levinas
   Mary Shanahan 43

4. The Woke Spirit: Teaching John Coltrane to Examine What Lives Inside
   Susan Browne and Yvette Onofre 63

PART II

5. Enabling Those Becoming Teachers of Young Children to Nurture Spiritual Growth: Challenges, Dilemmas, and Opportunities
   Tony Eaude 89

6. "Who Am I Now?": Spirituality in a Faith-Based Teacher Education Program in Canada
   Allyson Jule, Carolyn Kristjansson, Yu-Ling Lee, and Kevin Mirchandani 107

7. Connecting the Heart and Soul of Teaching Through Service-Learning
   Vickie E. Lake, Ithel Jones, Christian Winterbottom, and Miranda Lin 127

8. Havens for Acceptance, Faith, and Affirmation: The Spiritual Dimension of Reflection in Teaching for Democracy
   Rob Martinelle 143

9. Spiritual Expression in Historical Narration: Implications for History Teacher Education
   Travis L. Seay 169

10. Spiritual Underpinnings of a Teacher Education Program
    Ann Mary Roberts and Thomas Lucey 199

About the Authors 219

PREFACE

Rekindling Embers of the Soul: An Examination of Spirituality Issues Relating to Teacher Education is deeply rooted in the belief that preparing and supporting K–12 classroom-based educators and students is a spiritual and human endeavor that surpasses the external life—imposed criteria, standards, and licensure requirements. It is, as Parker Palmer has taught us, for those who have chosen the field of education for reasons of the heart and seek to strengthen one's inner life.

For all of us engaged in teacher education, balancing the institutional demands with the whole being of teacher candidates and K–12 teacher educators is often challenging, and at times, one of our persistent dilemmas. The constant swirl of deprofessionalizing and dehumanizing the professional educator, the field of education, and the lives of students may, at times, easily sweep us away from the true purposes of education and of preparing outstanding educators. This book sheds lights on a variety of ways in which spirituality abounds within teacher education. Readers will be challenged to rethink and reexamine their positionality, practices, and the purposes of teacher education—this is a great thing!! As Lin and Lucey write in their introduction, "the essentialness of this alternative lens to teacher education relates to the integrity of the profession's identity." This book is for those who seek to continue in the work of real teaching and learning with meaning, passion, and persistence.

Schooling reflects society, and teacher educators alone cannot fix the turbulent inequalities and injustices that face education. Many of us, for years, have drawn upon the seminal works of Parker Palmer, Nel Noddings, Marilyn Cochran-Smith, John Dewey, and numerous others to anchor our souls and to provide a framing of the inner life for teacher candidates

---

Rekindling Embers of the Soul:
An Examination of Spirituality Issues Relating to Teacher Education, pp. vii–viii
Copyright © 2024 by Information Age Publishing
www.infoagepub.com
All rights of reproduction in any form reserved.

and professional K–12 educators. The examination of spiritual issues in teacher education goes beyond the cursory consideration of spirituality as a personal issue and draws upon the notion of spirituality as a yearning to connect to something larger than oneself. Readers of this book will find themselves renewed with a reinvigorated pedagogy of the soul (Palmer, 2003) and ways in which to continue to connect the heart and soul through teaching and mastering the inner life (Palmer, 2003).

Cheryl A. Torrez
The University of New Mexico

REFERENCE

Palmer, P. J. (2003). Teaching with the heart and soul: Reflections on spirituality in teacher education. *Journal of Teacher Education*, *54*(5), 376–385.

ACKNOWLEDGMENTS

I am grateful to work with many teacher educators who enlightened us through their wisdom, practice, and research about the essence of human connections with one another and the universe over the past 15 months. Their contribution to truth-seeking/inquiry is often underrated and unrecognized. I would like to take this opportunity to thank the authors who demonstrate tremendous compassion and love for what they believe. This book's accounts surely spark further dialogues about the purpose of education and what teacher preparation entails. I hope you will find the richness of the discourses contributes to your inquiry into human existence and the science of spiritual knowledge. Last but not least, I want to dedicate this volume to my spiritual master, who opened my eyes with the torch of knowledge as I was born in the darkness. I offer my respectful obeisances'

Miranda

It is very difficult to articulate the full extent of my appreciation for the efforts of scholars who have persevered in studying spirituality and its relationship to education and teacher education. Especially in a climate of science and materiality, research of the invisible often represents a pursuit of faith—its truth to be realized when our applications of science fail. I appreciate the efforts of all those who contributed manuscripts for consideration towards this volume. Even those not selected inform the story of this work, just as the evaluation process informed the directions of these manuscripts. Finally, I appreciate the environments of compassion gifted to me by the faith communities that have nurtured me during my journey. They are primary sources of evidence for the endurance of grace, peace, and hope.

Tom

Rekindling Embers of the Soul:
An Examination of Spirituality Issues Relating to Teacher Education, pp. ix–ix
Copyright © 2024 by Information Age Publishing
www.infoagepub.com
All rights of reproduction in any form reserved.

INTRODUCTION

Miranda Lin and Thomas Lucey

Teacher education represents a profession of standards. A 21st century setting rooted in scientific knowledge governed by corporate leadership determines the parameters that shape teachers for classrooms. As determined by CAEP, these standards call within five areas ranging from the effects of the program to clinical partnerships and practice. This sense of boundaries or standards represents a system of contrived measurement constructed to serve the needs of those creating the standards (e.g., Piccanio & Spring, 2013; Van Hover et al., 2010). This environment exudes a climate of "positive" emotions that rewards those accomplishments based on the needs of those who create the standards. Success carries a material definition, quantified, and measured. This measured sense of success carries an inherent element of bias as measurement represents a sense of valuing based on the ideals of those creating the measure. Measuring possession and application of knowledge depends on those principles considered to be valuable to those shaping the standards.

Spirituality represents a field largely neglected or hidden in teacher education. Kurtz and Ketchum (1992) describe spirituality as being a condition that "has nothing to do with boundaries" (p. 24). From a human perspective, one may view spirituality as the external world through an alternative lens from the material (Taylor, 1993). The essentialness of this alternative lens to teacher education relates to the integrity of the profession's identity. Realizing, acknowledging, and affirming the spiritual element of teacher education provides a sense of wholeness for its participants that is independent of the standards imposed on their daily practices. Spirituality

---

Rekindling Embers of the Soul:
An Examination of Spirituality Issues Relating to Teacher Education, pp. xi–xiv
Copyright © 2024 by Information Age Publishing
www.infoagepub.com
All rights of reproduction in any form reserved.

may be complex to define because there is a lack of consensus in defining spirituality. Based on Fuertes and Dugan's (2021) findings, spirituality is a fluid concept to articulate. However, they encourage higher education to create spaces for students to express their conceptions of spirituality. This stance aligns with Trianna et al.'s (2020) suggestion that spirituality aids the development of the whole student and impacts student learning while shaping learners' perspectives and academic pursuits.

However, there are challenges that higher education face. For example, how can institutes integrate spirituality into the curriculum? As Chickering (2006) suggests, the core of human experiences might be the answer. When students have the opportunity to interact with each other, are involved in service, engage in conversations, and explore who they are, these everyday interactions with the people and the world around them help them understand better who they are. In other words, when students can immerse themselves in the community locally or globally, they get to reflect on the issues facing the community and the cultures that impact all aspects of everyday life. In turn, they learn to put meaning back to their experiences and make sense of their existence. Individually or jointly, college students create or cocreate the meaning of their growth, development, and inquiry into spirituality.

Our use of the word "rekindling" in the title of this book should not be viewed flippantly. The standards-ladened environment of teacher education represents a setting of darkness governed by the self-interests of an elite minority. The chapters in this book contain works that illuminate alternative ways of viewing teacher education from this environment of measure, specifically from the holistic view and ways of dealing with teacher candidates. We perceive spirituality as ingrained rather than a separate part of teacher candidates' identities. That is, one's behavior cannot be separated from his/her/their identity. Spiritual formation, therefore, is a needed conversation in teacher education as teachers' beliefs influence their classroom practice. Teacher education programs are responsible for encouraging and supporting teacher candidates by examining their identities and spiritual inquiry. The chapters in this book share many paths that enrich this conversation. There is no cookie-cutter approach to support spiritual formation in teacher education. Even though there are many paths, the ultimate goal is to have teacher candidates understand their true identity and relationship to the universe and each living being. Still, as revealed, some qualities such as compassion, kindness, and care are the common threads in all chapters. Every chapter deciphers a path that may be suitable in its specific sociocultural context. We encourage readers to be mindful of the context when trying to implement a similar program.

We organize this work into two sections, sequencing the chapters in a manner that both introduces the spiritual challenge faced by educational institutions and concludes with suggestions and a vision for hope. The first section contains four chapters that speak to conceptualizations of spirituality and its relationships to the classroom. It opens with the work of Eilidh Lamb, who presents the results of a study that relates spirituality to the conditions of professional work settings. Lamb illustrates that the fourth space created for inquiry is rooted in the values of relational exploration and connectedness with oneself and others and can be a powerful tool to help connect the researcher and participants. This research shed light on how higher education can facilitate various forms of education and learning opportunities for more significant reasons.

The first section also includes contributions that address spiritual understandings from non-Western perspectives, interpretations of philosophical moorings, and spirituality in children's literature. First, Shannon Leddy's work reminds us of the purpose of education and how the curriculum could be more inclusive, notably how to include indigenous ways of thinking and living in the curriculum and how to do it with respect, relevance, reciprocity, and responsibility. Next, drawing upon the accounts of spiritual development provided by Buber and Levinas, Mary Shannahan argues how religious education offers a space where teachers and students can develop their ethical and spiritual potential. Furthermore, Susan Browne and her collaborator elaborate on how they use children's literature to help teacher candidates examine themselves and their relationship with their students. In turn, teacher candidates can be ignited by spiritual inquiry that can extend into systematically thinking about the holistic nature of work with students and their communities.

The second section features six works that concern spirituality matters related to teacher education. It begins with Tony Eaude's research that concerns the empowerment of teachers in teaching children about spirituality. Eaude posits that young children's spiritual growth is essential to how their identities are shaped based on exploring existential questions related to identity. Hence, teacher education educators can model how to support learners' spiritual quests and identities. This was followed by work by Allyson Jule and colleagues concerning preservice teachers' views of spirituality. Given their assessment of its impact on identity formation, Jule and her colleagues firmly believe spirituality is integral to the activity of preparing teachers, engaging instruction, and developing programs in teacher education. Research by Vickie Lake and collaborators concerning spirituality and service learning ensues. They call for teacher education to focus on the heart and soul of teaching. They argue that service-learning provides a pathway for teacher candidates to think critically, develop moral reasoning skills and a sense of community and deeper meaning of purpose, and understand spiritual or religious identity.

Lake and colleagues' chapter is followed by a couple of contributions concerning social studies connections. Rob Martinelle offers a work that discusses spirituality and democracy, while Travis Seay considers spiritual narration. Martinelle's study offers teacher educators at the pre-and in-service conceptual and practical guidance for encouraging reflection in ways that honor the spiritual dimensions of their work. Meanwhile, Seay suggests teacher educators must recognize and problematize common moral imperatives that frame historical narration to help teacher candidates develop a holistic and authentic view of themselves/histories. Finally, this section concludes with Ann Roberts and Thomas Lucey's work that provides an alternative manner of spirituality, rooted in human psychology.

We believe this volume provides a collection of writings that offer a multidimensional enrichment to conversations about spirituality and teacher education. Also, it serves as a reminder for all of us who nurture and educate future teachers whose impact on the human race and humanity can be profoundly simple, humane, yet sophisticated. To conclude, we invite teacher education programs across the globe to consider whatever small or big step to be a daily practice and as a dance. So let's let the dance begin.

REFERENCES

Chickering, A. (2006). Every student can learn-if... *About Campus, 11*(2), 9–15. https://doi.org/10.1002/abc.161

Kurtz, E., & Ketcham, K. (1992). *The spirituality of imperfection*. Bantam Books

Fuertes, A., & Dugan, K. (2021). Spirituality through the lens of students in higher education. *Religions, 12*, 924. https://doi.org/10.3390/rel12110924

Piccanio, A. G., & Spring, J. (2013). *The great American education-industrial complex ideology, technology, and profit*. Routledge

Taylor, B. B. (1993). *The preaching life*. Cowley Publications.

Triana, C., Gloria, A., & Castellanos, J. (2020). Cultivating success for Latinx undergraduates: Integrating cultural spirituality within higher education. *About Campus: Enriching the Student Learning Experience, 24*(6), 4–9. https://doi.org/10.1177/1086482219896793

Van Hover, S. Hicks, D., Stoddard, J., & Lisanti, M. (2010). From a roar to a murmur: Virginia's history & social science standards, 1995–2009. *Theory and Research in Social Education, 38*(1), 80–113.

PART I

CHAPTER 1

COMPASSION AND TRANSFORMATIONAL PEDAGOGY

A Reflexive Approach

Eilidh Lamb
The University of Glasgow

ABSTRACT

This chapter aims to learn from and inquire into methods of positive wellbeing with a specific contemplation on the experiential underpinnings of spirituality in connection with the self. This chapter discusses the pertinence of caring for oneself despite established institutional demands and societal pressure in our ever-changing world.

This chapter concerns a theoretical and empirical inquiry into modes of educational practice, which might be defined in terms of their use of compassion to transform the self and others. The research question which guides the work throughout this chapter is: *can self-care or spirituality be a contagion for social change?*

The study here is concerned with nonformal educators in Scotland and their experiences of engaging in forms of self-care. In addition, practitioners who participated in this study are involved in the work of community development, youth work, social justice, and recovery from addictions with a specific lens on the Scottish context.

Keywords: Compassion, self-care, self-compassion, transformational learning, reflective practice, spirituality

INTRODUCTION

With compassion, one needs to be engaged, involved...

Dalai Lama (1992)

This chapter focuses on various disciplines, including theology, philosophy, critical theory, and pedagogy. This study recognized that these works were largely theoretical. There was an absence of educational "practitioners" voices to prompt a critical and dialogical conversation between different schools of scholarly literature. These subjects have been considered related to pedagogy, the self, experiential learning processes, and *whether self-care and spirituality can be a contagion for social change?* The attempt here is to connect with and compare comprehensive conceptual ideas philosophically. These approaches strive to cull the learner to develop, grow, and pursue humanizing and equitable living methods.

In transformational learning, one's values, beliefs, and assumptions create the gaze through which personal experience is negotiated, and life meaning is made. When "one's value base does not reflect positive life experiences and opportunities, it is through a process of transformational learning that a new outlook and opportunities may arise" (Mezirow, 2000, p. 7). Mezirow has described opportunities in learning which is transformational, as spaces that are "more inclusive, non-discriminating, open, emotionally capable of change, and reflective" (p. 7), in other words, more developed. With this idea in mind, the study discussed here was designed to inquire into what contributes to transformational learning practices (for ourselves and others) and if this means anything for practitioners working across multiple disciplines.

Compassion can be considered a variation of things and is not always a straightforward answer. However, there are connotations to kindness, kind-heartedness, empathy, care, and consideration for oneself and others. When considering compassion within education, Barbezat and Bush (2014) describe the moral and spiritual aspects of education as an inquiry into human nature, where practitioners and learners cultivate an empathetic relationship and social identification with others for compassion and connection in the world. Therefore, compassion can be considered a value, a practice, and an approach that can be used to create a positive relationship with ourselves and others. It is with this definition that this research was carried out.

This research inquires into the space where people hold their ideas, habits, and feelings. These can be concepts for people they were once unable to be untangled from. I have queried the motivation that people have to change their own challenging situations in life and how we as people can get support from another source. That source can be any manner of literature, script, or practice (physical or mental) that raises a person from being in a place they want growth from or from being in a challenging situation to a higher sense of self. These methods can focus one's attention on being inclusive and loving towards oneself and then also towards others (Nhất Hạnh, 1987). Development of self, or a change in how we treat ourselves, can be considered a process of disrupted thinking, where the foundations of thought are altered and reintegrated, thus shaping one's social character (Foster, 2017).

SPIRITUALITY AND PEDAGOGY

This study's interpretation of subjective searching is the definition this inquiry seeks to adopt. This concept is illustrated well by Foucault, who states:

> Philosophy, I think we could call "spirituality"—the search, practice, and experience through which the subject carries out the necessary transformations on himself in order to have access to the truth. We will call 'spirituality' then the set of these researches, practices, and experiences, which may be purifications, ascetic exercises, renunciations, conversions of looking, modifications of existence, etc., which are, not for knowledge but for the subject, for the subject's very being. (Foucault, 2005, p. 15)

The questions which resonated with me during the writing of this chapter ranged from personal and local to political and global. How do we connect, and what connects us? What are the phenomena that force the general population not to be isolated? What moves us to join purposefully, in gatherings, communities, ceremonies, groups, families, couples, and in contemporary times, on a virtual level, unprecedented in our mortal progress.

These questions can be related to concepts such as spirituality or oneness. This oneness is a connection to a higher power, a connection to "God," to nature, to one another, and, maybe most importantly, the connection to the self (Jung, 1947). This experience of oneness can also be described as a form of universal love (Darder, 2017). The definition of love and oneness is an interpretation of subjective searching and relational exploration. This inquiry seeks to adapt its approach. This notion of spirituality in connection to these ideas is related to a form of transformation, as put forward by Foucault (2005). As mentioned above, Foucault's framing of spirituality has been instrumental in framing what constitutes spiritual seeking and personal growth in this research project. This study seeks to engage with these concepts and includes the voices of community development educators, practitioners, and volunteers.

The Self and Transformation

I endeavored to inquire into the concept of transformation in connection to the concept of the self and what this practically means and looks like to nonformal educators. In order to find out how these concepts intersect, I first critically analyzed the academic literature and then explored the ideas in the realities and experiences of the participants. Consequently, the question which arose in my mind as a researcher into the social world was, "what then comes of these transformations of self, this change?" I also wondered how one's mind rearranges itself for new ideas and practices to fit together and operate newly, in harmony, once we engage in self-care practices. I wanted to find out what people did to make themselves feel better, their practices of self-preservation and rest, and how this impacted their work. The themes which were chosen for the inquiry were chosen to incorporate a variety of personal transformational experiences. The experiences I wanted to research come under the framing of exercise and practice. The term, exercises, was used to understand self-development exercises of the mind, engaging in exercise regimes for physical and mental change, and engaging in rituals connected to theology or spiritual enlightenment (like meditation). In short, the scope for the inquiry into self-care practices in this research was vast, wide, and highly subjective.

The phenomena of change within the self have been described by Foucault (1993) as cultivating methods and techniques that require individuals to monitor, transform, and, ultimately, act upon themselves. My quest with this research is to inquire *whether the self-development, care, and spirituality methods can be a contagion for social change for educational practitioners in pedagogical spaces*. Further questions drive the literature review to explore the relationship between knowledge, difference, and power. What does this relationship mean for individual and social transformation (Goldberger et al., 1996)?

East Meets West

Theorist and educator Eric Fromm and his colleagues have argued for the physical and mental benefits of esoteric and practical techniques carried out when humans engage in self-care practices. In addition to the discussion on how zen meditation has a profound impact on our ability to act and be in the world, Fromm and his colleagues develop ideas further in Zen Buddhism and psychoanalysis (Fromm et al., 1960), including the connection of this work to the practice of psychoanalysis and knowing oneself on a deeper level.

Fromm et al. (1960) frame "zen" as described by the Japanese school of Mahayana Buddhism, which emphasizes the value of meditation and intuition. They argued that Zen and psychoanalysis have much in common, including an abiding distrust in conscious thought and a belief that *self-knowledge leads to self-transformation*. They suggested that Zen practice may actually be better equipped than Western psychotherapeutic approaches in helping people more effectively manage the modern problems of emptiness and self-alienation.

In relation to these ideas and building upon the premise: *can self-care and spirituality be a contagion for social change*? I have found the work of Schuster (1979) helpful in connection to meditative awareness and compassion for oneself and others. In an article that makes an early link between empathy and meditation, Schuster argued that the deep awareness quality of mindfulness meditation and the Zen practice of *shikantaza* (just sitting) are likely to enhance the capacity for empathy within individuals. This study is not part of whether or not this is true for other forms of meditative practice, such as prayer, as having the same capacity to nurture empathy and compassion within people. However, the task in question with this research is to build upon the results of previous scholars as a mode of inquiry into various forms of self-motivated, spiritual practices for the good of oneself and others.

AWAKENED STRUGGLE: A CRITICAL REVIEW

Hattam (2004) discusses the concept of "awakening struggle," which has been supremely influential in the lens through which this research has been carried out. Hattam's work on the connection between Buddhist theory and critical social theory debates that true social change should be a duality of experiences, both an inner and outer world transformation. The awakened struggle consists of actions that create opportunities for the self and society, both the mind and social structure. Hattam's thoughts are that we must first have self-enlightenment for human enlightenment, and without enlightenment for all humans, we cannot be free (Hattam, 2004). The term "enlightenment" refers to human liberation from suffering and oppression, of social and individual wellbeing. These ideas struck me as critical when exploring the grounding principles people live and work by.

The reasoning behind engaging with Hattam's approach and utilizing this methodology within this research is due to his writings' theoretical and affective underpinnings in "Awakened Struggle." Hattam's (2004) book has highlighted a way forward in contemporary critical social theory. His book is engaging with flair, insight, and compelling literary examples. In this research project, I wanted to use the framework of marrying self-care practices to the experience of nonformal educators to inquire whether the quest for liberation of oneself through self-care motivates educators to work with others to do the same.

This study intended to study the tools, technologies, and wisdom the participants offered through the conversations in the interviews. As used in this text, the concept of self-care is connected to the later works of Foucault (2002). This has illustrated how the self, through history, has been constituted. In antiquity, the relation to self was intensified, and self-care was central (Giles, 1993). To work with oneself was connected both to ethics and freedom. It was seen both as a right and as a demand. Self-work required both an attitude and a set of actions where body care, health regimes, physical training, and restrained satisfaction were the main focus (Foucault, 2002). This research aims to work with these understandings to develop a contemporary insight into the lives of educators in a highly capitalized and individualized world—how *do* practitioners reflect on their experiences and work with themselves for their own good.

A Fourth Space

The inclusion of the practitioner's voice is lacking in the reading of Hattam's work, in his search for the "awakened struggle" for the middle ground between care for oneself and care for society. There seems no space in Hattam's literature, excluding only when Hattam reflects on his own personal meditation practice, for the practices of other educators to be included. Hattam includes a wide-ranging discussion and study of the various and vast forms of Buddhist practices and meditation (Hattam, 2004). This was hugely attractive as literature, yet it may not resonate with all educational practitioners. Hattam's work on the relationship between social theory and Buddhist theory argues that by having a third space between these two concepts of Buddhism and critical social theory, thus individuals can create a sharper focus for readers on the topics at hand. In this more profound connection, the reader can become the practitioner, and the quest for social justice at times parallels those seeking to create a more socially just world. The space I wish to create with this research has the noted addition of different ideologies and practices. Let me place here *the fourth space* to fill the gap in the literature and empirical research where the inclusion of practitioners is included and analyzed.

The justification for this approach of framing a "fourth space" lies in the structure in which this research is developed and carried out. The framework created for inquiry is rooted in the values of relational exploration and connectedness with oneself and others. This research has aimed to seek new spaces where we live and work, which help us thrive, know, and learn. The fourth space offered by this research actively uses the meaningful experiences of educators to understand the practical applications of self-care, compassion, and equity in a socially unjust world, provided with the critical, theoretical foundations of the literary work of Robert Hattam (2004).

The research introduced in this chapter is a conversation between educational practitioners, which seeks to map and involve the organic, distinct knowledge of the participants involved. The research process and findings have been brought forward in an attempt to find common ground, transferable skills, and approaches between people for the betterment of caring for oneself and caring for others, exploring a spiritual approach to education. Mannheim and Tedlock (1995) describe conversations as "wandering together with (others)" (p. 4), with Brinkmann (2014) stating that "conversation is used as the central tool to obtain knowledge about others" (p. 278). With these distinctions, I have approached the writing of this work and the research described above, adopting an approach that focuses on phenomenological approaches to learning. This is the gap in current literature.

The Commodification of Self-Care and Spirit

When contemplating Hattam's (2004) research, it is essential to avoid using Buddhist mindfulness practices without understanding the historical implications of the texts. It can become a damaging practice rather than restful when the onus for a mindful living and calmer life is put onto the individual and not society (Purser, 2019). Without a collective voice and shared opinion, there is a threat of a fragmented approach that does not challenge the power structures it seeks to pervade. Merely, it dances alongside them.

The research discussed in this chapter aimed to include the collective voices and reflections of practitioners in the field to prompt their thinking and understanding of self-care and whether self-care and spirituality practices motivate them to engage in practices rooted in social change. Foster (2017) raises essential points in the critique of self-development and social interdependence. His premise is that self-help genres and related texts have become central to our current neoliberal subjectivity. This is supported by Rimke (2000), who suggests that self-help literature trusts in the idea that people can exercise power and control of themselves, their behaviors, and their lives, deflecting the notion that we should help one another at the same time.

Confines of Compassionate Connection

This contemporary notion of self-care provided by Foster (2017) consequentially promotes a hyper-individualized notion of responsibility, where social dependencies and connectedness are thus obstructed from the processes of self and social and transformational change. This notion contrasts with the broader global interest in self-supporting, mindfulness-based training initiatives (Rimke, 2000). The rise in these initiatives may be partly due to psychosomatic symptoms of anxiety and stress. Some have seen these symptoms exist due to the amplified pace of life under the current neoliberal order to which the Western world is accustomed (O'Donnell, 2015). Therefore, it can be deduced that contemporary capitalism, as it is known, is pervasive throughout any attempt to engage in transformational practices or the search for our personal awakened struggle for the educators who took part in this research, no less (Hattam, 2004). Therefore, it is evident that there are consistent barriers to authentic connection and compassion in an attempt to understand the self with others.

Previous research has sought to elevate the ideas of compassionate Buddhist practices and combine them with Western approaches for positive transformational change (O'Donnell, 2015). However, there is a danger for these practices to be co-opted by the neoliberal pervasion of Western societies, bringing with it a de-authenticity of approaches, therefore demeaning the purpose of these methods of self-enlightenment. Therefore, caution is warranted when discussing these methods and approaches to self-care. Meditation, mindfulness, compassionate loving-kindness: these ideas and rituals become interwoven with their elation of wellbeing in the human mind, and their historical, cultural, spiritual, and sacred meanings can be diminished (Dowling, 2020).

Burned Out

Burned out is commonly found in many professions. However, Barford and Whelton (2010) offer insight when discussing the exposure that professional workers in the community development field (including both paid and unpaid workers) have to the idea of burnout. The concept of burnout, whereby individuals cease to be able to work due to over-working effectively, is one of many insidious effects that professional resiliency has on individuals.

Gormally et al. (2014) have undertaken a study focusing on neoliberalism's effects on youth and community workers. Their paper discusses how neoliberalism affects youth and community workers and their ability to engage fully with roles involving care. Their research has helped understand the depth in which the insidious effects of austerity policies have on youth and community workers, leaving access to self-development or the development of spirituality unattainable. Further, their research with youth and community workers provides the context of how community and youth practitioners have an insignificant opportunity to engage with their own feelings due to their over-bureaucratized roles. This lack of engagement with the self leads to the self-sacrifice of the professional to support and develop the individuals and groups they work with, leaving scarce room for personal care and growth under such pressurized workloads in the neoliberal agenda (Gormally et al., 2014).

The research from Gormally and colleagues (2014) further exemplifies the imperative need for educational practitioners to be supported to foster self-care methods in the environments in which they live and work. Dowling (2020) has warned that we need to explore how care, compassion, and responsibility are organized—for which groups of people, in which context, and to what benefit care or self-care is projected. Is it for the benefit of the community, the individual, the institution, or the corporate market? The ideology of care, writes Dowling, is ever-expanding and changing, as are the modes of rampant capitalism and guises in which methods of caring for ourselves and others are packaged and sold back to us at a high price.

A Connected Pedagogy

When we, as people, work alongside other people, there exists a relationship between the realities we feel throughout our lives. This intersection of realities is made up of feelings of pain, loss, and injustice alongside experiences that contain love, positive learning, and growth. This intersection can be difficult to navigate when engaging in educational practices in practicing strength against associated traumas while building and maintaining a sustainable practice (Bergman, 2002). I have found the writings of Boyd (2012) helpful in developing an evolved understanding of the work of Paulo Freire, providing critical insights into his notion of education as hope and as an act of freedom and connection (Freire, 1996). In his discussion on Paulo Freire, Boyd's work deeply references the impact that can be created in society when undertaking a nonformal approach to education and learning. The premise of nonformal education is to seek to overcome the challenges faced by sociopolitical and socioeconomic pressures, two overarching factors that impede Freire's education practice. Boyd believes Freire's lifework of engaging communities and citizens worldwide in education as a spiritual practice is a testament to progressive educators who seek to work for social justice and change. Boyd considers that those who engage in nonformal education have a site for developing their spirituality alongside their pedagogical and socially just practices. However, a note of attention for educators is warranted here, as Boyd's work does not allude to direct steps for nonformal educators to navigate their development or engagement with the spiritual self.

A Beautiful Pedagogy

Biesta (2014) adds to the literature that focuses on finding alternative spaces in the pedagogical terrain. Biesta clarifies that his thoughts on pedagogy are that education is teleological. Therefore, the purpose of education is the indefinite processes that learners and teachers undergo when engaging within it and in its many forms. The work of Gert Biesta goes on to share the purpose of educational spaces is to be one of connection, action, and emancipation. Thus, education can be considered an interactive space for learning and liberation in its contemporary sense. This can happen in its traditional sense, as within institutional environments, but it also reaches and encompasses more nonformal settings in communities and beyond (Goldberger et al., 1996).

Hayes (2012) argues that these nonformal settings ranged from indoor and outdoor spaces to online spaces. Ideas can be spread through mediums like books, the media, human connections, and, more recently, the internet. Areas that do not know many bounds. Books, literature, and stories are spaces where the hidden relics of understanding human nature and connection exist. Thus, stories, conversations, and dialogues have been the forbearers of gaining and appreciating differences in human connection and relationships with oneself and others (Horton et al., 1990). With the framing of a beautiful pedagogy, this research adopts its lens on education, spaces we connect within, act upon, and strive for emancipation.

Transformational Practice

Transformational learning is a concept that has been used and interpreted in various forms and is related to the internal and external experience of self-development and social change alluded to in this chapter. Within these interwoven markers, we shall consider this transformational learning existing through practices, dialogue, and conversations with one another (Giroux, 2004). Paulo Freire (2000) argued that individuals or groups who are going through acquiring or creating new knowledge could be considered students, no matter the formality of the education, the spaces education is delivered within, or those who are carrying out the educator's role, as we are all students of our own lives. This research has adopted the framing of the term "student" in the most holistic sense of the word to understand the purposes of transformational learning. Thus, the term "student" is not understood here as the academic or school student but as the *student of life* who *seeks to better themselves for the oneness of all beings*.

The experience of being a student of life relates to the experiences human beings create and engage with when they seek to better themselves. Therefore, this form of studentship and education is discussed in this research as the various physical or mental exercises which people take part in to improve compassion and wellbeing for themselves and others. These esoteric and physical practices can range from religious and non-religious prayer, positive worship, kindness for and towards others, physical meditations or physical fitness, a willingness to learn and share our skills, and the act of cultivating positive attributes towards the outer world and oneself (Goldstein, 1999). The literature studied here, a tapestry of disciplines intertwining together, offers the theoretical framework for this study that looks to fill the opening in the literature studied to involve the social and personal worlds of five community development pedagogues living and working in Glasgow, Scotland.

I have delved into the literary works of scholars and academics across a plethora of disciplines that seek to find the reasoning behind people working together for the good of others and themselves in the literature review. While the journey through the paths of these authors has been, at times, a momentous task, the realization that thinkers and educators can connect through theory is something of beauty. This approach to pedagogy is beautiful (Biesta, 2014), spiritual (Foucault, 2015), transformational (Giroux, 2004), liberated (Fromm et al., 1960), and awakened struggle (Hattam, 2004), and is more than a theory or an idea. Hattam (2004) carries out gracefully in his work the blending of theories on self and social change. I have endeavored to continue this blend in this research with the applicability of related skills in practice.

It is apparent from the literature studied that love, connection, and relationship are paramount to fostering positive social interaction in education and the world. There, this literature review inquired into another aim of the concept of what self-care actually is. In connection to this question, the literature discussed in this chapter offers philosophical and academic notions of self-care in relation to personal development methods. This review has been carried out to acknowledge that self-care practices mean various things for different people, and the literature review incorporates various concepts with this in mind.

The concluding point of this inquiry was to ask: What are the mechanisms between self-care, social change, and transformation? I initially focused on a book examining the connection between Buddhist and critical theory. What remains to be seen in the body of literature is incorporating the experiences of individuals who hold vital knowledge, which is paramount in understanding how the theories mentioned here interact with peoples' realities and lifeworld (Husserl, 1954). I have also included literature that critiques the methods of self-development and self-care and what this means in relation to transformational approaches to pedagogy and practice.

METHODS

Participants

The participants have been recruited through professional working relationships that have been upheld in previous work I have been involved in. I have introduced the participants using a pseudonym in the table of participants provided. The environments I have chosen to focus on in this research are of a statutory care nature and are based in institutional or community settings. These are places where institutional power structures and boundaries intersect. The spaces discussed also contained experiences for participants where power and boundaries have been exercised and imposed on the participants to varying degrees of difference and similarity. The professional working environments that participants engaged in involved people working as employed staff and supported volunteers. Table 1.1 deciphers the demographic information of the participants.

Procedure

This study employed a qualitative approach, using semi-structured, one-to-one interviews to capture the experiences of those working in the environments above and engaging participants in an inquiry into the relationship between self-care and social change (Punch, 2006). The premise of the interview dialogues with practitioners was to search for links between interview participants' narratives and life histories. Namely, I wanted to examine the overall stories told to illuminate a potential pattern concerning compassionate personal and pedagogical practices and how these shape people to live their lives (Freire, 2000). This piece of research thus became a space to refine and protect personal values, explore different practices in different contexts, and celebrate diverse lifeworlds in a safe setting.

Settings

The interviews were carried out in a private teaching space at an established university in west Scotland. They were carried out using a laptop

Table 1.1

Participants' Demographics

Name of research participant	Age	Gender	Years of working experience	Job Role & Profesional working environment
Riki	27	Male	12	Has a background in community development practice and has focused their professional career as a youth worker for both statutory and third-sector organizations
William	31	Male	5	Has experience serving custodial sentences for offenses committed while undergoing addiction issues. William* is now a volunteer in recovery communities/cafes across Glasgow prisons and is in recovery.
Robert	35	Male	10	Is a manager and researcher for the Scottish-wide initiative to review the care system within Scotland to provide more inclusive outcomes for young people experiencing a variety of care experiences.
Sophie	26	Female	6	Is a group facilitator and researcher for a Scottish University. Her role is to facilitate a focus group on the topic of 'Love' within the care system. Sophie* has experience in the care system and working as a professional with vulnerable people.
David	27	Male	9	Has a background in community education and facilitates community development training locally and internationally for both adults and young people, focusing on gender-based violence prevention.

and voice recorder. I took electronic notes during the interview and used the recordings to inform and illuminate the transcripts. Each interview lasted around an hour, and there were eighteen questions considered and answered by participants. The participants were invited into the space at times that suited them and their schedules. The room was light and spacious, with interviews being carried out in a relaxed manner in the form of a discussion. I arranged preconceived questions, which guided the shared dialogue as participant experiences are temporal, dynamic, and shifting (Cahill, 2007).

The research was designed to help the participants collaborate with the researcher to understand the topics and the terms used. The aim was to create a space in which the questions asked allowed the interview participants to delve into their psyche and unearth their reasoning and passion for the work they engage in (Pavey et al., 2012). The design of the research questions was imperative in the methodological strategy and process undertaken. The procedural development required me as the interviewer and the interviewees to think critically about the issues being studied and their own life experiences, which can be uncomfortable or had never been done before (Bryman, 2012). The questions were chosen to provide a pathway into the leading premise of this research: *can self-care and spirituality be a contagion for social change?* The questions did not assume that self-care is a contagion for social change. Instead, the questions were devised to inquire into this notion. Therefore, the questions (see Appendix A) asked were considered carefully, as they could evoke emotional responses or vicarious trauma, which was considered when developing the interview questions (Rapley, 2001).

All interviews took place after participants' informed consent was secured. This study was able to begin a dialogue focused on the meaningful approach. This was an approach practitioner took to engage in and facilitate various forms of education and learning opportunities for more prominent reasons.

Data Analysis

The interviews considered the relationship between trauma, compassion, and transformative pedagogy reflectively and broadly. The data collected for this study were analyzed using thematic analysis, whereby transcripts were color-coded using prominent themes and words and then were developed into narrative maps used for further analysis and discussion (Bryman, 2012).

The insights highlighted in the decoding of the data. The primary literature discussed (Hattam, 2004) offered an insight into the works of the scholar who has sought to combine critical theory approaches with those Buddhist approaches to living in the world (Hattam, 2004). Other theorists have incorporated the imperative to recognize the stories people hold and tell themselves (Connelly & Clandinin, 2006; Griffiths, 2003). However, their research did not include practitioners' voices. In connection with other theorists, namely Barford and Whelton (2010) and Gormally et al. (2014), the conversation on "burnout" is introduced, which is relevant to the themes gathered here. I had expected to be able to write about compassion and self-care more broadly, but in reality, in this sample, these concepts were kept mainly in the backdrop of more prominent topics.

I undertook a process of thematic analysis for decoding the data (Brauna & Clarke, 2013) in conjunction with using the literature to identify and seek commonalities. The main text discussed in the literature review, from the work of Hattam (2004), showed that themes of spirituality, social justice, and connection with others were prevalent and existed for community development practitioners in Glasgow. However, this was revealed more covertly. Through reading and rereading the interview transcripts, I found that participants connected with these themes through a form of *disconnection with them*. In undertaking a more organic thematic analysis rooted in my collected data, I looked for common words and phrases. I used colors to highlight and connect the participants' experiences. I used mind-maps and created a table to view the meanings derived from the coding process, allowing for an overview and analysis to be made with the data amounting to relational topics and themes. These shall now be discussed below.

FINDINGS

This section includes the participants' experiences, their understanding of their own lifeworld in relation to self-care practices, and how the critical educational work they engage in can impede their ability to stay well and nourished in body and mind. Three themes emerged from the data analysis.

Guerrilla Love

An influential aspect of this research study came from one of the research participants. While participating in this research project, Sophie discussed that she was able to think about compassion in a new light through the lens of her professional work. This was both in reference to herself and the people she worked with. Sophie described that she felt a distance between being a practitioner in the field and having the scope to practice self-care away from her job role. Working for the institutional establishment has offered the study insight into the practical field and the disconnect *between practitioners and institutional value bases*. We can see that there is much work still to do in recognizing and validating distinctive and meaningful methods of working in the world, involving the concepts of spirituality, compassion, and self-care.

Spaces for Change

There is a void space in workplaces where bureaucracy, targets, and pressure subsume compassion and empathy. This space is filled by the practitioners who spend their lives in these arenas. All five participants stated they felt the work they are involved in *is* compassionate, empathetic to others, or nurturing. Identifying the difference between the work practice and the work environment, Riki has stated that "the values that youth workers have and carry out are driven by compassion—just not sometimes by the organization."

Sophie works as a researcher and group facilitator for a Scottish university, investigating lived experiences of the care system in Scotland. She has described this practice as being a "love-led practice." Sophie added that her practitioner experience "surrounded gathering the stories and voices of others, providing evidence to organizations to learn from these stories ... to be able to humanize the way we do things, and strategically change things."

People hold different relationships, realities, and understandings, yet they meaningfully engage in their work-based practice for the care and benefit of others. The interviewees offered this research new, stirring, and moving accounts of their personal and professional experiences. For example, William describes this tenderly,

> I have a real desire to help others turn their lives around as I know firsthand the misery and pain that I have endured through difficult times. To see people slowly getting better a day at a time and using support networks fills me with a sense of satisfaction and keeps me going.

It is evident that practitioners want the spaces to be changed. They want to do their job with care, empathy, and compassion. Humanizing their practices is their goal.

The Self, the Institution, and Spirituality

The institutional powers that direct each participant's profession, workload, or employment (both paid and voluntary) have been seen to monopolize the terrain, leaving the practice of self-care or spirituality a second thought, a vital aspect of life that is neglected at times. Their connection with themselves has been impaired by their relationship to care for, and care with, others. This was outlined by Robert, who stated that:

> Being part of any organization which has funded or answerable commitments (either funding bodies or people in power) that you are responsible for has an impact on how you do your work. You can never really be free from work. There is a myriad of constraints, and this affects how you view yourself. There is definitely an impact on my wellbeing with pressure and stress from work. It is so there that I don't even think about it—it's so much a part of the system.

This statement (or mentality) was echoed by David, who stated that "I have worked in environments where working the bare minimum is not enough—in my job, going above and beyond is expected, and self-care is forgotten about." All five participants shared a similar view and highlighted how they held multiple jobs and roles, both in paid and voluntary work for various institutions, adding to the pressure of casualized work contracts that are generally part-time and fixed term with little benefits or security (Dowling, 2020).

DISCUSSION

This study's findings reveal that practitioners could not conclude that their own motivation for working in their chosen profession and role was because they showed compassion for themselves. Additionally, the need to practice self-care for the interviewees was determined by the pressure of their role and the broader institutions they work for, not by motivation from their own personal desire. This points to the overarching and subtle ways in which power and its' mechanisms pervade individuals' public and private lives.

Spirituality Disrupts Educators' Worldview

Each participant who took part found the space for disruption and healing in his/her working environment (hooks, 2000). Purely by presenting their views, the participants' voices in this piece challenge the hegemonic discourse taken by institutional establishments they have encountered in their personal and working lives. They aim to reimagine, reconceptualize, and refine what it means to engage in these environments alongside the pressures these environments create (Fisher, 2017). This work was purposely to engage with practitioners engaging in educational practices in different institutional environments and have an open conversation with them. The topics discussed were of interest, yet the participants were chosen as they had some connection to the question topics. At the point of inquiry, whether that connection was positive or negative was yet to be seen. However, patterns observed in the data have indicated that neither of these prospects—of having positive or negative experiences in relation to self-care and compassion- were true.

A Paradigm Shift

Within the roles discussed here, where workers are culturally responsive and work with reflexive criticality and a deep socioeconomic understanding, there is a stark realization for staff that the tides of poverty and inequity keep rising. For nonformal educators to remain critical in their approach while keeping their own safety paramount is a complicated and arduous task. To navigate our priorities to increase spirituality, honesty, commitment, and meaning requires fundamental institutional change, complemented by stages of professional validity and spirit rarely seen in contemporary Western culture.

The sentiments which arose for further empirical inquiry in a post-2020 world are related to concepts of compassion, care, and institutional wellbeing (Barford & Whelton, 2010; Evans & Curver, 2017). A subject that is pertinent to a paradigm shift in educational practice relates to the challenging circumstances within which teachers and educators—both formal and nonformal—operate within and how wellbeing for educational practitioners can be provided in these spaces. This is not only by the influence of educators working to look after themselves but also by how our places of work support this far-reaching mission. Can our institutions provide the critical research and reflection necessary for transformational pedagogy? This seems complicated when faced with the outside influences felt by educators who work to care for others. The pressures are almost entirely embedded in a global, hyper-capitalist economy reinforced by local and national corporations (Dowling, 2020). Therefore, the quest for educators is a new approach to living and working that celebrates rest, recovery, and healing as collective efforts for us all, not only as individuals.

To better understand these experiences after the research had been carried out, I have since looked to draw from Spooner and McNinch's (2018) work on dissident knowledge in higher education. They offer deep insights into the ideas behind the psyche of capitalist educational institutions and learning spaces, believing academics, students, and activists must adopt a knowledge democracy, which must pervade the forces co-opting knowledge and connection for capital (Hall, 2018). This work has helped develop a congruent understanding that without democratized access to education, elite forms of knowledge and knowledge production will pervade, rending forms of local knowledge out of the picture. In this form of knowledge production, this research has aimed to engage within, to value the experiences of all forms of educational knowledge in more abstract spheres than traditional tropes of education and pedagogy.

Sites for Transformation

Foucault (2005) explains the transformative potential of studying sites of personal and social experiences as an opening to construct the self differently and "to invite others to share an experience of what we are, not only our past but also our present ... in such a way that we might come out of it transformed" (p. 241). The findings of this study point to the practitioners disrupting the institution's influence and highlighting the importance of fostering compassion in nonformal spaces and in participants' work-based practice. The imperative to practice self-care for self-preservation has been alluded to here; this value is more to protect individuals from the pressures of institutional environments rather than being a motivator to work for social change.

The work of Feucht et al. (2017) is a helpful narrative for understanding ways in which educators can reclaim and repurpose their experiences of vocational burnout, as discussed by Barford and Whelton (2010). Feucht et al. (2017) discuss how "reflexivity and epistemic cognition" (p. 234) are paramount for teachers and educators to create a protective barrier for themselves against institutional demands. The study by Feucht and colleagues further states that "epistemic reflexivity becomes a powerful tool for teachers to facilitate meaningful and sustainable change in their classroom teaching" (p. 235). Therefore, the site for transformation and disruption exists within the self and out within the spaces in which educators learn, develop, and ultimately thrive.

The Fourth Space: Reflection on Compassion

The idea that volunteering and helping others is positive for an individual's wellbeing has been researched by Thoits and Hewitt (2001), whose investigation into volunteering experiences found a direct correlation between volunteering and enhanced six aspects of wellbeing. These six aspects of wellbeing included happiness, life satisfaction, self-esteem, sense of control over life, physical health, and depression. The trend in relation to participants' life experience being an influence on their own practice is then reiterated by Sophie. She explains,

> I have a belief in the transformational change that my work will create. This is because of my personal experience of growing up in care (for example)—the things that went wrong should not be repeated, and good experiences (in care) should happen for all young people.

The idea that institutional constraints impair the mobility of practitioners to be able to fully care for themselves is seen by this research as a simplistic narrative at best (Foucault, 1975). It is important not to get caught up in the dualism between spaces—for example, the institution's and practitioner's spaces. This research highlights that, although workplace environments have gaps in compassion, the practice of individuals in the workplace does not. It is the people, the human desire to work for change, that fill the cracks.

CONCLUSION

Developing a broader study on the power practitioners hold in de-escalating and mediating the relationship between the self and the institution is necessary, and indeed, not discovered, in relation to these topics discussed. The study discussed here allowed the researcher to understand the pressures of the field, entangled with the pressures of a modernist, post-capitalist society.

The findings of this research echo the studies by Barford and Whelton (2010), Gormally et al. (2014), and Goldberger et al. (1996), in the premise that local knowledge, social conditions, and their positionality (of community practitioners in Glasgow) recognize the constraints put upon the individuals by the institutions they work for. The impact of high workloads and complex experiences of operating in communities of high socioeconomic disadvantage in a climate of austerity has enormous implications for the wellbeing of these practitioners and their efforts to keep themselves mentally and physically healthy.

This chapter has provided a specialist lens to understand the experiences and development of nonformal educators living and working in Scotland. These educators operated in a wide variety of contexts, supporting a wide variety of vulnerable communities, displaying tenacity and compassion, and, at times, performing at the detriment of their own wellbeing to support the growth and development of others. Future research will offer this study the opportunity to qualitatively map different and new typologies, thus using this data to create a practical approach to the bureaucratic violence of the institution in partnership with other practitioners (Evans & Curver, 2017).

The bureaucratic violence put forth by Evans and Curver (2017) is pertinent to understanding the scope of this study and the real-life, personal constraints that can impact teacher education or teacher preparation, respectively (in both formal and nonformal spaces). The participant-educators in this study have discussed how their engagement within institutional structures can create a void in oneself to take care, look after and connect with their own wellbeing. This pressure to perform thus exists all the while the institutions that educators work for, more frequently than not, offer no respite from the daily challenges of learning and educating oneself and others.

LIMITATIONS OF THIS STUDY

The interviews were carried out with a small group of individuals who may not entirely represent all who engage in nonformal pedagogical practices. Therefore, a broader study, working with a more significant number of individuals over a more extended period, is necessary. In addition, I had intended to interview both women and men for the study. However, as mentioned, the initially identified participants' family and personal care commitments could not allow for their input in this sample. Instead, in addition to two males, another two male participants were asked to participate. I do not feel this impacts the research study other than the gender imbalance. Perhaps this highlights the constraints put on women, which can relate to caregiving responsibilities (Goldberger et al., 1996). However, this is merely an observation, which makes no difference to the outcome of this research.

For all five participants, the data's most prevalent and synchronized aspect was the direct relationship that working within institutional or care-focused environments has on each individual's capacity to look after themselves. However, the small sample size of this study makes the findings of the research discussed in this chapter challenging to define for all community-based educators, and a more extensive study with a broader analysis and larger group of participants is necessary.

IMPLICATIONS: PROGRESSIVE PRACTICE—
A HOPEFUL BEGINNING

A promising approach in this research seeks to cultivate future empirical studies seeking to disrupt prevailing hierarchies and unjust power constructs by creating the opportunity to engage in spaces that welcome and nurture another way of knowing and being using the work of Spooner (2018). At this stage, the real impact this research can offer is concrete evidence of hope, *despite the establishment*. The findings of this study suggest that progressive and engaged pedagogies must involve intervention and inquiry by practitioners, including how such pedagogical practice impacts their wellbeing.

The topics discussed in this chapter were of personal interest to me as the researcher. Yet, the participants were chosen as they had some connection to the questions asked. At the point of inquiry, whether that connection was positive or negative was yet to be seen. However, the research data have cemented that neither of these prospects—of having positive or negative experiences in relation to self-care and compassion—were true. People hold different relationships, realities, and understandings, yet they meaningfully engage in their work-based practice for the care and benefit of others. The participants offered this research with new, stirring, and moving accounts of their personal and professional experiences. As a result, their insights shed light on how the institutions should consider better care for employees in higher education, community-based organizations, and the like.

The findings of this study shed light on the importance of recognizing the difference between the work practice and the work environment and what kind of capital this affords practitioners. This study has begun a dialogue focused on the meaningful approach toward nonformal teacher education, preparation, and learning. This is an approach that practitioners take to engage in, and facilitate, a variety of forms of education and learning opportunities for reasons which are more significant than themselves.

REFERENCES

Barbezat, D. P., & Bush, M. (2014). *Contemplative practices in higher education: Powerful methods to transform teaching and learning*. Jossey-Bass

Barford, S. W., & Whelton, W. J. (2010). Understanding burnout in child and youth studies. *Child and Youth Forum, 39*(4), 271–287. http://dx.doi.org/10.1007/s10566-010-9104-8

Bergman, R. (2002). Why be moral? A conceptual model from developmental psychology. *Human Development, 45*(2), 104–124. https://doi.org/10.1159/000048157

Boyd, D. (2012). The critical spirituality of Paulo Freire. *International Journal of Lifelong Education, 31*(6), 759–778. https://doi.org/10.1080/02601370.2012.723051

Biesta, G. (2014). *The beautiful risk of education*. Paradigm.

Braun, V., & Clarke, V. (2013). *Successful qualitative research: A practical guide for beginners*. SAGE.
Brinkmann, S. (2014). Unstructured and semi-structured interviewing. In P. Leavy (Ed.), *Oxford handbook of qualitative research* (pp. 277–299). Oxford University Press. https://doi.org/10.1093/oxfordhb/9780199811755.013.030
Bryman, A. (2012). *Social research methods* (4th ed). Oxford University Press.
Cahill, C. (2007). Doing research with young people: Participatory research and the rituals of collective work. *Children's Geographies, 5*(3), 297–312. https://doi.org/10.1080/14733280701445895
Clandinin, D. J. (2006). Narrative inquiry: A methodology for studying lived experience. *Research Studies in Music Education, 27*(1), 44–54. https://doi.org/10.1177/1321103X060270010301
Dalai Lama. (1992). *Worlds in harmony: Dialogues on compassionate action*. Parallax Press.
Darder, A. (2017). *Reinventing Paulo Freire: A pedagogy of love*. Routledge.
Dowling, E. (2020). *The care crisis: What caused it and how can we end it*. Verso.
Evans, B., & Curver, T. (2017). *Histories of violence: Post-war critical thought*. Bloomsbury.
Feucht, F., Brownlee, J. L., & Schraw, G. (2017). Moving beyond reflection: Reflexivity and epistemic cognition in teaching and teacher education. *Educational Psychologist, 52*(4), 234–241. https://doi.org/10.1080/00461520.2017.1350180
Fisher, K. M. (2017). Look before you leap: Reconsidering contemplative pedagogy. *Teaching Theology and Religion, 20*(1), 4–18. https://doi.org/10.1111/teth.12361
Foster, R. (2017). Social character, Erich Fromm and the ideological glue of neoliberalism. *Critical Horizons, 18*(1), 1–18. https://doi.org/10.1080/14409917.2017.1275166
Foucault, M. (1975). *Discipline and punish: The birth of the prison*. Penguin.
Foucault, M. (1993). About the beginning of the hermeneutics of the self: Two lectures at Dartmouth. *Political Theory, 21*(2), 198–227. https://www.jstor.org/stable/191814
Foucault, M. (2002). *Archaeology of knowledge*. Routledge
Foucault, M. (2005). *The Hermeneutics of the subject: Lectures at the college de France, 1981–1982* (G. Burchell, Trans). Palgrave Macmillan.
Fourcault, M. (2015). Parrēsia. *Critical Inquiry, 41*(2). (Burchell, G., Trans.).
Freire, P. (1996). *Letters to Cristina: Reflections on my life and work*. Routledge.
Freire, P. (2000). *Pedagogy of the oppressed* (30th Anniversary Ed.). Continuum.
Fromm, E., Suzuki, D. T., & DeMartino, R. (1960). *Zen Buddhism and psychoanalysis*. Harper & Row.
Giles, J. (1993). The no-self theory: Hume, Buddhism, and personal identity. *Philosophy East and West, 43*(2), 175–200. https://doi.org/10.2307/1399612
Giroux, H. (2004). Cultural studies and the politics of public pedagogy: Making the political more pedagogical. *Parallax, 10*(2), 73–89. https://doi.org/10.1080/1353464042000208530
Goldberger, N., Tarule, J., Clinchy, B., & Belenky, M. (Eds). (1996). *Knowledge, difference, and power: Women's ways of knowing*. Basic Books.

Goldstein, L. S. (1999). The relational zone: The role of caring relationships in the co-construction of mind. *American Educational Research Journal, 36*(3), 647–673. https://doi.org/10.3102/00028312036003647

Griffiths, M. (2003). *Feminisms and the self: The web of identity*. Routledge.

Hall, P. A. (2018). Varieties of capitalism in light of the euro crisis. *Journal of European Public Policy. 1*, 7–30. https://doi.org/10.1080/13501763.2017.1310278

Hattam, R. (2004). *Awakening struggle: Towards a Buddhist critical social theory*. Post Pressed.

Hayes, N. K. (2012). *How we think: Digital media and contemporary technogenesis*. University of Chicago Press

hooks, b. (2000). *All about love: New visions*. William Morrow.

Horton, M., Bell, B., Gaventa, J., & Peters, J. M. (1990). *We make the road by walking: Conversations on education and social change*. Temple University Press.

Husserl, E. (1954). *Die krisis der europäischen wissenschaften und die tranzendentale phänomenologie* [The crisis of the European sciences and the transcendental-phenomenology]. Martinus Nijhoff.

Gormally, S., Hughes, G., Cooper, C., & Rippingale, J. (2014). The state of youth work in austerity England: Reclaiming the ability to care. *Youth and Policy, 113*(1), 1–14. https://doi.org/10.1057/9781137393593_1

Jung, C. G. (1947). *On the nature of the psyche*. Ark Paperbacks.

Mannheim B., Tedlock B. (1995). Introduction. In Tedlock B., Mannheim B. (Eds.), *The dialogic emergence of culture* (pp. 1–32).University of Illinois Press.

Mezirow, J. (2000). Learning to think like an adult: Core concepts of transformation theory. In J. Mezirow & Associates (Eds.), *Learning as transformation* (pp. 3–34). Jossey-Bass.

O'Donnell, A. (2015). Contemplative pedagogy and mindfulness: Developing creative attention in an age of distraction. *Journal of Philosophy of Education, 49*(2), 187–201. https://doi.org/10.1111/1467-9752.12136

Punch, K. (2006). *Developing effective research proposals*. SAGE.

Purser, R. (2019). *McMindfulness: How mindfulness became the new capitalist spirituality*. Repeater Books.

Pavey, L., Greitemeyer, T., & Sparks, P. (2012). "I help because I want to, not because you tell me to": Empathy increases autonomously motivated helping., *Personality & Social Psychology Bulletin, 38*(5), 681–689. https://doi.org/10.1177/0146167211435940

Rapley, T. J. (2001). The art(fulness) of open-ended interviewing: some considerations on analysing interviews. *Qualitative Research, 1*(3), 303–323. https://doi.org/10.1177/146879410100100303

Rimke, H., M. (2000). Governing citizens through self-help literature. *Cultural Studies, 14*(1), 61–78. https://doi.org/10.1080/095023800334986

Schuster, R. (1979). Empathy and mindfulness. *Journal of Humanistic Psychotherapy, 19*(1), 71–77. https://doi.org/10.1177/002216787901900107

Spooner, M., & McNinch, J. (Eds.). (2018). *Dissident knowledge in higher education*. University of Regina Press.

Thoits, P. A., & Hewitt, L. N. (2001). Volunteer work and well-being. *Journal of Health and Social Behavior, 42*(2), 115–131. https://doi.org/10.2307/3090173

APPENDIX A

Interview Questions

1. Do you consider the work you engage in to be of a compassionate nature?
2. Do you find the experiences you have had within institutional establishments to be ones driven by compassionate practice(s)?
3. Do you practice or engage in any form of self-compassion &/or methods of self-care? [This can include both physical and mental practices which allow you to look after yourself—e.g., meditation or prayer, sports or physical activities, writing down thoughts, speaking to a counselor/therapist, engaging in "alternative" therapies (like massage/acupuncture), reading literature related to self-care/development?]
4. What motivation do you have for using the practices/methods?
5. How do you understand the term resilience?
6. How would you define this in relation to the self/yourself?
7. Can you tell me a bit about the relationships between professionals and service users in the environment in which you work/volunteer?
8. What motivates you to engage in your professional/voluntary work?
9. Would you ever use the phrase 'transformational learning practice(s)?
10. What does 'transformational 'learning' mean to you?
11. Do you consider yourself to engage in transformational learning practice(s) in your work?

    1) If yes, is this for yourself/others?
    2) If no, is there a reason behind this answer?

12. How do you ensure that you look after yourself when working in institutional environments?
13. Has your experience of being in an institutional environment put constraints on your attitude towards yourself &/or taking care of your wellbeing?

    1) If yes, why?
    2) If no, is there a reason behind this answer?

14. Do you consider your practice to be emancipatory/empowering for yourself/others?

1) If yes, is this for yourself/others?
2) If no, is there a reason behind this answer?

15. Do you consider there to be a connection between practicing self-compassion/care and the role(s) you have engaged in (paid/voluntary) work?
16. To what extent do you think there is a gap (if any) in statutory institutional environments as having components of compassion and care for others?
17. Do you feel your practice positively impacts your wellbeing?
18. Do you feel your practice positively impacts other people's wellbeing?

CHAPTER 2

THE MANY WAYS TO TALK ABOUT SPIRIT AND SPIRITUALITY IN TEACHER EDUCATION

The Decolonizing Potential of Dialogues About Spirit

Shannon Leddy
University of British Columbia

ABSTRACT

In this chapter, I discuss three key discourses in decolonizing education that illustrate why conversations about spirit are necessary for teacher education classrooms. The first uses the Medicine Wheel (Bopp et al., 1989) as a framework for connecting learning to all aspects of a student's personhood. The second discourse links to the work of Kirkness (Kirkness & Barnhardt, 2001), whose discussion of the four Rs, respect, relevance, reciprocity, and responsibility, offers essential considerations for ensuring the intellectual and cultural safety of Indigenous students and faculty, rooted in Indigenous values. The third discourse comes from the work of Mi'kmaq Elders Murdena and Albert Marshall and their notion of two-eyed seeing (Bartlett et al., 2009). Finally, to provide a context for the consideration of these discourses, I offer the reader a window into a particular moment in my teaching practice that brought to the fore the importance of discussing spirituality in education.

Keywords: indigenous, spirit, Medicine Wheel, respect, relevance, reciprocity, responsibility, two-eyed seeing

NO TIME LIKE THE PRESENT

In the spring of 2021, as the global pandemic that began in 2019 seemed on the verge of receding, a new epidemic started to unfold in Canada with the discovery of 215 unmarked graves on the grounds of the former Kamloops Indian Residential School (IRS). As the months ticked by, more unmarked graves were found at former IRSs across the country, and the number of Indigenous deaths Canadians needed to reckon with kept growing. Seemingly in retaliation, a third epidemic emerged as several Catholic churches began to catch fire in communities across the country. First Nations, Inuit, and Métis folks who continue to practice Christianity, often right alongside traditional spiritual practices, found themselves targeted by angry community members for their participation in an institution that has inflicted so much damage on Indigenous peoples both in Canada and around the world. Of course, in most cases, those who continue to practice Christianity do so due to their own attendance, or their parents' attendance, at IRSs, also making them either survivors or intergenerational survivors.

While the complexity of this intersection definitely muddies the waters of talking about spirituality in teacher education classrooms, with the evidence of caustic outcomes so evident, I believe it is precisely within this space that such conversations are most important. In this chapter, I discuss three critical discourses in decolonizing education that illustrate why conversations about spirit are necessary for teacher education classrooms. The first is using the Medicine Wheel (Bopp & Bopp, 1989) as a framework for connecting learning to all aspects of a student's personhood. The second discourse links to the work of Dr. Verna Kirkness (Kirkness & Barnhardt, 1991), whose discussion of the four Rs, respect, relevance, reciprocity, and responsibility, offers essential considerations for ensuring the intellectual and cultural safety of Indigenous students and faculty, rooted in Indigenous values. The third discourse comes from the work of Mi'kmaq Elders Murdena and Albert Marshall and their notion of two-eyed seeing (Bartlett et al., 2012). In order to provide a context for the consideration of these discourses, I offer the reader a window into a particular moment in my own teaching practice that brought to the fore the importance of talking about spirituality in education. The approach of using stories in research is common in qualitative methods, most notably in Indigenous research methodologies. Indigenous scholars widely acknowledge the importance of stories in learning cultural histories and values (Archibald, 2008) and consider stories, in the general part of the education process (Cajete, 1994; Little Bear, 2000). In my own scholarship, I find stories helpful in illustrating the unity of theory and practice and the importance of reflection on practice.

Through these three Indigenous considerations for bringing discussions of spirit and spirituality into the teacher education classroom, I hope to offer an *ethical space* for engagement across differences. Willie Ermine (2007) defines ethics as "the capacity to know what harms or enhances the wellbeing of sentient creatures ... ethics entertains our personal capacity and our integrity to stand up for our cherished notions of good, responsibility, duty, obligation, etc." (p. 195). For Ermine and other Indigenous scholars, the notion of ethical space as a place of engagement is predicated on this view of ethics. It is intended to "trigger a dialogue that begins to set the parameters for an agreement to interact modeled on appropriate, ethical and human principles" (p. 202), aimed at deconstructing differences to facilitate moving forward.

MOVING FROM CLOSED TO OPEN STANCES

In my former life, I was a high school art and social studies teacher who also happened to teach a lot of English. In each of those discourses, issues of spirituality and the notion of spirit generally are not unfamiliar topics. As well, uncovering themes and biases in the work of writers, artists, and historians is a crucial aspect of learning in how social studies is taught. Raised by my white mother, and with 12 years of Catholic school under my belt as well as a growing practice in and understanding of Indigenous ceremony and spirituality linked to my Métis father and family, I felt well equipped to introduce the topic of spirituality as part of a holistic Indigenous framework in my postsecondary teacher education classroom. This might have been true if my class had only been comprised of teacher candidates in the arts and social sciences.

During my second year as an assistant professor responsible for my faculty's required course in Indigenous education, an illuminating dialogue unfolded during a class with several secondary science preservice teachers. I was discussing my work with the Medicine Wheel, moving through the Intellectual (North), Spiritual (East), Emotional (South), and Physical (West) aspects of self-hood, when one of the science educators raised his hand to express his discomfort with the notion of spirituality. A very interesting and sometimes spirited, if you will, discussion ensued. Together we raised a variety of ideas of spirit, including soul, zeitgeist, community feeling, emotional state, euphemisms for noncompliance, and distinctions between dogmatic religiosity and spirituality.

One student in particular found it challenging to unlink spirituality from connotations of Christianity and was concerned that such a concept had no place in a science classroom. In my experience, Indigenous spiritual traditions are quite distinct in practice from Judeo-Christian, Eastern, and other spiritual traditions in that they are generally not contained within purpose-built structures (although there are exceptions, such as sweat lodges) and are rooted in oral rather than textual modes of remembrance and transmission. Beyond these critical differences, there are also parallel but highly nuanced differences in notions of the divine, relative dogmatism, and animistic versus deistic worldviews, each worthy of deep exploration and none of which we had a lot of time for. In a moment of inspiration, I drew from my tiny bundle of scientific knowledge to ask the student if the earth was a closed system. The student agreed it was. I then asked if it was true that all energy was not lost. The student agreed it was. I then suggested that perhaps we could turn to the Greek notion of *animus*, the animating force of life and that we might name it "that which keeps your body from being a corpse" as a way to separate religious dogma from the notion of spirit. My goal was not to bring students to think as I do. Instead, I wanted to help them move from a closed stance on acceptable ontologies in a science classroom to an open stance where multiple ontological and epistemological positions offer enriched texture to scientific discourses and where students feel seen and welcome within these discussions.

Indigenous Discourses

Nehiyaw education scholar Cash Ahenakew (2017) offers a sound critique of Western and Indigenous ontology elements that require examination in the context of working in Indigenous education within faculties of education. He points to how Western perspectives, so dominant in curriculum, nurture in students the "desire for an ontological concrete: something solid, unchanging, unliving, that gives us meaning, purpose and control, as well as comforting notions of promise based on a linearity of past, present, and future" (p. 81). This positivist perspective is also pointed out in the work of Herman Michell (2018), a fellow Nehiyaw scholar, and in the work of Mi'kmaq scholar Marie Battiste (1998, 2013). Indigenous scholars raise these concerns because they form the locus for the exclusion of discussions about the spirit in both K–12 and postsecondary classrooms, except perhaps in those institutions rooted in the delivery of parochial curriculum. And for the many decades that Western and Eurocentric values and curriculum have dominated schooling, this exclusion has been accepted as good and right, and part of the larger project of moving towards a secular and capitalist social agenda. In fact, Donald (2019) offers a sharp critique of how recent Alberta curricular revisions manifest a plan rooted in capitalist economics, creating a new notion of the ideal citizen that leans sharply towards maintaining a colonial status quo.

The Many Ways to Talk About Spirit and Spirituality in Teacher Education 33

Now, however, with the advent of the United Nations Declaration on the Rights of Indigenous Peoples (2007), the Truth and Reconciliation Commission's Calls to Action (2015), and in the face of Canada's reckoning with a past that was hidden from all but Indigenous people, we need to rethink this position in relation to the impact it has, both historically and now, on Indigenous students in classrooms. These considerations are crucial where Indigenous students are present, obviously, but they are equally important in classrooms where no Indigenous students are present. Ethical space cannot emerge if one-half of the dialogue is not made aware that dialogue is required. In the following paragraphs, I unpack the three discourses suggested in the introduction to illustrate why incorporating spirituality in teacher education coursework and discussions is imperative.

From a very early age, I was aware of Medicine Wheels, both as archeological features of the Saskatchewan landscape, such as those around Waneskewin Heritage Park, just outside Saskatoon, but also as something that Indigenous people discussed as part of their cultural teachings. Some of these were shared with me when I was young, such as the notion of the four domains of holistic self-hood: Spiritual, Emotional, Physical, and Intellectual. I understood that the symmetry of the wheel was a reference to the need for balance between these quadrants and the parallels often drawn to seasons, directions, and so on. But as I grew and learned, eventually becoming a teacher, I began to understand on a much deeper level why these discussions are essential when thinking about the dynamics of a classroom. In fact, there is quite a lot written about the importance of this framework by authors such as Goulet and Goulet (2014), who build on the aspect of four to suggest the key relational elements in Indigenous education are "relationships with the student, relationships among students, connection to process, and connection to content" (pp. 86–87). Even earlier, Bopp et al. (1989) unpacked the Medicine Wheel and its teachings with the help of an extensive network of Indigenous Elders and Knowledge Keepers in their book, *The Sacred Tree*. These authors, and others who also rely on this framework, remind us that it is human beings we teach, not school subjects and that they are indeed prone to each of these elements of self-hood (Brendtro et al., 2005; Regnier, 1994). Over the decades, it has been challenging to include these conversations in schools and schooling, both because of a lack of capacity (we still do not have enough Indigenous people working as teachers) and because of the dominance of Western ontology. A curriculum that remains rooted in Christian and Eurocentric values and upholds whiteness as normative requires troubling; this is the aim of the dialogic creation of ethical space.

However, there have been some more recent successes in this arena, at least as far as theory is concerned. LaFever (2016) mapped Bloom's three domains of learning (cognitive, affective, and psychomotor) onto the Medicine Wheel to correspond with the intellectual, emotional, and physical, respectively, ultimately arguing that adding a spiritual domain to Bloom's framework offers a learning theory that is inclusive of both Indigenous and Western ontologies. Although her research clarifies that these two frameworks are compatible, securing students' understanding of this discourse within teacher education remains a challenge when their course work continues to be saturated with Western perspectives from educational psychology and subject area methodologies and curricular approaches. In many ways, this challenge remains rooted in the dominance of Western thought, which continues to hold Indigenous ontologies as inferior and even suspect. As Indigenous scholars point out, this is directly attributable to excluding Indigenous identities and histories from the Canadian curriculum (Battiste, 2000; Dion, 2009). These silences and erasures have paved the way for a grand ignorance in that it is easy not to care for those whom we do not know.

The Medicine Wheel offers students some insight into how Western and Indigenous ontologies differ. In addition to providing a holistic framework for considering a student as a whole person, Regnier (1994) suggests that the circle that forms the Medicine Wheel "symbolizes time as a form of the continual recurrence of natural patterns, such as the seasons, day and night, and life cycles from birth to death to rebirth" (p. 132). In other words, the circle *is* the spirit of the world.

In 1991, Verna Kirkness, the founder of NITEP (UBC's Indigenous Teacher Education Program), wrote, with Ray Barnhart, an exploration of the tension between the post-secondary educational institutions' tendency to say they welcome Indigenous students and Indigenous concepts while at the same time, maintaining a status quo that is determined to keep Indigenous people as subalterns. They introduced in this work the 4 Rs of Respect, Relevance, Reciprocity, and Responsibility. In addition to challenging the language of *coming* to the university, which implies a duty of hosting, versus *going* to university, which implies leaving home and community to attend, their discussion reveals the ways in which notions of hosting (and considering the obligations that role implies) are so important. In pointing to how universities often fail Indigenous students in this regard, they evoke an unpacking of the four Rs to illustrate that considering the impact of these critical values might also shift policy to be *actually*, rather than nominally, inclusive.

Respect, in this context, gets to the heart of why spirituality needs to be included in teacher education—it is a part of all Indigenous ontologies and often forms the backbone of our most fundamental teachings. Respect is the core of relational ethics, predicated on the understanding that we are all in this together—we are all related (Little Bear, 2000). It is one of the Seven Sacred Teachings (Bouchard, 2016) and discussions of respect are present in the work of all of the Indigenous authors cited thus far. So, a show of respect by the university would necessarily include consideration of this aspect of humanity. How can a student be expected to thrive if everything in the curriculum they are offered tells them they are wrong? How can Indigenous people form relationships with non-Indigenous people if they are also taught that Indigenous ways of knowing and being are wrong?

Relevance refers to the idea that the curriculum must be inclusive of Indigenous perspectives to be relevant to Indigenous students and highlight the relevance of Indigenous people in contemporary society. As suggested earlier, the exclusion of Indigenous voices, identities, and stories from the curriculum has paved the road for national ignorance and the profusion of stereotypes and mythologies that have prevented the formation of authentic and meaningful relationships between Indigenous and non-Indigenous people in Canada. Many Canadians have grown up with a curriculum that framed Indigenous peoples as "romanticized, mythical, victimized, or militant Other, [and] enable non-Aboriginal people to position themselves as a respectful admirer, moral helper, protector of law and order" (Dion, 2009, p. 331). A genuinely relevant curriculum must include Indigenous perspectives—most of which are tied to consideration of spirit.

This stance leads to the notion of reciprocity, in which receiving also requires giving back—that is, if universities wish to make space for the first two of these values by drawing on the knowledge of Indigenous peoples, then they must also be prepared to give something in return. For Kirkness and Barnhart (1991), learning goes both ways. Suppose students are willing to share their cultural knowledge. In that case, faculty are also responsible for sharing their institutional knowledge to genuinely encourage the success of Indigenous students by offering transparency. Celia Haig-Brown (2014) has further pointed to the need for non-Indigenous Canadians to acquire fluency in Indigenous ways of knowing and being. She notes that this is a step towards balancing the imposition of Western ways of knowing and being on Indigenous peoples through the ongoing process of colonization.

Administrators and faculty are responsible for participating through shifting policy and practice to be inclusive and consulting with Indigenous students and community members to determine what that means for them. Sharon Stein (2020) explicitly critiques the distance between declared institutional intentions towards inclusivity of Indigenous peoples and how such policies are actually enacted, or not enacted, in day-to-day operations. In particular, she notes that the burden of ensuring that inclusivity policies are followed most often falls on Indigenous peoples. Hence, there is a real need to ensure that this responsibility is shifted back onto the shoulders of non-Indigenous scholars and administrators. This concept is equally true of faculty, and Sheila Cote-Meek (2014), offers ample evidence of the damage caused to Indigenous students by Instructors who have not done their homework when it comes to working with Indigenous peoples, histories, and politics. She cites numerous experiences in which Indigenous students are left stunned by inaccurate and sometimes racist versions of Indigenous histories presented by ill-informed faculty and further abrogation of responsibility in shifting the burden of Indigenous representation onto students.

Each time I read Kirkness and Barnhart's (1991) work, I am reminded of another set of teachings that resonates strongly with their thinking. The Seven Sacred Teachings also offer a reference point for developing an ethical space framework: courage, love, wisdom, truth, honesty, respect, and humility (Bouchard, 2016). Imagine what it might mean if teachers and teacher educators actually considered these values each time they approached a classroom or the development of curricular resources for a classroom. Can any of these values be housed purely in the body or the intellect? Even the staunchest positivist may have difficulty arguing this.

I am also reminded here of the work of Teekens (2015), who speaks specifically about how each of these seven teachings is embodied in his practice as a powwow drummer. He shares the story of growing up as an urban Indigenous youth with little connection to his Ojibwe culture. However, his attraction to the work of a drum group when he went to his first powwow at the age of thirteen eventually led to joining a drum group as an undergraduate student. His discussion of the drum group's unconditional acceptance of him, and his gradual education about the relationship between drumming, the human spirit, and the seven teachings, speaks volumes about the importance of spirit in Indigenous lives. Further, as Teekens shares his story, it is clear that the absence of narratives such as his from the Canadian curriculum has left most Canadians with considerable gaps in their knowledge that continue to prevent the development of meaningful relationships with Indigenous peoples.

The third discourse, two-eyed-seeing, has been tremendously critical to my pedagogy in teacher education, especially in working with students who are resistant to moving beyond exclusively Western frames of thought. The notion that one can move to the third space in education informed equally by Western and Indigenous ways of knowing seems to offer comfort to those taking uncertain first steps. According to Mi'kmaq Elder Albert Marshall,

> Two-Eyed Seeing is the gift of multiple perspective treasured by many aboriginal peoples and explains that it refers to learning to see from one eye with the strengths of Indigenous knowledges and ways of knowing, and from the other eye with the strengths of Western knowledges and ways of knowing, and to using both these eyes together, for the benefit of all. (Bartlett et al., 2012, p. 335)

Perhaps more than the other two discourses discussed here, two-eyed seeing offers a clear invitation to non-Indigenous people. It is also a granting of permission to learn and to engage. It is an acknowledgment that we still have much to learn from one another. It is a reassurance that our ways of thinking and knowing are not mutually exclusive. It is the essence and realization of ethical space.

DIALOGUES ABOUT SPIRIT AS A DECOLONIZING DIALOGUES

The classroom moment described earlier has continued to resonate in my thinking about decolonizing teaching and learning in schools, and includes Indigenous voices, worldviews, and pedagogies in meaningful and respectful ways. Equally important is consideration of how to ensure that schools are inclusive and welcoming places for Indigenous students and other students who may bring non-Western ontologies to their learning. While I do suggest, along with Battiste (2013) and St. Denis (2011), that discussion of spirit is perhaps most appropriate when linked primarily to Indigenous peoples in the context of Canada, an additional benefit to framing such discussions with an Indigenous lens is that Indigenous pedagogies tend to be fundamentally inclusive. Finding ways to navigate conversations that include spiritual dimensions is necessary to establish trust relations that support deep learning. It is essential to model an open stance towards ontological difference, open discussion, and how teachers can facilitate collaborative understanding rather than needing to be "right." Stopping such dialogues breaks trust, stops learning, and foments disengagement. For teachers, acknowledging this relational reality is vital as we know what it feels like to realize we have let a student down or hurt them through lack of consideration. Such moments belie the spirit of teaching.

TEACHING FROM AN OPEN STANCE

In synthesizing the work of these scholars with my own practice and reflection, I conclude with the work of Manulani Aluli-Meyer (2013) and her notion of triangulation. First, we teach who we are, so we must know who we are to teach. For Aluli-Meyer, this involves coming to know oneself in relation to the land one is raised on, the people one is raised with, and the cultural knowledge one is inducted into. It is to acknowledge the interconnection of all things and the practice of living in ways that honor those interconnections. And there is increasing evidence from the field of quantum physics that shows this to be true (Cajete, 2004).

Instead of creating curricular discourses that reify Western cognitive imperialism (Battiste, 1998, 2013), we must help preservice teachers soften their teaching stance towards other ways of being in, seeing, and knowing the world. Doing so does not mean giving up rigor or fundamental principles, but it does mean accepting that our students are not reproductions of us. It means peeling back the layers of colonial logic to detect how exclusively positivist thought limits our ability to connect with our students across differences. Making space in teacher education classrooms to include discussions of spirit and spirituality disrupts dominant narratives rooted in Eurocentric normativity and dislodges the mythology of education as a neutral practice. It evokes decolonizing dialogues and transformative learning moments, and we must persist.

I want to conclude this discussion by returning to the work of Celia Haig-Brown (2010) and the adoption of a secondary discourse. In her writing, Haig-Brown offers a sound rationale for why it has been vital to her to learn Indigenous ways related to each geographic context in Canada in which she has lived. Fundamentally, she demonstrates what it means to come to grips with being a white person living in a colonized country. In recognizing the privileges she holds, she also articulates the responsibility that privilege entails. She notes that "many Indigenous people in Canada are within one or two generations of having a First Nation language as their first language and their primary discourse" (p. 934). To her and those who take their privilege seriously, there is a duty to balance this equation by ensuring that self-education about Indigenous peoples remains a central priority. Perhaps one of the most profound revelations of her work is her observation that:

> Not only do the physical manifestations of languages persist but so too do deeper discursive structures that allow some speakers new to English either to resist full acquisition of standard English, which itself is always in flux, as a primary discourse and instead to learn it in such a way that pays homage to older language patterns and usages ... to maintain some (unconscious perhaps) allegiance to the foundational language, discourse, epistemology, and worldview. (p. 934)

That is, the spirit of the primary discourse is preserved in how the secondary discourse is taken up, a stunning testament to Indigenous cultural survivance and resilience.

Haig-Brown's (2010) work affirms that it is indeed possible to adopt new perspectives—to maintain a self that is strong enough to hold but flexible enough to expand. In her conclusion, she offers a powerful summation of her thoughts:

> I am never Indigenous to a particular place in Canada, but I am often in a social situation that allows a potential for some proficiency in a secondary Discourse, secondary only in terms of learning it in relation to the one we learned at our mothers' knees. I have found as I moved from Secwepemc Territory in British Columbia to those of the Anishinaabe and Haudenosaune, much of what I had been taught had currency, served as a form of cultural capital that has allowed at least some First Nation people in those new places to recognize and accept me. (p. 945)

Circling back to the story from the teacher education classroom at the start of this work, in many ways, the discussion that unfolded that day never really found a resolution. We did not decide on an absolute definition of spirit or spirituality. We did not decide on how to field such discussions with students or develop a reliable script for their introduction. Instead, we placed focus together on the reasons "teachers must so emphasize the importance of persons becoming reflective enough to think about one's own thinking and become conscious of one's own consciousness" (Greene, 1995, p. 65). In the context of Indigenous education, part of my job is to reveal to students how the colonial tendrils of their K–12 education function to hold a status quo that keeps Indigenous people separate from other Canadians. The rest of my work involves helping teacher candidates find ways to decolonize their thinking, detect colonial messages in curricular resources, ensure accurate Indigenous representation, and include pedagogical approaches drawn from Indigenous knowledge systems. I try to help them do so better. In this work it is not necessary to have a clear notion of spirit and a solid rationale for its existence. Perhaps a certain level of ambiguity is even helpful. Creating learning opportunities and spaces that offer students the room they need to be and grow without policing what they may or may not wish to explore is the ethical space we hope for. That is the spirit of the dance we must learn to dance together.

REFERENCES

Ahenakew, C. R. (2017). Mapping and complicating conversations about Indigenous education. *Diaspora, Indigenous, and Minority Education, 11*(2), 80–91. https://doi.org/10.1080/15595692.2017.1278693

Archibald, J. A. (2008). *Indigenous storywork: Educating the heart, mind, body, and spirit.* UBC Press.

Bartlett, C., Marshall, M., & Marshall, A. (2012). Two-eyed seeing and other lessons learned within a co-learning journey of bringing together indigenous and mainstream knowledges and ways of knowing. *Journal of Environmental Studies and Sciences*, *2*(4), 331–340. https://doi.org/10.1007/s13412-012-0086-8

Battiste, M. (1998). Enabling the autumn seed: Toward a decolonized approach to Aboriginal knowledge, language, and education. *Canadian Journal of Native Education/Revue canadienne de l'éducation*, *22*(1), 16–27.

Battiste, M. (2000). Maintaining Aboriginal identity, language, and culture in modern society. In M. Battiste (Ed.), *Reclaiming Indigenous voice and vision*. UBC Press.

Battiste, M. (2013). *Decolonizing education: Nourishing the learning spirit*. Purich Press.

Brendtro, L. K., Brokenleg, M., & Van Bockern, S. (2005). The circle of courage and positive psychology. *Reclaiming Children and Youth*, *14*(3), 130–136.

Bopp, J., & Bopp, M. (1989). *The sacred tree*. Lotus Press.

Bouchard, D. (2016). *Seven Sacred Teachings*. Crow Cottage.

Cajete, G. (1994). *Look to the mountain: An ecology of indigenous education*. Kivaki Press.

Cajete, G. (2004). Philosophy of native science. In A. Waters (Ed.), *American Indian thought* (pp. 45–57). Blackwell.

Cote-Meek, S. (2014). *Colonized classrooms: Racism, trauma and resistance in post-secondary education*. Fernwood.

Dion, S. D. (2009). *Braiding histories: Learning from Aboriginal peoples' experiences & perspectives*. UBC Press.

Donald, D. (2019). 5 Homo Economicus and Forgetful Curriculum. In H. Tomlins-Jahnke, S. Styres, S. Lilley, & D. Zinga (Eds.), *Indigenous education: New directions in theory and practice* (pp. 103–125). University of Alberta Press.

Ermine, W. (2007). The ethical space of engagement. *Indigenous Law Journal*, *6*, 193–203.

Goulet, L. M., & Goulet, K. N. (2014). *Teaching each other: Nehinuw concepts and Indigenous pedagogies*. UBC Press.

Greene, M. (1995). *Releasing the imagination: Essays on education, the arts, and social change* (The Jossey-Bass Education Series). Jossey-Bass.

Haig-Brown, C. (2010). Indigenous thought, appropriation, and non-Aboriginal people. *Canadian Journal of Education*, *33*(4), 925–950.

Kirkness, V. J., & Barnhardt, R. (1991). First Nations and higher education: The four R's—Respect, relevance, reciprocity, responsibility. *Journal of American Indian Education*, 1-15.

LaFever, M. (2016). Switching from Bloom to the medicine wheel: Creating learning outcomes that support Indigenous ways of knowing in post-secondary education. *Intercultural Education*, *27*(5), 409–424. https://doi.org/10.1080/14675986.2016.1240496

Little Bear, L. (2000). Jagged worldviews colliding. In M. Battiste (Ed.), *Reclaiming Indigenous voice and vision* (pp. 77–85). UBC Press.

Meyer, M. A. (2013). The context within: My journey into research. In D. M. Mertens, F. Cram, B. Chilisa (Eds.), *Indigenous pathways into social research: Voices of a new generation* (pp. 249–260). Left Coast Press.

Michell, H. (2018). *Land-based education: Embracing the rhythms of the earth from an Indigenous perspective*. JCharlton.

Regnier, R. (1994). The sacred circle: A process pedagogy of healing. *Interchange, 25*(2), 129–144. https://doi.org/10.1007/BF01534540

St. Denis, V. (2011). Silencing Aboriginal curricular content and perspectives through multiculturalism: "There are other children here". *Review of Education, Pedagogy, and Cultural Studies, 33*(4), 306–317.

Stein, S. (2020). 'Truth before reconciliation': The difficulties of transforming higher education in settler colonial contexts. *Higher Education Research & Development, 39*(1), 156–170.

Teekkens, S. (2015). Drumming 101. D. H. Taylor (Ed.), *Me artsy* (pp. 175–191). Douglas & McIntyre.

CHAPTER 3

THE ELECTRICITY OF THE RELIGIOUS EDUCATION CLASSROOM

Lessons From Buber and Levinas

Mary Shanahan
St Angela's College, Sligo

ABSTRACT

Drawing on Buber's well-known claim that "[w]hen two people relate to each other authentically and humanly, God is the electricity that surges between them" (Buber, 2004), I argue that the relationship between the teacher and student is essentially a spiritual one. Taking on board Buber's call for a reciprocal, ethical relationship between self and Other, I explore how the teacher and student enter into an ethically educational relationship, through which both experience the development of their spirituality. To counter Buber's insistence that the ethical human relationship must be reciprocal, I examine Levinas's powerful argument against reciprocity and in favor of absolute ethical responsibility. Drawing on the Levinasian appropriation of otherness, I investigate his presentation of the self-Other encounter in an educational context. To concretize my claims, I turn to the Irish education system by appealing to the provision of religious education as a repository of spiritual development at the high school level. Drawing upon the accounts of spiritual development provided by Buber and Levinas, I will suggest that religious

---

Rekindling Embers of the Soul:
An Examination of Spirituality Issues Relating to Teacher Education, pp. 43–62
Copyright © 2024 by Information Age Publishing
www.infoagepub.com
All rights of reproduction in any form reserved.

education offers a space where teachers and students can develop their ethical and spiritual potential.

Keywords: Buber, Levinas, Irish education system, reciprocity; religious, education, responsibility, spirituality.

INTRODUCTION

The relationship between the teacher and the student forms the bedrock of their interactions within the classroom. Particularly in the religious education classroom, these interactions have the power to shape both the teacher's and the student's moral and spiritual development. In this chapter, I seek to examine the spiritual dimension of this mutual development by appealing to the concept of reciprocity. This concept lies at the heart of the central claims of the philosophies of Martin Buber and Emmanuel Levinas; however, like the "two roads [which] diverged in a yellow wood" (Frost, 2015, p. 87), they each take a very different stance in relation to this reciprocity.

Buber makes the evocative claim that "[w]hen two people relate to each other authentically and humanly, God is the electricity that surges between them" (Buber, 2004). Drawing on this claim, I will argue that this "electricity" renders the relationship between the teacher and student a spiritual one. Taking on board Buber's call for a reciprocal, ethical relationship between self and Other, I seek to show how the teacher and student enter into an ethically educational relationship through which both experience the development of their spirituality. I will hold, alongside Buber, that reciprocity is the key to developing an ethical (and thereby spiritual) relationship. Going further, I will hold that, given the nature of the subject matter, the religious education classroom provides a particularly unique space to nurture both this relationship and the individuals who participate in it (that is, the teacher and the student).

Although Levinas has much to say about the ethical significance of education (particularly Jewish religious education), he counters Buber's insistence that the ethical human relationship must be reciprocal. Instead, Levinas makes a powerful argument against reciprocity in favor of responsibility. I will call this rejection of reciprocity into question by drawing on the Levinasian appropriation of education and investigating his presentation of the Other as a teacher. Furthermore, I will attempt to offer an alternative to Levinas's position regarding reciprocity by appealing to Buber's presentation of the self-Other relationship.

To concretize the claims I make here, I will turn to the Irish education system, focusing mainly on the provision of religious education as an examinable subject at the high school level. According to the then Department of Education and Science (now the Department of Education and Skills), a key aim of education is to "foster an understanding and critical appreciation of the values—moral, spiritual, religious, social and cultural—which have ... traditionally been accorded respect in society" (DES, 1995, p. 12). According to numerous government documents, religious education is best placed to focus on these values across all years of the high school curriculum (see DES, 2003). Concentrating on the spiritual dimension of religious education, I bring this subject into conversation with Buber and Levinas by focusing on the relationship between the religious education teacher and the student.

By drawing upon the accounts of spirituality—particularly in the context of relation(ship)s and education—provided by Buber and Levinas, I will suggest that religious education offers a space in which the spiritual potential of teacher and student can be developed. Holding the view, alongside Buber and contra Levinas, that the teacher-student relationship is reciprocal, I will argue that religious education is uniquely poised to provide both spiritual education and spiritual nourishment. As a subject "like no other" (Sullivan, 2017, pp. 7–24), religious education opens up a space in which spirituality is discussed and experienced by both teacher and student. By appealing to Buber and Levinas, I aim to highlight the depth of the spiritual encounter between the teacher and the student and the 'vast' complexity of the spiritual dimension of the religious education classroom.

SPIRITUALITY AND ETHICAL EDUCATION IN BUBER AND LEVINAS

Let me commence my investigation by considering the accounts of spirituality and education that Buber and Levinas provide. Indebted to their shared tradition, both thinkers draw heavily upon Jewish interpretations of both spirituality and education. Additionally, Buber and Levinas bring the Jewish tradition into fruitful conversation with philosophy, both arriving at nuanced readings of spiritually informed education's ethical and philosophical implications. However, despite their many points of convergence—notably the importance of a divinely informed and inspired connection between self and Other—there are significant points of conflict to be found between both "thinkers" presentation of the self-Other relation(ship).

Reading the Spiritual in Buber and Levinas

Buber and Levinas make it clear that the self and the Other (rendered as "I" and "thou/Thou" by Buber) are connected to one and other, and that this connection is rendered possible by God (or, as Levinas frequently writes, the Infinite). For both thinkers, this connection is the foundation for one's development as an ethical self, and, as such, it opens up the possibility of ethical education. However, while Buber describes the connection in reciprocal terms, Levinas is highly suspicious of the demands which may issue from a reciprocal relationship. As a result, Levinas rejects any form of reciprocity in the ethical connection between self and Other. Interestingly, and despite this significant point of divergence, both Buber and Levinas uphold God as the highest point of existence, which informs all of our human relations and opens up the possibility of our ethical existence alongside one another.

Like Levinas, Buber is fascinated by the relationship between self and Other, and self and God, and insists that the highest form of human relationship is an ethical one. Characterizing this ethical relationship as an "I-Thou" relationship, Buber emphasizes its reciprocal nature, contending that: "[r]elationship is reciprocity. My Thou acts on me as I act on it" (Buber, 2004, p. 67). In the "I-Thou" relationship, both the self and the Other relate to one another respectfully and ethically. This does not introduce a "competitive" element to the relationship, and neither does it, as Levinas suspects, render the self as a demanding or expectant participant. Instead, claims Buber, the ethical relationship between self and Other is a spiritual one that requires the participation of both parties to ensure their ethical development because "every particular *Thou* is a glimpse through to the eternal *Thou*" (Buber, 2004, p. 99). Interestingly, reciprocity aside, Levinas takes a similar view, commenting that: "[the] trace [of Infinity/God] lights up as the face of a neighbor" (Levinas, 1998, p. 12). Thus, for both thinkers, there is something intrinsically spiritual about the encounter with another person.

However, while inspired by Buber's spiritual presentation of the self-Other relationship, Levinas does not share his commitment to the reciprocal development of the self and the Other. For Levinas, there is a fundamental asymmetry to the self-Other relation, which reflects, to a certain extent, the asymmetry of the relationship between humanity and divinity. There can be no mutual development arising from, or participation in, the ethical relationship between self and Other because there is a "fundamental inequality of terms" (Levinas, 1969, p. 218). While, for Buber, I am not ultimately responsible for the other's spiritual or ethical development, for Levinas, my responsibility for this Other is all-consuming. It forms the heart of my ethical life. Thus, while

Levinas and Buber appear to operate with a similar starting point vis-à-vis God as the absolute Other and source of our ethical relation(ship)s with Others, their accounts of such relationships are dramatically different. The kernel of this difference would appear to be their very different readings of the related concepts of reciprocity and responsibility.

A Tale of Two Cities: Responsibility and Reciprocity

While Buber accepts responsibility as an aspect of the relationship between self and Other, contrary to Levinas, he argues that responsibility is reciprocal. For example, in *Between Man and Man*, he notes that "[g]enuine responsibility exists only where there is real responding" (Buber, 1955, p. 18). As far as Buber is concerned, both parties in the relationship retain responsibility for their own ethical development, but, at the same time, they are mutually invested in the work of helping one another to live an ethical and spiritual life. The self is not, however, *more* responsible for the other than they are for themselves.

Such a line of thinking is unacceptable to Levinas, who argues that the self is not only responsible for the Other, but absolutely so. Therefore, the self cannot, and should not, expect a reciprocal measure of responsibility from the Other. As Levinas (2001) puts it: "therefore, *I* am responsible, and may not be concerned about whether the Other is responsible for me. The human, in the highest, strictest sense of the word, is without reciprocity" (pp. 130–139). Such a claim contrasts Buber's claim that reciprocity, knitted together with responsibility, is part and parcel of the ethical interaction between "I" (self) and "Thou" (Other).

In Levinas's thinking, responsibility and reciprocity must be uncoupled, partly because of the phenomenological accounts of the self-Other relationship that Levinas seeks to move beyond. But, more than this, Levinas insists that the absolute difference between self and Other can never, and should never, be either diminished or overcome. As far as Levinas is concerned, reciprocity opens the floodgates to reducing the Other to a "sameness," which he finds morally reprehensible. Hammering this point home in *Time and the Other*, Levinas makes the following claim:

> To be sure, the other that is announced does not possess this existing as the subject possesses it; its hold over my existing is mysterious. It is not unknown but unknowable, refractory to all light. But this precisely indicates that the other is in no way another myself, participating with me in a common existence. (Levinas, 1987, p. 75)

Such an outright rejection of reciprocity (or a "common existence") is most certainly problematic for the claims I will be making about the spiritual development of the teacher and the student in the religious education classroom. As I will argue, a measure of reciprocity is key to the spiritual development (growth?) of both the teacher and the student. As Levinas would suggest, this does not reduce each individual's uniqueness, nor does it compromise their ethical responsibility for one another. Instead, as Buber has suggested, such reciprocity allows for the completion of the "circuit" through which the spiritual "electricity" of the classroom flows. It opens up the possibility of spiritual development (though not necessarily equal) that benefits both the teacher and the student and nourishes the religious education classroom environment in which they find themselves.

A QUESTION OF RELATION: TEACHERS, STUDENTS, AND THE SPIRITUAL DYNAMIC OF THE CLASSROOM

I move now towards the domain of the religious education classroom proper. I must, therefore, ask: what do Levinas and Buber have to say about teaching and learning? More pointedly, I must ask: "how do their comments about teaching and learning relate to the spiritual dimension of the religious education classroom?" In answering both of these questions, I will highlight their differing perspectives on the role and function of both the student and the teacher in the learning encounter. More particularly, I will pay close attention to the interrelatedness between ethical development and education, which is evident in both Levinas's and Buber's work. In both cases, such interrelatedness is intimately (and perhaps innately) correlated with spirituality.

The Call to Ethical Education

The question of education is one that inspired both Buber and Levinas, with each writing (to greater and lesser extents) on the theme and invariably merging the issue of education with that of ethical development (see Buber, 1955, 1965, 1980; Levinas, 1969, 1998). Both thinkers also view education as essential and cast it as playing a significant role in the ethical development of individuals. Furthermore, ethical development and thereby education, is deemed by Buber and Levinas to take place in a spiritual context given the implicit involvement of the divine in all self-Other encounters (irrespective of whether or not the individuals engaging in such encounters recognize or accept this). Yet, it is essential to note that, as is often the case in his writing and over-arching philosophical style, Levinas adopts a somewhat less structured or formalized account of education than Buber's.

This somewhat enigmatic description of education reflects Levinas's insistence upon the "unknowability" of the Other by the self. Unsurprisingly, the Other is the focal point in Levinas's account of education, but, strikingly, the Other is presented as a teacher. It is the Other who teaches me that I am responsible for her/him. Commenting on Levinas's characterization of the Other as a teacher, Tanja Staehler has written the following about the contents of the Other's teaching:

> What does it mean for teaching if the Good beyond Being is that which is ultimately taught? It means that the Other teaches me, but that the Other does not just teach me about himself or herself. The Other teaches me about ethics, about radical calling into question, and about that which exceeds all Being: the Good. (Staehler, 2010, p. 77)

Staehler (2010) correctly highlights the core links between the questions of ethics and alterity, which are found at the heart of Levinas's work. The good beyond being (a term which Levinas borrows from Plato) is a phrase used evocatively by Levinas and is closely connected to his thinking in relation to Infinity/God and responsibility. What I learn from the Other is that I am responsible for him/her, and I cannot escape from this. While I might well choose to ignore the responsibility to which the Other calls me, I remain responsible. More than this, the Other teaches me about the source of this responsibility: God. In other words, my encounters with the Other are not simply reminders of my ethical responsibility for them or opportunities for moral development; they are more than this: they are encounters with the divine.

Yet, while this is a highly significant educational encounter, it is rarely described in terms that we might delineate as positive by Levinas. Instead, we read that, as a consequence of my encounters with the teacher-Other, I learn that I carry the weight of ethical responsibility. This debt can never be repaid, and this responsibility is mine long before I engage in a face-to-face encounter with the Other (cf. Levinas, 1998). Levinas describes such responsibility in very stark terms, who writes that "[t]he self is *sub-jectum*; it is under the weight of the universe, responsible for everything" (p. 116). While this description is not offered during a discussion of education, Levinas holds firm to this view of the responsible self across his *oeuvre*. From the religious education classroom perspective, such a view is troubling, given its potential to overwhelm the student. In addition, there appears to be a lack of concern for the mutual development of self and Other, which Levinas has already intimated in his denial of ethical reciprocity.

Buber, on the other hand, while most certainly ascribing a weighty significance to the encounter between self and Other, casts the educational potential of such in quite different terms. With his emphasis on dialogue, the "Between," and the need for a reciprocally responsible relationship between self and Other, Buber (2004) presents an account of education that highlights the importance of both parties (student and teacher) in the educational encounter. As he writes, "all real living is meeting" (p. 17). So each encounter presents the teacher and the student with an opportunity for growth and development—ethically and spiritually—because "every particular *Thou* is a glimpse through to the eternal *Thou*" (p. 99). As Buber points out in his famed essay "Education," such development cannot occur to an equal extent for the teacher and the student, given the asymmetrical nature of their relationship does not negate its significance (cf. Buber, 1955).

Notably, the spiritual is much at the heart of the I-Thou relationship in the classroom as it is outside of it. Emphasizing this point, Buber (1955) writes that the teacher "is set in the *imitatio Dei absconditi sed non ignoti* [the imitation of a God hidden but not unknown]" (p. 103). The teacher, it would seem, thus carries a grave responsibility to his/her student, and s/he must recognize this if they are to bring about dialogue within the classroom, for such dialogue successfully leads to ethical development on the part of the student. Bringing his point to bear more forcefully, Buber goes on to make the following claim regarding the teacher's role in the classroom: "[m]an, the creature, who forms and transforms the Creation, cannot himself create; but every person can expose himself and others to the creative spirit" (p. 103). This creative spirit (which, in its openness to God, opens the self to the ethical) is nurtured in the student by the teacher via dialogue, the basis of which is reciprocity. In Buber's framework, there can be no ethical or spiritual development without reciprocal dialogue. Put differently, the I-Thou relation(ship) is necessarily dialogical (cf. Buber, 2004, p. 20). What better place to nourish this dialogical relationship than the classroom?

The Teacher and the Student: A Spiritual Circuit Board?

The proximal space of the classroom is an interesting domain for both the teacher and the student. As I have noted, Buber highlights a fundamental asymmetry inherent to the teacher-student relationship. Therefore, it seems reasonable to assert that this asymmetry also properly extends to the classroom environment. Similarly, Levinas emphasizes the fundamental asymmetry at the heart of the teacher-student encounter (though, as I have shown, his asymmetry account is somewhat more extreme than that of Buber). How, then, when both thinkers propose a fundamental asymmetry in the relationship/encounter, can I hold the teacher-student relationship as a "spiritual circuit board?"

Indeed, in general, a "circuit" or "circuit board" implies a certain level of completion, which is not my intention to invoke here. But, like Buber and Levinas, I believe a relationship can never be deemed fully "complete" or "completed." There is always something more, something ineffable, which informs but exceeds the limits of the self and the Other engaged in the encounter. This includes the educational encounter between a teacher and a student. Nevertheless, there is a sense of spiritual continuity at the heart of self-Other (or I-Thou) encounters which bespeaks a certain circularity. Let me turn to Buber first to explain better the point I am trying to make here.

Earlier, I cited Buber's (2004) interesting remark: "every particular *Thou* is a glimpse through to the eternal *Thou*" (p. 99). In other words, when I am engaged in an "I-Thou" encounter, I engage not only with another human person as "Thou" but also with the ultimate and absolute "Thou," God. In responding to their student as "Thou" rather than as "It," the teacher recognizes the otherness of the student and the spiritual significance of the encounter as a genuine "I-Thou" relation. Commenting on this, Buber observes that: "[s]pirit in its human manifestation is man's response to his Thou ... it [the spirit] is the response to the Thou that appears from mystery and addresses us from the mystery" (Buber, 2004, p. 36). Therefore, there is a mystery at the heart of the "I-Thou" relation between the teacher and the student. And the relation is informed by such. Notably, this mystery is not a solvable one, nor is it meant to be. Both the mystery of the human Thou who presents themselves to their teacher as Other and the mystery of the divine being which renders such an encounter possible retain their mysteriousness at all times. Of course, it must also be noted that while the divine remains a mystery to us, and there is something inherently mysterious in the self-Other connection, our relationships and selves are not a mystery to God.

Yet, it is the ultimate mystery that, in Buber's (2004) own words, connects us to one another. As he writes in the "Postscript" to *I and Thou*, the I-Thou relation highlights "the close connection of the relation to God with the relation to one's fellow man" (pp. 123–124). In a rather circuit-like manner, the self is confronted by the mystery of the Other in the I-Thou relation. In like manner (and here we see the centrality of reciprocity in Buber's work), the Other is confronted by the mystery of the self. Additionally, the more deeply they engage in the I-Thou relation, the more both self and Other are confronted by the divine mystery (or "electricity" which flows between them. Importantly, and this is key to the educational rendering of the I-Thou relation, the self and the Other (or the teacher and the student) do not have to experience an equal sense of either the mystery of one another or the ultimate mystery of the divine in order to be connected by it. That they relate to one another as I and Thou, as mysterious and mystery-informed beings, is sufficient for their encounter to be deemed spiritual and ethically potent. Thus, the possibility of spiritual and ethical development remains open to both the teacher and the student (even if to unequal extents).

Deeply inspired by Buber, many of Levinas's initial steps in his description of the self-Other encounter mirror his predecessor's. Like Buber, in the Levinasian face-to-face encounter, there is a strong emphasis on the mystery of both the human Other and the absolute Other (God), which informs it. For example, when attempting to describe the indescribable mystery of the transcendent, Levinas writes, "Infinity is characteristic of a transcendent being as transcendent; the infinite is the absolutely other. The transcendent is the sole *ideatum* of which there can be only an idea in us" (Levinas, 1969, p. 49). Here, Levinas characterizes the divine as both infinity and a transcendent being, the absolutely other. Importantly, and again similarly to Buber, Levinas places this absolute Other (God) above the human Other I encounter daily. Through my encounter with this human Other, my spirit is struck by something of this infinity. In other words, I am deliberately invoking Buber here; the mystery of divinity that is opened up to me by the Other's face brings me to an awareness of the connection between the Other who stands before me and the Other *par excellence*, "the being above being" (Levinas, 1969, p. 218). In *Totality and Infinity*, Levinas (1969) writes: "[t]here can be no 'knowledge' of God separated from the relationship with men. The Other is the very locus of metaphysical truth and is indispensable [*indispensable*] for my relationship with God" (p. 78). Yet here, we also reach the critical point of divergence from Levinas's Buberian inspiration, which is rooted in the question of asymmetry.

Levinasian asymmetry is of fundamental importance to the 'structure' (and I use this term very lightly here) of the self-Other relation. The asymmetrical nature of the relation renders reciprocity both unethical and impossible, as far as Levinas is concerned. In such relations, the self must exponentially give while the Other continuously receives; there can be no reversal of these terms, and thus there cannot be any form of reciprocity (see Levinas 1969). Such inequality is fundamental, including in self-Other educational encounters between teachers and students. As Levinas economically puts it, "[t]he face-to-face is not a co-existence" (Levinas, 1969, p. 305).

In addition, Levinas argues that the self-Other relation is not completable as a relationship because of the persistent gap (ontological, epistemological, and ethical). However, I am compelled to ask, "Does incompleteness necessarily close off the possibility of a reciprocal relationship?" Returning to Levinas's claim that there can be no knowledge of God separated from the relationship with men, I am reminded of Buber's emphasis on the importance of reciprocity and the abiding mystery at the heart of the I-Thou relation. Allow me to elaborate.

As Levinas clearly states that one cannot know God (absolute transcendence) apart from his/her relationships with others, then is it not the case that others cannot know God apart from their relationship with the individual? Surely Levinas does not wish to argue that the Other is necessarily prevented from coming to intuit God. No doubt this is not what he intends, but it remains the case that he refuses to discuss such possibilities for the Other here. What can we make of this appeal to the fundamental importance of relationships (and, by implication, reciprocity) by the thinker of non-reciprocity *par excellence*? Is it the case that, against his better judgment, Levinas has left a space open within his theory for reciprocity? If this is so, it may be reasonable to assert that Levinas has not departed quite as drastically from Buber as it might initially appear.

Further, if I am invoking my earlier reference to Staehler's (2010) work, I can be taught by the Other. The content of that teaching is God/the Good (about whom I can only know because of my relationships with other persons). Indeed, there is something akin to the reciprocal occurring between us. To explore this idea further, I will now turn to my consideration of the religious education classroom proper.

THE IRISH WAY: RELIGIOUS EDUCATION, LEVINAS, AND BUBER IN CONVERSATION

To begin, I want to consider how Irish high school religious education syllabi have attempted to take account of the spiritual potential of the classroom and the impact of such on the teacher-student relationship. In so doing, I will note the effect of recent changes to the approach being brought to religious education at the high school level and consider the extent to which these changes support the spiritual development of students. Finally, I will conclude by suggesting how Levinas's and Buber's perspectives on the spiritual nature of the teacher-student relationship can be positively brought to bear on the Irish religious education classroom.

An Irish Approach to Spiritual Education: Religious Education, Spirituality, and the Classroom

Modern Ireland is a pluralistic and liberally democratic society that is undergoing a period of rapid change. Though still very much connected to its predominantly Roman Catholic Christian past, several recent political moves have further separated the state's business from the Church (the 2015 Marriage Equality Referendum and the 2018 Abortion Referendum, for example). In the sphere of education, however, the "battle" continues to rage between those who wish to establish a fully nondenominational system and those who want to retain the roughly 50–50 split between denominational and multidenominational schools at the high school level (Houses of the Oireachtas, 2020). Unfortunately, religious education is caught up in this rather intense situation due to its historical association with Catholic denominational provision and formation. Furthermore, because of this challenging context, it will not be surprising to learn that the question of spirituality—particularly spiritual development—in the religious education classroom is contentious.

The first point to note regarding this matter is that "spiritual development" is used several times in Irish Government documents pertaining to the entire education system and religious education specifically. The 1995 white paper on education, *Charting Our Education Future* states that the role of education is to: "foster an understanding and critical appreciation of the values—moral, spiritual, religious, social and cultural—which have ... traditionally been accorded respect in society" (DES, 1995, p. 12). When focusing on the junior years of the high school curriculum, the document clearly states, "[t]he Junior Certificate Programme also contributes to the moral and spiritual development of students" (p. 46). The same document highlights that, during these junior years, students "will have achieved or experienced ... formative experiences in moral, religious, and spiritual education" (DES, 1995, p. 50). It is important to note, however, that while the Christian heritage of the Irish education system is acknowledged in this white paper and religious education syllabi documents, the issue of students' spiritual development and experiences does not align with any particular religious denomination.

Regrettably, the Irish Government has not published an updated white paper on the education system. Despite this, much has changed in the Irish educational landscape since 1995, particularly in relation to religious education. The introduction of the new *Framework for Junior Cycle* (to replace the somewhat outdated Junior Certificate program) in 2015 ushered in a new curriculum for junior students in high school. Interestingly, rather like the 1995, the *Framework* document highlighted the importance of spirituality in the curriculum, listing being spiritual as one of the elements of the critical skill, "Staying Well" (DES, 2015). In addition, in 2018, a new syllabus for religious education in the junior years of high school was launched: *Junior Cycle Religious Education Specification* (DES, 2018). The new *Specification*, like its predecessor, the *Junior Certificate Religious Education Syllabus* (DES, 2000), emphasizes the importance of the spiritual development of the students. Most interestingly, the new *Specification* also includes a glossary of terms that offers the following careful definition of the term spiritual:

> Indicates a sense of relatedness to something bigger than the self. For some, this may be in relation to their understanding of the Divine. For others the relationship is with a power or presence. All religions seek to foster a spiritual life, although spiritual can also refer to something other than religious affiliation. It refers to a quality beyond the material and the mundane that strives for inspiration, reverence, awe, meaning and purpose. (DES, 2018, p. 29)

The last line of the definition is of particular significance when considered in the context of the Buberian and Levinasian frameworks I have been discussing: "[i]t refers to a quality beyond the material and the mundane that strives for inspiration, reverence, awe, meaning and purpose" (DES, 2018, p. 29). While the glossary definition provides this line as a point of clarification regarding non-theistic and/or non-religious conceptions of the spiritual, the language used is reminiscent of the various ways Buber and Levinas have described both the divine and the spiritual nature of the self-Other encounter. What might this mean in the context of the religious education classroom?

Undeniably, the spiritual encounter between the teacher and the student is complex and lies at the heart of the religious education classroom. It is undeniable that there are many forms of spirituality (religious, secular, or somewhere in between the two) and that spirituality is itself defined in many different ways (cf. Council of Europe, 2014, p. 29; see also Lipiäinen et al., 2020). However, despite my focus on Jewish spirituality, which is clearly at play in Buber's and Levinas's work, it is not my intention in this chapter to privilege one form of spirituality over another. Indeed, what strikes me about the definition in the *Specification* is its openness. The definition would seem to concur with the recent work of Watson (2009a, 2009b, 2010), who holds that a spiritual education approach rooted in interfaith dialogue opens up the religious education classroom to all. Like Byrne (2021), I hold that the new *Specification* provides ample opportunities for the spiritual development of students. Such work is continued in the senior cycle, with a core aim of the *Leaving Certificate Religious Education Syllabus* being: "[t]o contribute to the spiritual and moral development of the student" (DES, 2003, p. 5). Yet, this can only be the case if the religious education teachers concerned acknowledge and commit themselves to this task.

Recognizing the enormity of the task faced by the religious education teacher, Michael Grimmitt, outlines various approaches to teaching and learning about religions and beliefs. Identifying three fundamental approaches—learning religion, learning about religion, and learning from religion—Grimmitt emphasizes learning from religion as the most appropriate approach to teaching and learning in the religious education classroom (see Grimmitt, 1981, 1987, 2000, 2010; see also Teece, 2010). Notably, Grimmitt (1987) highlights the spiritual dimension of religious education as a critical component of the learning from religion approach. For Grimmitt, the best kind of religious education classroom is one in which students are encouraged to discern "signals of transcendence" and be able "to discern a spiritual dimension" (p. 225). Meanwhile, Dermot Lane builds upon the learning from religion approach by developing a "learning into" approach which places spirituality at the core of the religious education classroom (see Lane, 2013). Such openness to the spiritual dimension and the signals of transcendence is unmistakably present in the student-teacher relation(ship)s outlined by Buber and Levinas.

Learning With and From Buber and Levinas: Concluding Remarks on the Spiritual Relation as Learning Encounter

Thus far, I have shown that, for both Buber and Levinas, the connection between one person and another is necessarily a spiritual one that is opened up by the divine. I have also demonstrated that in their conceptions of the teacher-student encounter, and despite their differences regarding the role of reciprocity, Buber and Levinas emphasize the spiritual nature of the encounter. Further, I have highlighted that, in Ireland, the Government documents pertaining to religious education emphasize spirituality and spiritual development as the subject's core elements. In so doing, I have raised the question of the extent to which the spiritual dimension of the classroom and the spiritual development of the student and the teacher is sufficiently recognized.

It strikes me that, with the rolling out of the new *Specification* and its renewed emphasis on spiritual experiences and development, Irish religious education teachers have an opportunity to commit themselves more deeply to entering into spiritual encounters with their students (both religious and not). How this might be achieved, I would wager, can be gleaned from a close examination of Buber's and Levinas's descriptions of the self-Other education encounter. For one thing, both Buber and Levinas highlight the importance of recognizing the significance of the encounter with the Other's radical difference or alterity. For both thinkers, there is something sacred about the encounter with the Other, including the encounter between teacher and student. Lee (1985a) captures something of this line of thinking in his consideration of the spirituality of the religious education teacher. He writes, "the scope of the content of religious instruction is the religious instruction act itself because it is in this total concrete existential situation that the learner's religious experience occurs" (pp. 1–2). Borrowing from the language of the *Specification*, what I am suggesting is that Buber's and Levinas's emphasis on the magnitude of the self-Other encounter in the educational setting opens up the classroom as a space in which the teacher and the student can actively consider their mutual "sense of relatedness to something bigger than the self" (DES, 2018, p. 29).

If religious education teachers are to provide an adequate spiritual education for their students, then these Buberian and Levinasian "lessons" cannot be overlooked. Practically speaking, this will require the selection of content and pedagogies which both recognize and value difference, otherness, and dialogue. Student-centered pedagogies such as debates, learning centers, jigsaw group work, peer teaching, role plays, and simulation games will be critical to this endeavor. With each of these pedagogies, the student's voice and ability to engage in dialogue are essential. Additionally, these pedagogies largely require the creation of smaller sub-groups within the main class group, providing even safer spaces for sharing spiritual beliefs, values, and attitudes. Naturally, the teacher has a key role to play here too, as s/he understands their class dynamic.

Additionally, the selection of content can influence the extent to which the student's spiritual development is facilitated. Moreover, spiritual development does not occur in isolation from other forms of development. As we have already seen in Buber and Levinas, for example, there is a fundamental link between spiritual growth and moral development. Thus, the content that teachers select to facilitate their students' spiritual development will also support their moral and academic development. The point, however, is that teachers must make a conscious effort to ensure that lessons are not *solely* focused on students' academic development, for this is a grave disservice to all concerned.

It is perhaps helpful to consider an example of how academic content may be taught in a way that supports students' spiritual and moral development. Currently, along with my Team Ireland colleagues from the School of Education at the National University of Ireland Galway (NUIG), I am developing some senior high school religious education modules as part of our work on the Erasmus+ project, *Life 2: Learning Interculturality from Religion* (LIFE 2, 2022). I will comment briefly on one of these modules—"Learning from Religion"—to illustrate my point concerning the importance of selecting content and pedagogies.

Throughout the Learning from Religion module, senior high school students will study four key areas over eight religious education lessons. These key areas are: (1) Words Matter (e.g., religious language and literacy); (2) The Modesty Question (e.g., religious codes of dress and conduct); (3) An International Faith Community (e.g., expressions of faith in different countries); and, (4) Walk a Mile in my Shoes (e.g., what does it mean to live as a member of a faith community?). Regarding content, a particular religious tradition is selected as the focus point by the teacher, and the research team guides them in selecting content and pedagogies. (In the case of the draft module, the team selected Islam, and draft lessons on this theme were presented to and discussed during teacher focus groups.)

While students' academic understanding of the content is a core aim of the module, developing their sense of interculturality—specifically their spiritual and moral application of such—is the priority. To facilitate this, the team employs a range of student-centered pedagogies in the draft module. These include paired thought shower, mind mapping, structured class discussion, case study, poster creation, learning centers, group work, peer teaching presentations, simulation games, and reflection activities. In addition, key questions are posed by the teacher during each lesson in order to stimulate discussion and dialogue. In particular, these questions focus on students' spiritual and moral values to compare and contrast them with their peers and those of the religious community being studied. The key point here is that the teacher leads out on various respectful student-centered activities with the clear aim of contributing to their students' spiritual and moral development and supporting their academic development.

Regarding our lessons from Buber and Levinas, the teacher here recognizes the significance of the encounter with the other's alterity while actively encouraging and supporting his/her students to do likewise. In addition, by choosing such student-centered pedagogies, the teacher demonstrates his/her trust in and respect for the students, thereby acknowledging the sacredness of the encounter between teacher and student. The content and pedagogies employed in the draft module referred to above accord well with these Buberian-Levinasian lessons and correlated with the core aims of junior and senior high school religious education in Ireland. More particularly, the module contributes to the students' spiritual awareness of their relatedness to something more significant than the self (DES, 2018). While this is just one example, it draws attention to the many spiritual education possibilities presented to the religious education teacher by Buber and Levinas (at least as I read them).

CONCLUSION

Many scholars have been at pains to articulate that religious education is distinctive and unique (e.g., Gearon, 2013; Groome, 1982, 1998, 1999, 2001, 2021; Hull, 2002; Sullivan, 2017). In the majority of such scholars' articulations of the uniqueness of the subject, the question of spirituality is also raised, either in relation to the subject matter being taught, the experience of the student and the teacher, or some combination of the two (see Bellous, 2007; Durka, 1994, 2002; Lee 1985a, 1985b). One such articulation is that of Groome (1999), who stated in an important interview:

> The point is that education can never, and should never, be value free; it must always propose ways of making and keeping life human. So why not draw upon the great spiritual values of humankind—and the core values are generally common to all—as the grounding of our education? (p. 127)

Groome's appeal to "the great spiritual values of humankind" echoes, I think, something of what both Buber and Levinas attempted to elicit in their description of the educational incantation of the self-Other relation(ship). In order to ensure that we "[keep] life human," as Groome puts it, we must engage with one another at a spiritual level. Sidestepping the thorny issue of reciprocity, it is the case for both Buber and Levinas that it is only by engaging with one another at such a level that we can develop ethically. In the Irish school setting, it is difficult to envisage a subject more apt to explore such spiritual engagement than religious education.

What has been learned from Buber and Levinas, then, is that such a task is inescapable. Specifically, with Buber, I highlighted that such inescapability is positive. Through it comes the possibility of the mutual (though unequal) commitment of both the teacher and the student to the ethical task. On the other hand, with Levinas, I showed that this task is incompletable, and thus ethical and spiritual development does not end at the conclusion of each religious education lesson. This is because, as Zhao (2016) suggests, teaching and learning "are about encountering the new and strange, about being interrupted and called into responsibility to the Other" (p. 324). Thus, the responsibility of the religious education teacher is not limited to confinement in the classroom.

I have also attempted to show that the task of ethical development is necessarily also one of spiritual development. This point would seem to accord with Government documents and syllabi pertaining to religious education. As Durka (1994) puts it: "[r]eligious educators are teachers of spirituality because of the religious education process" (p. 58). It would then seem that the religious education teacher has a critical job to do, a position which (as demonstrated by Buber) will also entail their own ethical and spiritual development. The religious education teacher not only provides the student with an opportunity for religious education but also provides the student with an opportunity for spiritual education, too (see Morgan & Guilherme, 2014). Such a responsibility "behooves the religious educator" (Lee, 1985a, p. 257) and should not be taken lightly. Moreover, it opens up the possibility of moving towards a religious education otherwise (Strhan, 2012) in which both teacher and student are spiritually and ethically nourished (see Durka, 2002).

REFERENCES

Bellous, J. (2007). The educational significance of spirituality in the formation of faith. In M. De Souza, K. Engebretson, G. Durka, R. Jackson, & A. McGrady (Eds.), *International handbook of the religious, moral and spiritual dimensions of education* (pp. 171–182). Springer.
Buber, M. (1955). *Education: In between man and man* (R. Gregor-Smith, Trans.). Beacon Press.
Buber, M. (1965). *Daniel: dialogues on realization* (M. Friedman, Trans.). McGraw-Hill,
Buber, M. (1980). *Besod siach (in the secret of dialogue)*. Bialik.
Buber, M. (2004). *I and thou* (R. Gregor-Smith, Trans.). Continuum.
Byrne, G. (2021). Investigating the spiritual and religious dimension of life with young people in Catholic second-level schools in Ireland. *Review of Religious Education and Theology, 1*(1), 2–17.
Council of Europe. (2014). *Signposts: Policy and practice for teaching about religions and non-religious worldviews in intercultural education*. Council of Europe Publishing.
Department of Education and Skills (DES). (1995). *Charting our education future: white paper on education*. Stationery Office.
Department of Education and Science (DES). (2000). *Junior certificate religious education syllabus*. Stationery Office.
Department of Education and Science (DES). (2003). *Leaving certificate religious education syllabus*. Stationery Office.
Department of Education and Skills (DES). (2015). *Framework for the junior cycle*. Stationery Office.
Department of Education and Skills (DES). (2018). *Junior cycle religious education specification*. Stationery Office.
Durka, G. (1994). Religious educators as teachers of spirituality. *The Way, 84*, 58–66.
Durka, G. (2002). *The teacher's calling: A spirituality for those who teach*. Paulist Press.
Frost, R. (2015). *The road not taken and other poems* (100th anniversary edition). Penguin.
Gearon, L. (2013). *Master class in religious education: Transforming teaching and learning*. Bloomsbury.
Grimmitt, M. (1981). When is a commitment a problem in religious education? *British Journal of Educational Research, 29*(1), 42–53.
Grimmitt, M. (1987). *Religious education and human development: The relationship between studying religions and personal, social and moral education*. McCrimmons.
Grimmitt, M. (2000). The captivity and liberation of religious education and the meaning and significance of pedagogy. In M. Grimmitt (Ed.), *Pedagogies of religious education* (pp. 7–23). McCrimmonds.
Grimmitt, M. (2010). Contributing to social and community cohesion: just another stage in the metamorphosis?' In M. Grimmitt (Ed.), *Religious education and social and community cohesion* (pp. 260–317). McCrimmons.
Groome, T. (1982). *Christian religious education: sharing our story and vision*. Harper.
Groome, T. (1998). *Sharing faith: a comprehensive approach to religious education and pastoral ministry*. Wipf and Stock.

Groome, T. (1999). Interview with Thomas Groome. *Catholic education: A Journal of Inquiry and Practice*, *3*(1), 124–136.
Groome, T. (2001). *Educating for life: A spiritual vision for every teacher and parent*. Herder and Herder.
Groome, T. (2021). *What makes education Catholic: Spiritual foundations*. Orbis Books.
Houses of the Oireachtas. (2020). *Education in Ireland: Statistical snapshot*. https://data.oireachtas.ie/ie/oireachtas/libraryResearch/2020/2020-04-03_l-rs-infographic-education-in-ireland-a-statistical-snapshot_en.pdf
Hull, J. (2002). The contribution of religious education to religious freedom: A global perspective. In P. Schreiner H. Spinder, J. Taylor, & W. E. Westerman (Eds.), *Committed to Europe's future: Contributions from education and religious education* (pp. 107–110). Comenius Institute.
Lane, D. (2013). *Religion and education: Re-imagining the relationship*. Veritas.
Lee, J. M. (1985a). *The content of religious instruction: A social science approach*. Religious Education Press.
Lee, J. M. (Ed.). (1985b). *The spirituality of the religious educator*. Religious Education Press.
Levinas, E. (1969). *Totality and infinity: An essay on exteriority* (A. Lingis, Trans.). Duquesne University Press. .
Levinas, E. (1987). *Time and the other* (R. A. Cohen, Trans.). Duquesne University Press.
Levinas, E. (1998). *Otherwise than being, or beyond existence* (A. Lingis, Trans.). Duquesne University Press.
Levinas, E. (2001). Being-toward-death and "Thou Shalt Not Kill." (A. Schmitz, Trans.). In J. Robbins (Ed.), *Is it righteous to be?* (pp. 130–139). Stanford University Press.
LIFE 2. (2022). *Learning interculturality from religion*. https://www.lifetwo.eu/
Lipiäinen, T., Halafoff, A., Mansouri, F., & Bouma, G. (2020). Diverse worldviews education and social inclusion: A comparison between Finnish and Australian approaches to build intercultural and interreligious understanding. *British Journal of Religious Education*, *42*(4), 391–402.
Morgan, W. J., & Guilherme, A. (2014). *Buber and education: dialogue as conflict resolution*. Routledge.
Staehler, T. (2010). *Plato and Levinas: the ambiguous out-side of ethics*. Routledge.
Strhan, A. (2012). *Levinas, subjectivity, education: Towards an ethics of radical responsibility*. Wiley-Blackwell.
Sullivan, J. (2017). A space like no other. In M. Shanahan (Ed.), *Does religious education matter?* (pp. 7–24). Routledge.
Teece, G. (2010). Is it learning about and from religions, religion or religious education? And is it any wonder some teachers don't get it? *British Journal of Religious Education*, *32*(2), 93–103.
Watson J. (2009b). Responding to difference: spiritual development and the search for truth. In M. de Souza, L. J. Francis, James O'Higgins-Norman, D. Scott (Eds.), *International handbook of education for spirituality, care and wellbeing* (2 vols). Springer.

Watson J. (2009a). Science, spirituality, and truth: Acknowledging difference for spiritual dialogue and human well-being. *International Journal of Children's Spirituality, 14*(4), 313–322.

Watson J. (2010). Including secular philosophies such as humanism in locally agreed syllabuses for religious education. *British Journal of Religious Education, 32*(1), 5–18.

Zhao, G. (2016). Levinas and the philosophy of education. *Educational Philosophy and Theory, 48*(4), 323–330.

CHAPTER 4

THE WOKE SPIRIT

Teaching John Coltrane to Examine What Lives Inside

Susan Browne and Yvette Onofre
Rowan University

ABSTRACT

This chapter is a content analysis of the picturebook *Spirit Seeker: John Coltrane's Musical Journey* (Golio, 2012) that examines how John Coltrane's spirit emerges in the text and how his spirituality can be used to support preservice teachers in exploring their own spirituality and that of the future students they will teach. The Reading of *Spirit Seeker* was rooted in culturally responsive, critical trauma, and critical spirituality theoretical frames. Our close analysis provides an in-depth discussion of three major themes: locating what lives inside, sources of internal trauma, and spiritual transformation while providing conceptual implications for using the critical literacy picturebook as a resource in teacher education classrooms.

Keywords: spirituality, preservice teachers, teacher education, critical literacy, culturally relevant education, picturebooks

INTRODUCTION

The role of spirituality is integral to work committed to sustaining the cultures, experiences, and communities that accompany P–12 students to school. Starratt (2002) and Shields (2005) assert that spirituality connects individuals to the most profound realities of life, thereby playing a vital role in education. For preservice and established teachers to help students manifest what is inside of them, they must first tap into their own spirituality to support their students' dreams and set the tone for the trajectory of their lives. How then does a preservice teacher embody what we will refer to as a "Woke Spirit?" According to Babulski (2020), "the term 'woke' emerged from the twentieth-century black American vernacular and popularized in William Melvin Kelley's 1962 *New York Times* essay" (p. 74). His essay, "If You're Woke, You Dig It," initially indicated an awareness of the specific injustices and abuses targeting the African American community. He discusses the recent use of the word woke across various venues in American society to describe an antiracist or anti-oppressive stance. Artist Erykah Badu's *New Amerykah Part One* musical album helped inscribe woke into political vocabulary with the song "Master Teacher" and its refrain "I stay woke." Hunt (2020) explains that "woke extends to conversations around art, politics, economic and social class, gender inequality, trans rights, and environmentalism" (n. p.). Babulski argues that "woke has become synonymous with dispositions related to equity, diversity, and inclusivity, regardless of whether [teacher] candidates engage in any form of anti-oppressive praxis to address specific inequities, promote diversity, or meaningfully include marginalized individuals and communities" (p. 74). This notion of being woke connects to spiritual discourse. Aside from preservice teachers being or becoming woke in equity, diversity, and inclusion, it is equally important to become conscious in the area of spirituality.

Drawing from the seminal work of Thurman (1963) and the scholarship of Starratt (2002), Shields (2005), Boyd (2012), McCray et al. (2012), and Gardner (2016), spirituality refers to looking inward and is constructed by connectedness to unseen forces emitting creativity, power, hope, and energy during good times and uncertain times. Shields (2005) points out that teachers must be in touch with their own spirituality to foster opportunities for its potential in the classroom. Like Shields's work, this study does not use the term spirituality and religion interchangeably but rather ascribes to the use of spirituality in teacher education, asserting:

> (1) that spirituality connects us to the most profound realities of life and, thus, has an integral role to play in education; (2) that engaging spirituality

is distinct from the teaching of or expression of religion; and (3) that public education and spirituality are not mutually exclusive. (Shields, 2005, p. 610)

Based on an understanding of being woke and the scholarly literature around spirituality in education (Boyd, 2012; hooks, 1999; Gardner, 2016; Mata, 2014; McCray et al., 2012; McLoughlin, 2003; Mulalić, 2017; Shields, 2005; Starratt, 2002), being spiritually woke might begin with attempts to be what Boyd (2012) refers to as being "authentically human." To be spiritually woke involves recognizing and acknowledging one's own spirituality and, in turn, recognizing and acknowledging the spirituality of others. For teachers, a woke spirit involves a deep self-awareness reflected in decision-making and actions. These practices relate to education in spirituality that is not explicitly tethered to religion; the aim is "to engage in exploration, discussion and critical assessment of the spiritual domain and issues of meaning, truth and value relating to it" (McLoughlin, 2003, p. 193). From this stance, how teachers see and interact with students stretches beyond pedagogical moves to include influences such as truth and values. Practice makes no distinctions between teaching and social justice as it draws on intangible life forces to apply meaning and purpose to the work of classrooms. Therefore, we posit that to support each student holistically throughout their K–16 academic journey, spirituality must be included in the curriculum, and preservice teachers must reflect on their own spirituality to meet students' needs.

Spirit Seeker: John Coltrane's Musical Journey (Golio, 2012) is a critical literacy tool that can allow preservice teachers to both learn about the life and music of saxophonist John Coltrane and encourage teacher candidates to examine spirituality inside them and those of the students they will teach. Golio (2012) provides a creative and compelling biography of Coltrane's life, music, and spirituality enhanced by illustrations by Rudy Gutierrez inspired while listening to Coltrane's music (Kustanczy, 2012). Described as a "picturebook for older readers ... that anyone can read anew and fall in love with again and again" (Davila & Graff, 2013, p. 72), the text explains how Coltrane, over 40 years, recognized and ultimately acknowledged his spirituality. The compound word "picturebook" indicates the union between text and illustrations (Wolfenbarger & Sipe, 2007). The text portrays Coltrane's humble beginnings and home culture filled with spirituality and music, followed by childhood grief and trauma. Further, the text is an evocative pedagogical resource for considering the potential of addressing spirituality in teaching and learning.

This chapter provides a content analysis of Golio's (2012) text that is conceptual in nature in its work to understand what the text is about. This analysis process involves close readings of portions of text that are interpreted and then contextualized in new narratives (Krippendorff, 2003) with emergent themes related to spirituality. The study is framed by intersecting critical theories to support analysis and generate practical implications for using the picturebook as a culturally centered practice to examine spirituality. As a critical text, *Spirit Seeker* (Golio, 2012) has a profound ability to offer new perspectives and promote deeper understandings. The content analysis provides insight into themes of spirituality in *Spirit Seeker* (Golio, 2012) and implications for using the text in preservice teacher education classrooms to connect its content to candidates and the multiple lived realities of children in their future classrooms.

THEORETICAL FRAMEWORK

Four theories work together to frame this textual analysis and the assertions regarding the text's potential to introduce and prepare preservice teachers for self-reflection regarding spirituality: 1. critical spirituality, 2. critical trauma theory, 3. critical literacy, and 4. culturally relevant education. Together these theories provide a lens for understanding *Spirit Seeker* (Golio, 2012) and using the text for building holistic connections with P–16 students. The following section describes these theories and their relationships (see Table 4.1).

Table 4.1

Framework for Analysis of Spirituality in Spirit Seeker (Golio, 2012)

Critical Spirituality Theory		Critical Trauma Theory		Critical Literacy		
Recognizing individuals holistically (Gardner, 2016; Boyd 2012; McCray et al 2012)	+	Acknowledging and addressing the impact of trauma on individuals (Nelson, 2019, as cited in Hatch, 2021)	+	Advocating to transform dominant ideologies (Freire, 1983)	↔ support ↔	Nurturing the whole person/P–16 student

↓ support ↑

Culturally Relevant Education

Advancing pedagogies committed to working against oppression in schools (Ladson-Billings, 1995; Gay, 2010; Paris & Alim, 2014; Aronson et al. 2016)

Critical Spirituality

Freire (1997) and hooks (1999) argue for including spiritually responsive pedagogy in classrooms. Freire's critical consciousness framework focuses on self-reflection, cultural awareness, transformative learning, and social justice, as well as defining spirituality in an educational context. hooks (1999) points to teachers entering the classroom with hope. She further describes teaching as a profession deeply rooted in the hope that students will learn, share, and seek knowledge. hooks links hope to spirituality in its ability to ignite work toward change and social justice throughout schools and communities. In situating critical spirituality, McCray et al. (2012) point out that "critical spirituality combines aspects of African American spirituality and critical theory" (p. 100). Gardner (2016) further explains, "critical spirituality means seeing people holistically, seeking to understand where they are coming from and what matters to them at a fundamental level; the level that is part of the everyday but also transcends it" (p. 180). Boyd (2012) examined critical spirituality from the lens of Paulo Freire, stating "awareness of Freire's spiritual perspective invites those who have embraced his pedagogical philosophy to examine how their own spirituality may have shaped their perspective and approach to their work" (p. 761). Critical spirituality is a practical tool for preservice teachers to learn in their educational program to critically reflect on their own individual and collective community spiritual experiences and examine how to respect and address their students' spiritual experiences in the classroom. This framework generates principles and strategies for transforming practice and, through practice, the world (Gardner, 2016). Critical spirituality can be understood across multiple disciplines to discuss holistic care and overall well-being.

From a holistic perspective, it would be necessary for preservice teachers to look within themselves in the areas of mind, body, and spirit to evaluate their own understanding of what aligns with their students' needs. Senreich (2013) gives an example of how the field of social work provides an inclusive definition saying that "Spirituality refers to a human being's subjective relationship (cognitive, emotional, and intuitive) to what is unknowable about existence, and how a person integrates that relationship into a perspective about the universe, the world, others, self, moral values, and one's sense of meaning" (p. 553). Tan and Wong (2012) point out that ideas surrounding spiritual ideals are not new. Drawing on the work of Carr (1995), Tan and Wong describe these ideals as derived from spiritual education perspectives that make distinctions between religion and spirituality. These ideas concern aspects of human experience beyond the mundane and move towards the transcendent.

Boyd (2012) also notes, "however, in recent years, scholars have begun to speak of spirituality in broader and more eclectic ways" (p. 760). Spirituality has become a more inclusive term that is not connected to any specific religion or institution, spiritual beliefs, or practices and respects students' spiritual belief systems and practices. Incorporating critical spirituality as part of teacher education programs can help preservice teachers reflect on specific events in their lives, create meaning-making about events, understand who they are holistically, and shape their teaching philosophy through deliberate invitations to invoke spiritual identity. Both school teachers and school leaders can participate in critical spirituality to create a more transformative experience for their students and school. Dantley (2014) posits that "critical self-reflection calls upon that conscience to consider ways in which the behaviors of schools and their leadership marginalize those who, because of race, class, gender, or other markers of difference are outside the hegemony of public schools" (p. 509). Critical spirituality offers insight into the significant role of schools in acknowledging the personal and social identities of those inhabiting them.

Critical Trauma Theory

There is a substantial knowledge base of the impact of trauma on learning. Along with hindering academic growth, trauma prompts a debilitating sense of hopelessness that is also often present. Critical trauma theory (CTT) is an anti-oppressive, socially-just micro theory that analyzes behavioral health symptoms, prevention and treatment approaches, organizational and institutional policies and practices through critical race theory (CRT), intersectionality and cultural, cumulative, and collective trauma theories (Nelson, 2019, as cited in Hatch, 2021). Major tenets of CTT include:

1. Radically acknowledging that oppression-centered structural and institutional barriers to education access exist for Black, Indigenous, students of color (BISOC) and other decentered identities (Crenshaw, 1989; Delgado & Stefancic, 2017; Ladson-Billings, 1998; Solórzano & Yosso, 2001; Yosso, 2005).
2. Taking into account that exposure to oppression and subsequent risk for trauma is ever-present (Goodwin, 2014; Jordan et al., 2014; Kucharska, 2018; & Nadal, 2018) where nascent literature links trauma with restricted academic outcomes (Arnekrans et al., 2018; Bernat et al., 1998; Cantrell, 2016; Jordan et al., 2014; & Walker, 2015).

3. Contending that oppression-based trauma is cumulative, cultural, and collective thereby requires its own critical micro-theoretical perspective that delineates it from individual trauma to address oppression-based trauma in educational contexts.
4. Centering experiential knowledge evidences the existing presence of students' posttraumatic growth, healing, resilience, and resistance in the face of oppression (Yosso, 2005).
5. Recognizing CTT as a vital socially-just micro-theoretical addition to CRT that educators and educational leaders must consider applying to their work (as cited in Hatch, 2021).

CTT provides practical implications for educational settings that embrace opportunities to support success for students of color (Hatch, 2021). Important to the work of teacher education programs is the recognition that trauma-sensitive and supportive school environments require holistic approaches to enable necessary instruction and interventions.

Critical Literacy

Critical literacy argues that education is never a politically neutral process while offering a lens to examine, critique, and transform dominant ideologies and institutions. Freire (1970) offers critical literacy as a process of problem-posing that unfolds in dialogic classrooms where mutual learning (teacher and student) is obtained through conversation, questioning, and deconstructing interpretations. Critical dialogue grows out of learners' consciousness (teacher and student) and gives voice to their questions and wonderings. In order for preservice teachers to teach students how to become critically literate, they must first do the work themselves. Preservice teachers must examine their own bias, power, and privilege through a critical literacy lens. Critical literacy calls for preservice teachers to become involved in advocating for access, equity, and inclusion to become socially woke and to take action for social justice. As a powerful pedagogical approach, critical literacy looks at power and privilege and teaches students to seek the truth about what they read and see in the world. Critical readers have a heightened awareness that language and power influence the world as they work on unpacking texts, the world, and their own biases (Kelly et al., 2020). Kelly et al. (2020) discuss critical literacy as "both a framework for our teaching and a way to view the world that illuminates everything that is read, viewed, heard, or written. It is an awareness, a consciousness about perspective, power, and intention" (p. 298). Lankshear and McLaren (1993) assert that opportunities to be critically literate are presented through a close analysis of ideas present in texts. "To become critically literate is to develop the ability to see and think about the story not told, the voice not honored, the information withheld, the message muted" (Kelly et al., 2020, p. 298). Critical texts provide content that develops readers' knowledge about the nature of texts and supports reading from critical perspectives (Albers et al., 2011). In doing so, critical texts establish a pedagogical relationship between literacy and social justice.

Culturally Relevant Education

This discussion uses culturally relevant education (CRE) to describe the synthesis of work produced by scholarship on culturally relevant pedagogy (Ladson-Billings, 1995; Ladson-Billings & Tate, 2016); culturally responsive pedagogy (Gay, 2010); funds of knowledge (Hogg, 2012; Moll et al., 1992) and culturally sustaining pedagogy (Paris & Alim, 2014). Guided by its predecessors, CRE emphasizes teaching beyond monocultural and monolingual approaches to education (Aronson et al., 2016). It examines the importance of including cultural backgrounds and life experiences in the curriculum and school environment. As noted by Aronson et al. (2016), "CRE represents a wide collection of pedagogies of opposition by teachers to oppression in schools and holds a commitment to collective empowerment and social justice" (p. 140). They argue the need for educators to have discourse about religious and spiritual diversity as a way to support all students and inclusion in schools. Educators and academic institutions must consider funds of knowledge that students bring, such as spirituality, as well as their perspective on the meaning and purpose of life to nurture them as whole human beings. Miller (1996) asserts that human beings are connected to structures that are inclusive of biology, ecology, psychology, and ideology, along with cultural, environmental, and religious systems; thereby indicating that educational systems must work to coexist with these elements of humanity.

LITERATURE REVIEW

As early as 1934, Dewey explicitly argued for the relevance of spirituality in democratic societies. To view a student holistically requires that educators acknowledge their spirituality. Despite the existing tendency in public schools to disengage from the relevance of spirituality, it would be unrealistic to ask students to hide all spiritual parts of themselves before entering the school building or classroom. Lingley (2016) further points out that "scholars such as Dantley (2005), Dillard (2006), Miller (1997),

Palmer (1998, 2011), and Bai (2001, 2009) have addressed the political implications of schooling in democratic societies that do not explicitly acknowledge the spiritual dimension of learning" (p. 3). It is imperative for educators to holistically acknowledge students' spirituality—especially those who have been marginalized and have experienced trauma as a way to support self-awareness and transformative learning.

Theoretical and pragmatic discussions regarding spirituality have been addressed by Dewey (1934), Freire (1997), Noddings (2006), and hooks (2010) to support teachers in incorporating spiritual references in the classroom. Halford (1999) suggests that addressing spirituality has the potential to meet the needs of diverse learners, promote critical cultural literacy and attend to existential wonderings. Noddings argues for spirituality in public education by connecting spiritual issues to educational goals, such as promoting opportunities for students to engage in critical thinking.

Spirituality in education can bring about the interconnectedness between students, teachers, schools, and communities. Norton (2014) specifies three connections of spiritualities which include:

1. Connections of people's minds-spirits-bodies to (un)seen forces.
2. Connection of people's minds-spirits-bodies to the other entities created by and/or related to those (un)seen forces.
3. Connections are enacted through spiritual practices to manifest, sustain, and develop spiritualities through activities such as meditating, praying, chanting, exercising, reading, and writing to support their mind-body-spirit (Anzaldua, 1999; Bridges, 2001; Sams, 1994).

For example, students can use writing to express their life experiences and spirituality and communicate with their higher power. In Norton's (2014) study, students used hip-hop writing to communicate with God. The students' hip-hop writing allowed them to make others see their personal connection with a un(seen) force they call God. Norton reported, "during our time together, in this research, young children repeatedly identified themselves as spiritual beings who demonstrated spiritual practices that included manifesting spiritual content in their hip-hop writing" (p 341). The students were able to connect their own spirituality by way of hip-hop writing while in the classroom.

In order for preservice teachers to engage in spiritual reflection, they must first understand spiritual tenets. In a study conducted by Mata (2014), she asked her teacher candidates to define what spirituality meant to them so they could be open to the possibility of having discourse with children in the classroom. Some teacher candidates described spirituality as a way to center themselves or a crucial part of themselves. As a result of the conversation amongst preservice teachers, Mata found that teacher candidates who shared their understanding of spirituality agreed that there were differences between spirituality and religion. Furthermore, they also agreed that spirituality belonged in early childhood education classrooms.

Meanwhile, McCray et al. (2012) explored ways to integrate critical spirituality in an urban school setting while addressing systemic issues prevalent in these contexts. Their study acknowledged how African Americans have historically experienced years of trauma and have relied on religion and spirituality to cope. Their work relates to what West (2008) refers to as "tragicomic hope," which is the view that tomorrow will be a better day than yesterday and today. This view is what Holmes (2017) describes as the blessed legacy of African ancestors that carries hope and empowerment. Grounding their work in those mentioned above African American traditions, McCray et al. concluded with four elements of critical spirituality for educational leaders: critical self-reflection, deconstructive interpretation, performative creativity, and transformative action. Although their study focused on school leaders, their elements of critical spirituality can be applied equally to P–16 educators and preservice teachers. Their notion of critical self-reflection and transformative action particularly resonate with the themes identified in *Spirit Seeker* (Golio, 2012) and support the text as an instrument for exploring spirituality with preservice teachers.

This study examines spirituality as an integral part of John Coltrane's life through the lens of the critical text *Spirit Seeker* (Golio, 2012). Our focus is to conceptually build on existing research devoted to the pedagogical implications of spirituality through content analysis that describes *Spirit Seeker* (Golio, 2012) as a powerful tool for initiating spiritual discourse with preservice teachers. This work provides entry points for engaging preservice teachers in examining the pedagogical potential of exploring their own spirituality and, thereby, the spirituality of the students they will teach using Golio's text. We have identified the picturebook as significant in illuminating Sipe's (2001) assertion that "The ultimate purpose of analysis and criticism should be to assist us in returning to any given picturebook with the power of seeing and feeling more intensely, thereby increasing our pleasure and capacity for wonder (p. 39). We further suggest that as an evocative critical test, *Spirit Seeker* (Golio, 2012) offers both windows and mirrors (Bishop, 1990) for spiritual inquiry.

METHODOLOGY

This study uses content analysis to systematically interpret the text *Spirit Seeker* (Golio, 2012). Content analysis is an appropriate tool for nonnumerical documents such as literary text. It is a qualitative methodology based on "identifying, coding, and categorizing the primary patterns in the data" (Patton, 1990, p. 381). White and Marsh (2006) further describe content analysis as a "flexible" methodology for analyzing texts. It involves making inferences from texts using their contexts, with researchers adapting the methodology to research question(s) and approaches for textual analysis (Krippendorff, 2003). The research questions guiding the content analysis of *Spirit Seeker* ask, How does John Coltrane's spirit emerge in the text? How can John Coltrane's spirituality be used to support preservice teachers in exploring their own spirituality and that of the future students they will teach?

Data Analysis

The analysis was approached using a deductive, inductive, two-step inquiry process (Johnson et al., 2016). In the deductive phase, we brought a set of a priori concepts to the reading of the text rooted in critical spirituality, critical literacy, critical trauma, and culturally responsive theoretical frames. Simultaneously, new thematic discoveries emerged through a more traditional inductive approach (Willig, 2013). *Spirit Seeker* (Golio, 2012) was interpreted through a process of coding and identifying themes that involved close reading and interpretive analyses. To establish trustworthiness, there was a lengthy engagement with the picturebook. It was read repeatedly over time to enable new discoveries related to spirituality. The content analysis of the picturebook enabled the emergence of three major themes. Each theme illustrates how John's Coltrane's spirituality emerged in the text and how his spirituality can be used in the college classroom to support preservice teachers in developing a "wide - awakeness" (Greene, 1977) regarding the role of spirituality in connecting with self and supporting students.

FINDINGS AND DISCUSSION

Our analysis of *Spirit Seeker* (Golio, 2012) provides an in-depth discussion of the textual themes: (1) locating what lives inside, (2) sources of internal trauma, and (3) spiritual transformation. Our content analysis revealed that each emerging theme was clearly embedded in Golio's text. For example, in his discussion of Coltrane, Golio (2012) presents how spirituality, trauma, and transformation are integral to defining Coltrane, and each theme significantly contributes to his musical journey. The sections below use the text to illustrate the emergence of each theme, its connections to our theoretical framework, and its implications for spiritual discourse in preservice classrooms.

Locating What Lives Inside

Spirit Seeker (Golio, 2012) opens by introducing readers to Coltrane's life in 1938, High Point, North Carolina. Readers immediately learn that Coltrane grew up in the church where his mother played the organ, and his grandfather was a pastor. The text describes how Coltrane was a spirit seeker soaring to new heights with the choir's songs from a young age while imagining angels with brass horns and golden harps. He was intrigued by the words his grandfather Reverend Blair spoke:

> Preaching from the Gospel, the Reverend spoke about the power of the Spirit to guide and heal each human being—no matter what. This was a promise John would never forget. (Golio, 2012, n.p.)

According to Boyd (2012), spirituality is most often thought of as a dimension of life that is both private and inward. He also notes that spirituality is commonly linked to one's "cultural background and milieu" (p. 763). Coltrane is first introduced to spirituality as part of a religious experience in the church, where the notion of the spirit emerges as an internal force capable of guiding human behavior and healing. The text suggests that through his grandfather, Coltrane is provided with a deep understanding of the spirit's transcendent nature, aligning with Starratt's (2002) assertion that spirituality is *present in the most profound realities of one's world*. Thus, the spirit was being formed as an innate part of Coltrane's being.

The strength and stability of the family were essential to Coltrane's childhood. His early world existed in an extended family that included his mother, father, Grandfather Blair, Aunt Bettie, and Cousin Mary. Golio writes of Coltrane's joyful childhood filled with play and plenty of time with his family. Just as kinship was significant to Coltrane's childhood, music was also a substantial part of his life from an early age. His existence was shaped by his mother's organ playing, the church choir, and his father's ukulele playing. His early relationship with music provided the foundation for an evolving relationship between feelings and sound. Gardner (2011) points to the importance of recognizing people and communities holistically to understand where they are from and what matters to them. This "critical perspective asserts the importance of living harmoniously and respectfully at an individual, family, and community level" (p. 77). Recognizing Coltrane's roots is integral to an examination of his spiritual journey.

After experiencing a series of devastating losses, Coltrane found solace in the radio and Black band leaders such as Duke Ellington and Count Basie. Tenor saxophonist Lester Young became his favorite musician, with a sound that expressed both the laughter and tears that connected Coltrane to his father's voice. Also, around this time, Coltrane received his first alto saxophone from the church and then began playing in the high school band. Nurtured by his community, his relationship with his horn was born, allowing it to be his voice.

> Playing made John come alive. Now he was filling the house with sound— mellow love songs or spunky swing music, it didn't matter. (Golio, 2012, n.p.)
>
> *Different songs for different moods.* Papa would have understood. (Golio, 2012, n.p.)

Coltrane was developing his unique relationship with music that was not based on the tangible influence of his family. He was listening to new artists and taking his horn everywhere "John felt the sax becoming more a part of him (Golio, 2012, n.p.). His sax was the beginning of a new journey that allowed him to move towards becoming part of something bigger than himself. According to Tisdell (2000), spirituality is shaped by an awareness of self, and its task is to enable making sense of one's actions and the decisions one makes. Coltrane was finding new meaning in life and his way through the traumas that had profoundly impacted him.

Sources of Internal Trauma

The sweet life Coltrane's family provided unraveled when he was left to face the deaths of close family members.

Two Weeks before Christmas, Reverend Blair died. He was the head of the family, and everyone felt lost without him. Then, three weeks later, J. R. died of cancer. Now the family was in shock.

> That spring, Grandma Blair died. Mary's father, too, would be gone the following year. It seemed like the sweetness of life had vanished forever. (Golio, 2012, n.p.)

His mother and aunt took in boarders and worked at a White-only country club because of the family's financial difficulties. The absence of those things that had been so uplifting and nurturing now shifted Coltrane's emotional responses to the series of unfortunate events that profoundly impacted his life. Responses to trauma can manifest in many ways, and as Thurman (1963) posits, human suffering can violate the dignity of the human spirit. His spirit was being impacted by death, disruptions in family structure, a sense of up-rootedness, unacknowledged pain, economic strife, and racial oppression. In Coltrane's last year of high school, his mother and aunts left North Carolina searching for work. Missing his family, he wrapped himself up in his music and began drinking alcohol to cope with his loneliness.

> But loneliness only grew. John even started to wonder if God really was there—watching over him and listening—and he wanted an answer.
>
> Out in the backyard, late one night, he raised his horn to the dark, distant sky. Notes went flying upward, shot at the stars if to say, Look here I am, trying to light my way with this horn! But the stars went silent. (Golio, 2012, n.p.)

After high school, still trying to cope with sadness and loneliness, Coltrane moved to Philadelphia to live with his mother, Aunt Bettie, and cousin Mary. There, his mother bought him his alto saxophone, and he began taking lessons, leading to playing around town. He was soon hired to tour with well-known bands and started to spend weeks on the road. "Staying in one dark hotel room after another, he found each new city cold and lonely" (Golio, 2012, n.p.). He also felt unease by a white gaze as he was undeniably a black man traveling through many of these places. "Sad and tired, John soon stopped going to church or reading his Bible. He drank alcohol with other musicians at the clubs and bars where they played" (Golio, 2012, n.p.). By age 24, Coltrane was playing with Dizzy Gillespie's renowned bebop band, yet so much on the inside was keeping him in the dark place. Around this time, a friend gave him a book about world religions and the idea of the human body as a sacred place. These books offered Coltrane new insights and hoped to move out of the darkness.

> Still, the sadness he'd known for years hung over him, dark and heavy, like an overcoat he couldn't take off. He even tried using drugs to remove his painful feeling, quiet his thoughts, and numb his body. But drugs could not do that. And John couldn't stop using them. (Golio, 2012, n.p.)

During this time, he fell asleep on stage and lost his job. Here, the trauma had become debilitating through its accompanying hopelessness. In his fight with his suffering, Coltrane was at war with what Thurman (1963) describes as a sense of being or the "is-ness" of personality. In this private terrain, his battle with suffering and the sanctity of his spirit would be lost or won.

Spiritual Transformation

Jazz trumpeter Miles Davis asked Coltrane to join his group, which seemed to be a new beginning. Davis provided Coltrane with musical freedom, but Davis would not accept drug use as a former user. Unable to quit as Davis had, Coltrane lost his job and once again lost direction. However, when Coltrane met and married Naima, he felt hopeful again, and her devotion to him is credited with helping him find his way back.

> Moving back to Mama's house in Philadelphia, John saw his world come to a sudden stop. His body was sick, and his pockets were empty. Now he had to choose between the dead end of drugs or a life rich with music. Waking one morning, John remembered his grandfather's words—the promise of the spirit, and of healing. He asked Mama and Naima for help. With nothing to eat and only water to drink, he stayed alone in his room, resting and praying, as the drugs slowly left his body. (Golio, 2012, n.p.)

Golio's text goes on to say that it was a painful process, but Coltrane felt that he was being cleansed and renewed, and a few days later, he emerged free from drugs. Here, Coltrane's journey connects to Emmons (1999) description of spirituality as the "search for meaning, for unity and connectedness, for transcendence, and for the attainment of a human being's highest potential" (pp. 92–93). He describes spirituality as personal beliefs and practices that are "designed to facilitate a relationship with the transcendent" (pp. 92–93). Emmons's views are reflected in the new freedom emanating from Coltrane's music. "His spirit was set loose, and it flowed through his hands and mouth like the wind filling a sail" (Golio, 2012, n.p.). He rejoined Miles Davis's group and found deep inspiration and innovation. He read about world religions, found meaning in them all, and how his music could be a messenger. "Like his grandfather before him, John wanted to wake people up and call them to worship" (Golio, 2012, n.p.). He became dedicated to sharing the transcendent power of music with everyone.

> Meditating at home one night, John felt the spirit take hold of him. Later, he would tell Mama of his vision, and of the music that came to him. It would become the ultimate expression of his spiritual search. (Golio, 2012, n.p.)

Coltrane called his creation that was to become a masterpiece, *A Love Supreme*. Serving as one of the most significant recordings ever, *A Love Supreme* represented Coltrane's past and profound spiritual transformation. According to *The Wisdom Daily* article by Gindin (2018), John Coltrane wrote in the liner of the *Love Supreme* album:

> *During the year 1957, I experienced, by the grace of God, a spiritual awakening which was to lead me to a richer, fuller, more productive life. At that time, in gratitude, I humbly asked to be given the means and privilege to make others happy through music. I feel this has been granted through His grace.* (n.p.)

The textual themes in *Spirit Seeker* (Golio, 2012) invite readers to think about what made John Coltrane who he was spiritually across his life span. In addition, the biography invites readers to consider the multiple manifestations of spirituality in Coltrane's life. In this way, it can support readers such as future teachers in examining themselves internally while encouraging serious reflection on personal funds of knowledge that cannot readily be seen but are intrinsically significant to each individual. This self-reflection related to *What Lives Inside,* has substantial implications for recognizing the spiritual lives of the students emerging teachers will teach and ultimately can influence developing classroom practice.

Critical trauma theory (Hatch, 2021) calls for teacher education to recognize the need for trauma-sensitive and supportive school environments. The textual theme, *Sources of Internal Trauma,* is particularly significant to BISOC populations. They experience trauma at alarming rates brought on by factors such as underserved schools, food insecurities, violence, and other underlying issues related to poverty. Lingley (2016) states that the spiritual domain has the potential for human growth and can exist as an intentional space for pedagogical interventions that counter dehumanizing and/or undemocratic school practices. Attending to the spiritual domain can reverse trauma's often challenging and immobilizing consequences. McCray et al. (2012) call "deconstructive interpretation" an integral aspect of critical spirituality. Examining the incidents causing trauma in Coltrane's life illuminates what can be learned from the deconstruction and interpretation of traumatic events. This process opens a window into ways to view students holistically. It further represents a significant source of knowledge for teachers working with students who have had their traumatic experiences marginalized and even ignored. As an aspect of the reflective nature of critical spirituality, deconstructive interpretation is a starting point for a transformative practice that enacts processes for negotiating trauma.

Finally, the theme, *Spiritual Transformation,* corresponds with what McCray et al. (2012) identified as transformative action. Coltrane is a powerful example of what confronting personal struggles and transforming them looks like. As a unique symbol, he represents a cultural treasure who reached the pinnacle of his musical craft and spiritual attainment. Reaching these heights happened through struggle and, ultimately, spiritual growth. Thurman (1963) describes growth as an orderly process of development. Thurman explains that this process can find its counterparts in the mind and spirit as we grow and develop. Critical spirituality illuminates how the "raw materials" of growth can be spiritual in nature and provide opportunities for spiritual transformation. It is disheartening to imagine a world in which John Coltrane had not undergone a spiritual awakening leading to his unprecedented contributions to jazz and spiritual discourse. Conversely, it is heartening to imagine an educational system that images nothing less for its students.

CONCLUSION

Most John Coltrane purists will likely contend that the picturebook *Spirit Seeker* (Golio, 2012) captures only segments of Coltrane's life. Although we would agree, we believe that the picturebook importantly and powerfully depicts Coltrane as seminal in exploring one's personal spiritual journey. Coltrane's early life experiences presented in Golio's text are framed by Starratt's (2002) link between spirituality and being present with the most profound realities of one's world. Golio helps readers see how Coltrane's spirituality evolved from suffering enduring trauma and longing for internal freedom. Drawing on the textual themes, locating what lives inside, sources of internal trauma, and spiritual transformation, this chapter possesses conceptual knowledge related to spirituality of value to teacher educators and preservice teachers. The themes allow for profound discoveries involving critical spirituality through critical self-reflection (McCray et al., 2012). We encourage teacher educators to engage teacher candidates in discourse about spiritual identity and self-transformation beliefs. We maintain that three major themes identified in the critical text, *Spirit Seeker* (Golio, 2012), are a noteworthy resource for this engagement.

Wolfenbarger and Sipe (2007) describe picturebooks as a "unique visual and literary art form that engages young readers and older readers in many levels of learning and pleasure" (p. 273). They discuss contemporary picturebooks as "new forms, images, and intersections" that serve as critical spaces for inquiry that are central to the work of teaching, learning, and research. Literature such as *Spirit Seeker* (Golio, 2012) can be essential in nurturing new understandings regarding spirituality and contemplating this knowledge.

Although spirituality remains a primarily avoided topic outside of religious schools, there are unutilized opportunities for the kinds of discoveries it can lead to. In much the same way that Moore (2010) discussed the absence of discussions about religion in public schools and how this avoidance hinders respect for diversity and peaceful coexistence, we apply the same to discussions on spirituality. In its 2021 position statement, the National Council for the Social Studies (NCSS) urges departments of education and school districts to adopt "deliberate and thoughtful study of religion in historical and cultural contexts" to prepare citizens for religious plurality. We further conclude that the absence of spiritual discourse in teacher education represents a failure to prepare teachers to recognize the criticality in assuming a culturally responsive social justice teaching stance.

IMPLICATIONS FOR TEACHER EDUCATION PROGRAMS

Spirit Seeker: John Coltrane's Musical Journey (Golio, 2012) is significant in its capacity to impart spiritual knowledge. As a critical text, it provides both windows and mirrors (Bishop, 1990) for future teachers to examine the role of spirituality in a holistic social justice teaching stance. As preservice teachers are invited to explore Coltrane's spiritual life, they are invited to examine themselves, which has further implications for the students they teach. It is critical to prepare preservice teachers to look at students' faces, races, cultures, genders, abilities/disabilities, and equally necessary to include the deeper essence of each child. This offers hope for transforming learning for children owed what Ladson-Billings (2006) terms an educational debt. Boyd (2012) argues for a link between spirituality and a commitment to both social action and social change. Noddings (2006), Freire (1997), and hooks (2010) are among scholars who make the distinctions between religion and spirituality and point to spirituality as a strategy for classrooms. Implicit here is that critical spiritual workers need to include their own spirituality to give meaning to practice (Gardner, 2011; Shields, 2005). hooks (1999) argues that the connections between spirituality and hope are vital to working with students facing challenges brought on by issues such as food insecurities, violence and/or housing crises. Preparing teachers to act as agents of social change can be ignited by spiritual inquiry that can extend into systematically thinking about the holistic nature of work with P–12 students and their communities.

In his own words, Coltrane expressed that he wanted to point out "the divine in a musical language that transcends words," and he wanted to speak to the soul. We hope that preservice teachers will be afforded the opportunity to explore *Spirit Seeker* (Golio, 2012) to examine themselves and what it means to work to recognize their future students fully. We encourage teacher educators to use Golio's picturebook to nurture a woke spirit in preservice teachers and layer it with other texts (Muhammad, 2020). We recommend the 2020 film, *Concrete Cowboy,* in which a young man Cole, named after Coltrane, experiences the existential threat of gentrification in an urban community of Black cowboys as his coming-of-age experience provides deep insight into himself and others. Other recommended texts for layering include the 2016 Netflix documentary, *Chasing*

Trane, which captures Coltrane's life and music, and John Coltrane's 1964 album and spiritual declaration, *A Love Supreme*.

REFERENCES

Albers, P., Harste, J. C., & Vasquez, V. (2011). Interrupting certainty and making trouble: Teachers' written and visual responses to picturebooks. *60th Yearbook of the Literacy Research Association*, 179.

Anzaldua, G. (1999). *Borderlands, la frontera: The new mestiza*. Aunt Lute Books.

Arnekrans, A. K., Calmes, S. A., Laux, J. M., Roseman, C. P., Piazza, N. J., Reynolds, J. L., Harmening, D., & Scott, H.L. (2018). College students' experiences of childhood developmental traumatic stress: Resilience, first-year academic performance, and substance use. *Journal of College Counseling, 21*(1), 2–14. https://doi.org/10.1002/jocc.12083

Aronson, B., Amatullah, T., & Laughter, J. (2016). Culturally relevant education: Extending the conversation to religious diversity. *Multicultural Perspectives, 18*(3), 140–149. https://doi.org/10.1080/15210960.2016.1185609

Babulski, T. (2020). Being and becoming woke in teacher education. *Phenomenology & Practice, 14*(1), 7–88.

Bai, H. (2001). Cultivating democratic citizenship: Towards intersubjectivity. In W. Hare & J. P. Portelli (Eds.), *Philosophy of education: Introductory readings* (3rd ed.). (pp. 307–320). Detselig Enterprises.

Bai, H. (2009). Contemplative pedagogy and revitalization of teacher education. *Alberta Journal of Educational Research, 55*(3), 319–334.

Beach, R., Enciso, P., Harste, J., Jenkins, C., Raina, S. A., Rogers, R., & Yenika-Agbaw, V. (2009). Exploring the "critical" in critical content analysis of children's literature. In K. M. Leander, D. W. Rowe, D. K. Dickinson, M. K. Hundley, R. T. Jimenez, & V. J. Risko (Eds.), *58th yearbook of the National Reading Conference* (pp. 129–143). National Reading Conference.

Bernat, J. A., Ronfeldt, H. M., Calhoun, K. S., & Arias, I. (1998). Prevalence of traumatic events and peritraumatic predictors of posttraumatic stress symptoms in a nonclinical sample of college students. *Journal of Traumatic Stress, 11*(4), 645–664. https://pubmed.ncbi.nlm.nih.gov/9870219/

Bishop, R. S. (1990). Mirrors, windows, and sliding glass doors. *Perspectives, 6*(3), ix–xi.

Boyd, D. (2012). The critical spirituality of Paulo Freire. *International Journal of Lifelong Education, 31*(6), 759–778. https://doi.org/10.1080/02601370.2012.723051

Bridges, F. W. (2001). *Resurrection song: African American spirituality*. Orbis Books.

Cantrell, A. M. (2016). *Understanding posttraumatic stress and academic achievement: Exploring attentional control, self-efficacy and coping among college students* [Masters Theses and Specialist Projects. Paper 1618]. http://digitalcommons.wku.edu/theses/1618

Carr, D. (1995). Towards a distinctive conception of spiritual education. *Oxford Review of Education, 21*(1), 83–98.

Crenshaw, K. (1989). Demarginalizing the intersection of race and sex: A Black feminist critique of antidiscrimination doctrine, feminist theory, and antiracist politics. *University of Chicago Legal Forum, 1989*(1), 139–167. http://chicagounbound.uchicago.edu/uclf/vol1989/iss1/8

Dantley, M. E. (2005). The power of critical spirituality to act and to reform. *Journal of School Leadership, 15*(5), 500–518. https://doi.org/10.1177/105268460501500502

Davila, D., & Graff, J. M. (2013). Take 5: The legacy of jazz in picturebooks. *Journal of Children's Literature, 39*(2), 68–77.

Delgado, R., & Stefancic, J. (2012). *Critical race theory: An introduction* (2nd ed). New York University Press.

Dewey, J. (1934). *A common faith*. Yale University Press.

Dillard, C. B. (2006). *On spiritual strivings: Transforming an African American woman's academic life*. State University of New York Press.

Emmons, R. A. (1999). *The psychology of ultimate concerns: Motivation and spirituality in personality*. The Guilford Press.

Freire, P. (1970). *Pedagogy of the oppressed*. Herder & Herder.

Freire P. (1983). The importance of the act of reading. *Journal of Education, 165*(1), 5–11. http://10.1177/002205748316500103

Freire, P. (1997). *Pedagogy of the heart* (D. Macedo & A. Oliveria, trans.). Continuum.

Gardner, F. (2011). *Critical spirituality: A holistic approach to contemporary practice*. Ashgate.

Gardner, F. (2016). Critical spirituality in holistic practice. *Journal for the Study of Spirituality, 6*(2), 180–193. https://www.researchgate.net/publication/309272469_Critical_Spirituality_in_Holistic_Practice

Gay, G. (2010). *Culturally responsive teaching*. Teachers College Press.

Gindin, M. (2018, July). *How John Coltrane set his spirit free*. The Wisdom Daily. http://thewisdomdaily.com/how-john-coltrane-set-his-spirit-free/

Golio, G. (2012). *Spirit seeker: John Coltrane's musical journey*. Clarion Books.

Goodwin, E. I. (2014). *The long-term effects of homophobia-related trauma for LGB men and women* [Counselor Education Master's Thesis]. http://digitalcommons.brockport.edu/edc_theses/160

Greene, M. (1977). Toward wide-awakeness: An argument for the arts and humanities in education. *Teachers College Record, 79*(1), 119–125.

Halford, J. M. (1999). Longing for the sacred in schools: A conversation with Nel Noddings. *Educational Leadership, 56*, 28–32.

Hatch, T. (2021, February 10). Resilience, oppression & liberation: A conversation with Anna Nelson. *International Education News*. https://internationalednews.com/2021/02/10/resilience-oppression-liberation-a-conversation-with-anna-nelson/

Hogg, L. (2012). Funds of knowledge: An examination of theoretical frameworks. *New Zealand Annual Review of Education, 21*(21), 47–76.

Holmes, B. A. (2017). *Joy unspeakable: Contemplative practices of the black church*. Fortress Press.

hooks, b. (1999). Embracing freedom: Spirituality and liberation. In S. Glazer (Ed.), *The heart of learning: Spirituality in education* (pp. 113–129). Putnam.

hooks, b. (2010). *Teaching critical thinking: Practical wisdom*. Routledge.

Hunt, K. (2020). How 'woke' became the word of our era. *The Guardian.* https://www.theguardian.com/books/2020/nov/21/how-woke-became-the-word-of-our-era

Johnson, H., Mathis, J., & Short, K. G. (Eds.). (2016). *Critical content analysis of children's and young adult literature: Reframing perspective.* Routledge.

Jordan, C. E., Combs, J. L., & Smith, G. T. (2014). An exploration of sexual victimization and academic performance among college women. *Trauma, Violence, and Abuse, 15*(3), 191–200. http://dx.doi.org/10.1177/1524838014520637

Kelly, K., Laminack, L., & Gould, E. (2020). Confronting bias with children's literature: A preservice teacher's journey to developing a critical lens for reading the word and the world. *The Reading Teacher, 74*(3), 297–304. https://doi.org/10.1002/trtr.1949

Krippendorff, K. (2003). *Content analysis: An introduction to its methodology.* SAGE.

Kucharska, J. (2018). Cumulative trauma, gender discrimination and mental health in women: Mediating role of self-esteem. *Journal of Mental Health, 27*(5), 416–423. https://pubmed.ncbi.nlm.nih.gov/29260963/

Kustanczy, C. (2012, November 28). Rudy Gutierrez paints the stories behind the music. *Digital Journal.* http://www.digitaljournal.com/article/332361#ixzz2UkYAZzBe

Ladson-Billings, G. (1995). Toward a theory of culturally relevant pedagogy. *American Educational Research Journal, 32,* 465–491.

Ladson-Billings, G. (1998) Just what is critical race theory and what's it doing in a nice field like education? *International Journal of Qualitative Studies in Education, 11*(1), 7–24.

Ladson-Billings, G. (2006). From the achievement gap to the education debt: Understanding achievement in US schools. *Educational Researcher, 35*(7), 3–12.

Ladson-Billings, G., & Tate, W. F. (2016). Toward a critical race theory of education. In G. Ladson-Billings (Ed.), *Critical race theory in education* (pp. 10–31). Routledge.

Lankshear, C., & McClaren, P. (Eds.). (1993). *Critical literacy: Radical and postmodernist perspectives.* SUNY Press.

Lingley, A. (2016). Democratic foundations for spiritually responsive pedagogy. *Democracy and Education, 24*(2), Article 6. https://democracyeducationjournal.org/home/vol24/iss2/6

Mata, J. (2014). Sharing my journey and opening spaces: Spirituality in the classroom. *International Journal of Children's Spirituality, 19*(2), 112–122.

McCray, C. R., Beachum, F. D., & Yawn, C. (2012). Educational salvation: Integrating critical spirituality in educational leadership. *Catholic Education: A Journal of Inquiry and Practice, 16*(1), 90–114.

McLoughlin, T. H. (2003). Education, spirituality and the common school, In D. Carr & J. Haldane (Eds.), *Spirituality, philosophy, and education* (pp. 186–199). Taylor and Francis Group.

Miller, J. (1996). *The holistic curriculum.* OISE Press.

Miller, R. (1997). *What are schools for? Holistic education in American culture.* Holistic Education Press.

Moll, L. C., Amanti, C., Neff, D., & González, N. (1992). Funds of knowledge for teaching using a qualitative approach to connect homes and classrooms. *Theory into Practice, 31*(2), 132–141.

Muhammad, G. (2020). *Cultivating genius: An equity framework for culturally and historically responsive literacy*. Scholastic Incorporated.

Mulalić, M. (2017). The spirituality and wholeness in education. *Journal of History Culture and Art Research, 6*(2), 13–24. http://dx.doi.org/10.7596/taksad.v6i2.692

Nadal, K. L. (2018). *Microaggressions and traumatic stress: Theory, research, and clinical treatment*. American Psychological Association. http://dx.doi.org/10.1037/0000073-000

National Council for Social Studies. (2021). *The study of religion in the social studies curriculum*. https://www.socialstudies.org/position-statements/studyof-religion-in-social-studies

Noddings, N. (2006). *Critical lessons: What our schools should teach*. Cambridge University Press.

Norton, N. E. L. (2014). Young children manifest spiritualities in their hip-hop writing. *Education and Urban Society, 46*(3), 329–351. https://doi.org/10.1177/0013124512446216

Palmer, P. (1998). *Courage to teach: Exploring the inner lives of teachers*. Jossey-Bass.

Palmer, P. (2011). *Healing the heart of democracy: The courage to create a politics worthy of the human spirit*. Jossey-Bass.

Paris, D., & Alim, H. S. (2014). What are we seeking to sustain through culturally sustaining pedagogy? A loving critique forward. *Harvard Educational Review, 84*(1), 85–100.

Patton, M. (1990). *Qualitative evaluation and research methods*. SAGE.

Rogers, R., Mosley Wetzel, M., & O'Daniels, K. (2016). Learning to teach, learning to act: Becoming a critical literacy teacher. *Pedagogies, 11*(4), 292–310.

Sams, J. (1994). *The 13 original clan mothers: Your sacred path to discovering the gifts, talents, and abilities of the feminine through the ancient teachings of the sisterhood*. HarperCollins.

Senreich, E. (2013) An inclusive definition of spirituality for social work education and practice, *Journal of Social Work Education, 49*(4), 548–563. https://doi.org/10.1080/10437797.2013.812460

Shields, C. M. (2005). Liberating discourses: Spirituality and educational leadership. *Journal of School Leadership, 15*(6), 608–623.

Sipe, L. R. (2001). Picturebooks as aesthetic objects. *Literacy,* Teaching *and Learning, 6*(1), 23.

Solórzano, D. G., & Yosso, T. J. (2001). Critical race and LatCrit theory and method: Counter-storytelling. *Qualitative Studies in Education, 14*(4), 471–495.

Starratt, R. J. (2002). La spiritualité, thème émergent en education [Spirituality, an emerging theme in education]. In L. Langlois & C. Lapointe (Eds.), *Le leadership en education: Plusieurs regards, une même passion* [Leadership in education: Many perspectives, one passion] Chenelière-McGraw/Hill.

Tan, C., & Wong, Y.-L. (2012). Promoting spiritual ideals through design thinking in public schools. *International Journal of Children's Spirituality, 17*(1), 25–37. https://doi-org.ezproxy.rowan.edu/10.1080/1364436X.2011.651714

Tisdell, E. (2000) Spirituality and emancipatory adult education in women adult educators for social change. *Adult Education Quarterly, 50*(4), 308–335.
Thurman, H. (1963). *Disciplines of the spirit*. Friends United Press.
Turner, R. (1975). John Coltrane: A biographical sketch. *The Black Perspective in Music*, 3–29.
Walker, L. (2015) *Trauma, environmental stressors, and the African American college student: Research, practice and the HBCUs*. Penn Center for Minority Serving Institutions. https://cmsi.gse.upenn.edu/sites/default/files/Walker%20Research%20Brief%20%28final%29.pdf
West, C. (2008). *Hope on a tightrope: Words and wisdom*. Hay House.
White, M., & Marsh, E. (2006). Content analysis: A flexible methodology. *Library Trends, 55*(1), 22-45.
Willig, C. (2013). *Introducing qualitative research in psychology*. McGraw-Hill Education (UK).
Wolfenbarger, C. D., & Sipe, L. (2007). A unique visual and literary art form: Recent research on picturebooks. *Language Arts, 83*(3), 273–280.
Yosso, T. (2005). Whose culture has capital? A critical race theory discussion of community cultural wealth. *Race, Ethnicity and Education, 8*(1), 69–91. http://10.1080/1361332052000341006

PART II

CHAPTER 5

ENABLING THOSE BECOMING TEACHERS OF YOUNG CHILDREN TO NURTURE SPIRITUAL GROWTH

Challenges, Dilemmas, and Opportunities

Tony Eaude
University of Oxford

ABSTRACT

This chapter considers how those learning to become teachers of young children (up to about 11 years old) can be helped to understand and nurture children's spiritual development and growth. Five key challenges about spirituality are considered: uncertainty about what it means and what provision entails, too fixed an understanding, whether it involves only joyful, life-enhancing experiences, whether it is mainly individualized and internal, and not knowing where and how spiritual development and growth fit into the curriculum. A context of performativity and a relentless focus on literacy and numeracy is problematic in making provision for spiritual growth. Distinctive aspects of how young children learn, primarily through actions and visually, rather than mainly through language, are discussed, emphasizing the importance of example, relationships, and environments that provide time and space for reflection. Teacher educators should try to enable teachers,

Rekindling Embers of the Soul:
An Examination of Spirituality Issues Relating to Teacher Education, pp. 89–106
Copyright © 2023 by Information Age Publishing
www.infoagepub.com
All rights of reproduction in any form reserved.

whether preservice or in-service, to consider what spiritual growth can entail and how to provide suitable opportunities across the curriculum. Drawing on the idea of signature pedagogies, teacher educators' own pedagogies should help model how teachers can enable children's spiritual growth.

Keywords: spirituality, identities, relationships, teacher education, signature pedagogy

INTRODUCTION

This chapter considers how those learning to become teachers of young children (up to the age of about 11) can be enabled to understand and nurture children's spiritual growth, seen as a lifelong and holistic process. It highlights, and does not underestimate, the challenges and dilemmas teachers and teacher educators face in how spirituality is understood, and spiritual growth can be encouraged, and others more specific to teacher educators. Opportunities for how young children's spiritual growth can be nurtured are considered based on how young children learn and avoiding a programmatic, "tips-for-teachers" approach. Providing such opportunities and experiencing how children respond is one of the great joys of teaching young children.

The language used to describe how children change over time in relation to their spirituality is problematic. This chapter uses the term growth rather than development, following Priestley's (2000) and Smith's (1999) argument that the process is less even and linear than cognitive or physical development. Growth suggests a more organic, less tidy process, which requires nurturing. As Smith writes, "we should think ... in terms of creating spaces where spirituality is affirmed, and spiritual growth can happen" (p. 4). Similarly, the metaphor of a spiritual journey conjures up a process, often with no definite route or endpoint. Using such metaphors helps one see spiritual growth as a dynamic process that is neither predictable nor measurable. The fluidity and elusiveness of spirituality tend to prompt a wish to reify it, making it static, but this tendency should be resisted if provision for spiritual growth is not to be reduced to a set of activities, however worthwhile these may be.

Another significant issue relates to defining spirituality and, more broadly, deciding what provision for spiritual growth should entail. There is a difficulty for any author to base an argument on a specific understanding of spirituality while arguing that teachers or other adults should be open to different interpretations and views since doing so inevitably makes various assumptions. However, I try to present a view of how teacher educators can enable those learning to become teachers to enhance young children's spiritual growth while remaining open to varying understandings of what this might entail. Teacher education is a career-long professional development process, though this chapter focuses mainly on initial teacher education (ITE). The terms preservice and in-service teachers are used to distinguish between those in ITE and those teaching after qualification. While mainly drawing on the English policy context, the implications are applicable in most contexts and systems.

The next section considers some key challenges, followed by an exploration of research related to young children's spirituality. This leads to discussions of how spiritual growth can be nurtured and enabled or may be constrained in the primary/elementary classroom, the implications for teachers and those in initial teacher education, and the implications for teacher educators. Finally, the conclusion draws together the threads of the argument.

CHALLENGES TO ADDRESS

This section highlights five key challenges in relation to spirituality for teachers and, by extension, for teacher educators, namely:

- an uncertainty and, in some cases, suspicion or scepticism about spirituality and what it entails;
- too fixed a sense of spirituality, especially associating it mostly or entirely with organized religion;
- the view that spirituality only involves joyful, life-enhancing experiences;
- seeing spirituality as mainly individualized and internal; and
- not knowing where and how provision fits into the curriculum.

The first reflects the difficulty—and desirability—of defining spirituality (see Bregman, 2004; Priestley, 1996; Westerlund, 2016) and suspicion about it from some people, notably those who associate it mainly with religious affiliation and are wary about indoctrination. The second, which is more likely in those from a religious background and a strong personal faith, may result in an understanding of spirituality only, or mostly, in terms of religion or a set of practices designed to strengthen religious faith. Seeing spirituality as only related to positive, life-enhancing experiences is common among those working with young children. However, I shall argue that spiritual growth must entail people addressing puzzling and possibly painful questions. Understanding spirituality as mainly individualized and internal, taking little or no account of the external, societal factors which affect children and their spiritual growth, is a commonly held view. I shall argue for a more relational approach, which seeks to extend children's perspectives and enable them to be critical of some cultural and societal norms that they—and their teachers—may take for granted.

The fifth, more practical challenge is that many teachers are unsure where and how spirituality fits in the curriculum. In some systems, its place is explicit in policy, as with spiritual, moral, social, and cultural development (SMSC) in England and Wales, but this is frequently underplayed in practice in a climate of performativity where success is judged mainly in terms of measurable outcomes. As a result, the spiritual dimension of SMSC is often seen as mainly within the remit of religious education and personal, social, health, and citizenship education, or a similar subject or area of learning. I shall argue against this, suggesting that a curriculum designed and considered mainly in discrete subjects makes it harder to see how to make provision for spiritual development (or growth). In other systems, the word spiritual may not even appear, though I shall suggest that children's spiritual growth must be addressed, nevertheless.

The following two sections set out a view of spirituality and spiritual growth, which tries to address some of the challenges outlined in this section, with later sections addressing the more practical challenges.

EXPLORING SPIRITUALITY

One of the few areas in which there is broad agreement about spirituality is that it is hard to define and often elusive. There is no one universally accepted definition. Priestley (1996) argues that to try to define spirituality is to limit it and that it should only be described. I agree with Bregman (2004) that "the quest for the true essential meaning of spirituality is a fool's errand because its meaning keeps slipping, whether deliberately or not, even though, and perhaps because, the term continues to be fuzzy, confusing and yet widely appealing" (p. 157). While spirituality is frequently associated with what is not tangible, exotic, or mysterious experiences, and transcendent aspects of religion, this section outlines some fundamental research on children's spirituality to argue for a broader, more inclusive, and everyday understanding.

A brief historical discussion of how the term has been used in educational legislation and policy in England, while potentially parochial, may help to illustrate the importance of the context in which the word spiritual is interpreted. The 1944 Education Act (HMSO, 1944) stated that "it shall be the duty of the local education authority for every area, so far as their powers extend, to contribute towards the spiritual, moral, mental and physical development of the community." What spiritual meant was not defined, although the assumption was that it mainly referred to religious, predominantly Christian belief—and interestingly to the community rather than the individual. A similar slightly changed list was included in the 1988 Education Reform Act. This looseness of definition meant that the term could be interpreted differently or ignored in some cases. There was little call for what it involves being more clearly explained until the demand in the early 1990s that spiritual development be inspected. This resulted in a series of documents (e.g., National Curriculum Council [NCC], 1993; Office for Standards in Education [Ofsted], 1994; School Curriculum and Assessment Authority [SCAA], 1995, 1996; and Qualifications and Curriculum Authority [QCA], 1997) that sought to describe what spiritual development involves and the implications for provision. As a result, spirituality was associated in many teachers' minds with terms such as "awe and wonder," widely used by those working with young children, and qualities such as imagination and creativity. However, the association with religion remained a matter of debate.

The 1944 and 1988 Acts and writers such as Hyde (2008) and Eaude (2020) suggest that "spiritual" should not be seen as a separate aspect or dimension of a person's identity but as overlapping with others such as physical, mental, social, emotional, cognitive, moral, cultural, and aesthetic. It must be considered in the context of the whole child and the groups and cultures to which he or she belongs. However, the emphasis on performativity (see Ball, 2003)—the idea that success is mainly about measurable outcomes in decontextualized, high-stakes tests based on attainment in skills associated with literacy and numeracy—has meant that SMSC development has usually been seen to matter less, in practice, than these aspects.

An inclusive understanding must take account of children's diverse religious backgrounds, including members of a faith community and those who are not. McLaughlin (2003) suggests that spirituality can be "tethered" to religion or not. This idea, which I find compelling, was influential in my argument (Eaude, 2003) that the spiritual dimension involves exploring existential questions related to identity, meaning, and purpose—such as who am I? where do I fit in? why am I here?—whether within a religious framework or not, and often in ways other than using words. Such a search necessarily includes seeking answers to puzzling and possibly difficult and painful questions related to rejection, loss, and domestic violence, not just life-enhancing experiences.

From a sociological perspective, Hull (1996, 1998) suggests that spirituality should not just be seen as an interior, individualized process and makes a fierce critique of contemporary capitalist societies' spirituality(ies) based on materialism, consumerism, and sexualization. Hull (1998) argues that spirituality is not the cultivation of the inward or universal and that an authentic spirituality exists not inside people but between them and seeks to recreate community through participation in the lives of others, a relational rather than an internal view. Hull writes, somewhat counterintuitively, that "a true spirituality will not seek to become more and more spiritual but will seek to become more and more embodied, more significantly in touch with our bodily existences" (p. 65). The emphasis on embodiment resonates with the ideas of Hart (2017) and others who argue that young children, especially, express and experience spirituality mainly through their senses and actions rather than language.

We have seen that the meaning of spirituality is contested and often hard to grasp and paradoxical. As Love and Talbot (1999) suggest, "the paradox of spirituality is that its experience is personal and unique, but only finds its fullest manifestation in the context of an ever-broadening, mutually supportive community" (p. 619). This stance again emphasizes the spaces and environments in which children are nurtured and educated—linked to the relationships within these, which are very important when working with young children.

TRYING TO UNDERSTAND CHILDREN'S SPIRITUALITY

Hay and Nye (1998) set out an understanding of children's spirituality based on "relational consciousness." While the emphasis on consciousness makes this term, in my view, not entirely satisfactory, the relational aspect emphasizes that any child should be seen not just as an individual but as part of a broader ecology. Spiritual growth involves how individual children learn to relate to other people, to the world around and to transcendent experience, which (for some people) is described in terms of God or a divine being. As Nye (2013) writes, "in childhood, spirituality is especially about being attracted to 'being in relation,' responding to a call to relate to more than 'just me'—i.e. to others, to God, to creation or to a deeper sense of self" (p. 6). Her focus on relatedness is reflected in the emphasis of scholars such as Hyde (2008) on connectedness, though many scholars and practitioners tend to focus more on internal processes.

Hay and Nye (1998) argue that children's spirituality involves three overlapping elements: values-sensing, mystery-sensing, and awareness-sensing. The emphasis on values highlights that spirituality is not neutral, ethically, about what matters, that mystery suggests that there is a dimension of experience beyond what appears to be immediately apparent, and that awareness-sensing implies being attentive to details, even those which may seem unimportant, rather than relying on language and consciousness.

Corbett (2007) suggests that "children are particularly receptive to numinous experience because their sensitivity has not yet become blurred by exposure to social expectations. They lack the prejudices of adulthood and are permeable to transpersonal experience" (p. 27). Young children seem to have access to some types of experience and a level of insight that adults no longer have, maybe because adults are more dominated by cognitive processes and concerned with protecting their power and status.

One key issue is how spiritual growth occurs naturally and how much it can be enhanced or inhibited by other people. For example, Hyde (2008) identifies two main factors that inhibit children's spirituality: material pursuits in consumerist societies and trivializing by avoiding issues of meaning and value in life.

The materialism of contemporary capitalist culture, emphasizing consumption and children as consumers, echoes Hull's critique of capitalism and modern culture. Consumerism tends to discourage children from exploring more serious questions (see Westerlund, 2016). In addition, contemporary culture tends to reflect, emphasize, and encourage individualism and narcissism—and an overemphasis on the self. Therefore, the cultures within which young children—and those learning to become teachers—grow up and the values and beliefs these reflect and encourage must not be ignored.

Trivialization often results from adults not taking children and their ideas, insights, and questions seriously. Rather than infantilizing or looking down on them, adults should see children from a very young age as active creators of meaning, albeit inexperienced ones, and enable them to become so. This will involve adults, including teachers, observing, listening, allowing, and waiting, rather than transmitting, delivering, compelling, and thereby dominating the discourse.

The last two sections have suggested many intertwined and overlapping aspects or dimensions of how children grow. The spiritual dimension needs to be nurtured since it contributes significantly to a broader sense of identity and personhood beyond academic and cognitive attainment. Children's spirituality often seems elusive, puzzling, and mysterious. However, it is best understood as a relational process rather than reified or seen only as a set of practices. This process is neither internal nor reliant on exotic experiences but often manifested and encouraged, as we shall see, in everyday situations and actions.

There are many reasons why teachers, especially inexperienced ones, may avoid addressing children's spirituality. Among these may be a wish to protect both children and themselves, fear of indoctrination, and a perceived lack of time and pressure to cover a full, overloaded curriculum. However, we now turn to how teachers can nurture young children's spiritual growth.

ENABLING SPIRITUAL GROWTH IN THE PRIMARY/ ELEMENTARY CLASSROOM

As Berlak and Berlak (1981) indicate, dilemmas are integral to teaching in the primary/elementary classroom. In Alexander's (1995) words, "teaching is essentially a series of compromises" (p. 67). Similarly, Kennedy (2006) argues that teachers constantly try to reconcile six competing concerns: covering desirable content, fostering student learning, increasing students' willingness to participate, maintaining lesson momentum, creating a civil classroom community, and attending to their own cognitive and emotional needs. There are often difficult choices and judgments to be made. However, it seems hard to argue against the view that young children's long-term well-being and how they learn should be prime considerations in making provision for spiritual growth.

There are both advantages and difficulties in the meaning of spirituality, and what provision should entail, being elusive and hard to pin down. This can encourage teachers to take a broad view of how children learn. Still, there is a danger that opportunities may easily be overlooked in the busy world of the primary/elementary classroom. This section considers some practical implications for teachers.

Many researchers (e.g., Donaldson, 1982) have emphasized the centrality of context and relationships in whether and how young children engage with learning opportunities. This is particularly so in relation to spiritual growth when this is an active process based on search and questioning, especially in areas where answers are not definite. Such a view implies that adults should encourage varied ways of working and reflecting and seek to strengthen qualities such as curiosity, creativity, openness, and empathy—all of which require time, space, and guidance.

Spirituality is not a subject or an area of learning to be covered during specific days or lessons but is more like a thread that runs through every aspect of what children experience. Spiritual growth is enhanced or inhibited throughout a child's life and may occur at any time, in any context, and not always deliberately or consciously. It frequently seems to occur through apparently ordinary, everyday experiences, such as a comment which prompts a child to consider his or her place in the world or an action where one child helps another feel included.

Teachers can encourage and promote spiritual growth but cannot ensure it. Some activities, such as play and first-hand encounters with the natural world, and some subject areas, notably the humanities and the arts, including music and drama, provide abundant opportunities. For example, seeing an egg hatching or experiencing a beautiful building or landscape can evoke a sense of surprise, wonder, and new perspectives, which may have a profound, long-lasting impact on children. Similarly, for a child, or group, to discuss an issue that is significant to them, discover a previously unseen pattern, or create a new understanding of oneself and the world around them may do so. Seeking to expand children's horizons by providing such opportunities is increasingly vital in a globalized, diverse world. It is particularly beneficial for those with a limited range of prior experience (see Eaude, 2019, 2020).

Chances for celebrating what is wonderful and reflecting on existential questions may occur in almost any subject area or activity. Reflection can be scheduled for specific times, but opportunities for a child to reflect on his or her own or with other people are possible throughout the curriculum. Provision for spiritual growth must, therefore, not be considered only in relation to religious education or personal and social education, but in science, mathematics, the arts, and the humanities—and in many other respects outside the school curriculum. Such opportunities often occur unexpectedly, though this does not mean that they cannot be planned for, but that planning must be imaginative and flexible. By encouraging an exploratory and not-too-definite mindset in children (and themselves), teachers can open up other opportunities for spiritual growth.

Spiritual growth is not directly observable and takes place at a deeper level than completing a series of activities depending on the questions these evoke. While programs such as Godly Play and those involving mindfulness often provide good opportunities, there can be a danger of these becoming bolt-on activities unless a holistic view is adopted, which opens up opportunities for children to explore ideas beyond the boundaries of the activity or program. Finding ways to make connections between subject areas and with children's own experiences is likely to be helpful.

Since spirituality is closely bound up with what is regarded as being of value, provision should enable children, especially as they approach adolescence, to explore and critique aspects of what they may take for granted in contemporary cultures. This includes images of success based on appearance and possessions or behavior which may seem amusing but is hurtful. Therefore, spiritual growth entails questioning social and cultural norms and potentially addressing risky rather than cozy, warm issues. However, teachers should be aware of the dangers of indoctrinating, exerting undue influence, and over-protecting children. This presents a dilemma, especially for young children, in that teachers may be wary of challenging norms and expectations associated with children's culture, community, and family. In addition, there is a danger of teachers making assumptions based on their own culture and background and imposing these on children rather than recognizing that children may bring different beliefs due to their social, cultural, or religious backgrounds and experiences.

While children should, where possible, take the lead, they, particularly young children, need some guidance. So, teaching that nurtures spiritual growth will likely involve guided inquiry within a safe but challenging environment, more than instruction and "delivery." Eaude (2014) explored the idea of "hospitable space," arguing that this must be welcoming and inclusive, but creating such space is very difficult in hyper-competitive environments. Doing so requires relationships based on mutual trust between children and between child and teacher and environments where children feel safe to take risks and grapple with challenges without the fear of the emotional cost of failure. However, such relationships and environments are not as easy to create as one might assume in a system dominated by individual attainment, interpersonal competition, and performativity. Children may be over-trusting, and the asymmetry of power between teachers and young children means that there is a significant danger of children's search being inhibited rather than enhanced by adults, especially teachers, whether intentionally or not.

This section has suggested that young children need appropriate relationships and environments that provide opportunities, space, and time to explore questions of identity, meaning, and purpose for their spiritual (and other types of) growth to be nurtured. The following section considers the implications for those preparing to become teachers of young children.

IMPLICATIONS FOR THOSE PREPARING TO BECOME PRIMARY/ELEMENTARY CLASSROOM TEACHERS

The previous discussion indicates that what provision for spiritual growth entails is hard to grasp and may not have a high priority for those embarking on a course to qualify as a teacher of young children in a policy context that emphasizes performativity in a narrow range of subject areas. When working with young children to enable their spiritual (and other types of) growth, teachers should concentrate more on creating appropriate relationships and environments that provide space and time to explore questions of identity, meaning, and purpose rather than simply imparting information.

Some will see spirituality and spiritual growth as essential and exciting. Others may shy away from it and find discussing this and its provision extremely challenging. There may seem to be good reasons for teachers who lack confidence, especially inexperienced ones, to avoid addressing spirituality-related issues. But learning to teach, particularly with young children, requires an understanding of the broader, particularly emotional, aspects of the role, and the interactions between children and adults, rather than, as is sometimes assumed, being primarily concerned with cognitive learning. Such considerations extend far beyond children's spiritual growth but matter especially in making provision for this.

There is no one method of teaching young children to be slavishly copied. Instead, professional development requires teachers to decide on and practice their own pedagogies, drawing on their own values and beliefs, guided and supported by those with greater experience or different insights. This will involve recognizing and finding ways to resolve practical dilemmas such as those between:

- providing both haven and challenge;
- curriculum coverage and allowing time for reflection; and
- being sensitive to and respecting children's cultural backgrounds enables them to explore and question these and their beliefs (see Eaude, 2019).

Whatever their level of experience, teachers need to recognize that the spiritual dimension of children's growth and development matters, wherever it is placed (or not) in the formal curriculum and even if they are unsure what provision should involve. Moreover, a consideration of the spiritual and other overlapping dimensions of children's experience, such as moral, cultural, and aesthetic, may encourage preservice teachers to think deeply about the purposes of education. In turn, they will develop a broader, more holistic view of the purpose of children's education, learning, and educational priorities from one related mainly to performativity. However, adopting such a fluid and holistic approach is likely to be easier for those preparing to teach young children (up to 5 or 6 years old) than those preparing to teach older primary/elementary children. This is partly because such an approach usually fits more closely with how the curriculum is organized in broad areas of learning rather than separate subjects. In contrast, older age groups often focus more on knowledge acquisition and measurable outcomes in separate subjects.

Those preparing to become teachers of young children must be able to address the five challenges identified previously. Preservice teachers can be encouraged to do so by:

- discussing different views and cultural perspectives on spirituality in relation to young children, preferably in diverse groups;
- thinking about what is distinctive about young children and how they learn;
- watching, listening, and being attentive to children's responses and questions;
- considering examples where opportunities to foster children's curiosity, imagination and creativity have arisen or can do so in their practice;

- providing opportunities for children to question and expand their range of experiences and horizons across the whole curriculum;
- enabling children to raise and consider difficult, potentially distressing questions, realizing that many teachers, including themselves, may find addressing such topics hard, not least because there are no definite answers;
- reflecting on their own values and beliefs about what really matters and their own spiritual journeys and the influences which have helped to shape these, for instance experientially by exercising their own creativity and imagination and through discussion and personal journals;
- questioning their own assumptions, for example, by recognizing that planning must allow for what may be unexpected and that measuring spiritual growth is of doubtful validity;

This so potentially challenging other aspects of how teachers they are expected to teach. To learn to act in these ways, teachers on preservice courses require time and space, just as children do, and a willingness, and encouragement, to address personal and challenging issues.

IMPLICATIONS FOR TEACHER EDUCATORS

This section considers the implications for teacher educators, particularly those working with preservice teachers. In addition to the challenges previously mentioned, teacher educators face four further ones which are not specific to spirituality. These may make it hard to enable preservice teachers to understand why they should nurture young children's spiritual growth—and how to do so. First, most preservice teachers will have grown up and gone to school within a neoliberal, performative system where education relates mainly to "core subjects" and outcomes can be measured in tests. This is exacerbated by the expectation that teacher education should concentrate on a narrow "core curriculum," thus limiting the time and space available for more discursive but essential aspects of education. A second is how to enable preservice teachers to learn how to teach in a wide range of contexts, not just the current one. The third is that the thinking and practice of those preparing to become teachers must have a sound theoretical basis, but it is often difficult to relate theory to practice. The fourth is how to influence inexperienced teachers in terms of practice—procedural knowledge—when the pedagogy involved is hard to articulate or demonstrate, particularly since teacher educators work most of the time away from the classroom and children.

Becoming a teacher with a high level of expertise is a continuum, taking several years after qualification (see Berliner, 2001). Therefore, an initial teacher education course is only the start of a longer process. Continuing professional learning is necessary to build up the varied knowledge and qualities such as confidence and empathy required in a teacher. Inexperienced teachers need confidence and the courage to trust their intuition about what may be appropriate to allow or follow up as they teach. This is difficult when, inevitably, they are unlikely to have as much case knowledge as more experienced ones so that they can decide what to do when in an unfamiliar situation.

Teachers are likely to deepen their understanding of spiritual growth and how to nurture this as they become more experienced and gather the necessary case knowledge to judge when to intervene and when not. Much of this will probably be learned after qualification once they work with groups of children. Preservice teachers cannot reasonably be expected to acquire a deep understanding of spirituality and how to enable spiritual growth in a short course. However, they need to understand aspects of children's development other than cognitive attainment to "sow the seeds" for a deeper understanding of these. Therefore, teacher educators are responsible for ensuring that those they teach are at the leaset aware of and pay attention to the whole range of children's needs.

All teachers benefit from the support of professional learning communities. This is true both in preservice courses and after qualification when there are significant dangers of feeling overwhelmed, isolated, and demotivated. Such professional learning communities may be of various types, in person or online, but the most influential one is likely to be the school where a teacher works. (Eaude, 2018; Lieberman, 2007).

I have argued that the spiritual dimension should be understood as one aspect of children's development and growth rather than separately. Opportunities for spiritual growth can happen in any context and at any time. Therefore, while one or more specific days or modules to address such issues may be valuable, such considerations should be part of and threaded into all taught modules as far as possible. Provision is not just about setting up activities or experiences that evoke awe and wonder or encourage creativity and imagination. However, these may provide a good starting point. Instead, preservice teachers should be encouraged to consider *why* and *how* to set up and lead activities and programs, thinking about how these may benefit a specific group of children.

The practicum, or field placement, is a chance to try new ideas. At the least, preservice teachers should seek to encourage, rather than inhibit, children's curiosity, imagination, and creativity; and set up opportunities for reflection and discussion. However, there is an understandable tendency to focus on delivering narrow aspects of the core curriculum, and there may be few opportunities to teach other areas. The practicum also has the potential for preservice teachers to watch more experienced teachers at work as an essential way to learn from them. Since watching a range of other teachers, and preferably discussing this in groups, is unlikely to be much possible in person, video is probably the best alternative.

The idea of "signature pedagogies" can help teacher educators consider why and how to demonstrate ways of working as a teacher. Shulman (2005) uses this term to describe the main ways in which those new to a profession are taught and expected to learn three fundamental dimensions of professional work to *think*, *perform*, and *act with integrity*. He argues that those teaching any group of professionals should model the ways of working associated with that profession. So, doctors learn much of their practical knowledge by working alongside more experienced doctors; and lawyers learn mainly by examining cases and judgments under the supervision of a more experienced lawyer. All of these are based, in varying ways, on the idea of apprenticeship, where the necessary knowledge, skills, and values are gradually learned over time by watching and internalizing how other, more experienced professionals think and act (see Eaude, 2018).

Thomson and Hall (2015) argue that signature pedagogies are:

- epistemological, dealing with things that we have to know and know how to do;
- axiological, about ways of working; and
- ontological, about the way we are in the world and how we orient ourselves to being and making meaning in the world,

They continue that while these elements cannot be separated in practice, this distinction provides a helpful way of understanding what those new to the profession and teacher educators should concentrate on.

By using signature pedagogies, teacher educators can model the ways of working that primary/elementary classroom teachers should adopt. For example, by asking open questions, being reflective, curious, and open to what is wonderful but often overlooked, and by doing so, both implicitly and explicitly. Such an approach is valuable in helping teachers internalize procedural knowledge and understand elusive ideas such as spiritual growth.

CONCLUSION

Recognizing that there is no universally agreed definition of spirituality, this chapter has argued that young children's spiritual growth is essential to how their identities are shaped and strengthened, based on exploring existential questions related to identity, meaning, and purpose. Teachers should enable such a search whether the questions raised, or the experiences and responses involved are named "spiritual" or not. Spiritual development or growth should not just be seen as a legal requirement in systems where it is, but as an aspect of education that enriches children's and teachers' lives and enables the latter to gain a more profound understanding of children. However, teachers and teacher educators face significant challenges and dilemmas, especially in systems and contexts where performativity dominates how teachers are expected to teach.

Growth is a more appropriate metaphor than development since the spiritual dimension needs nurturing and tending, emphasizing the importance of contexts, spaces, and environments. Spiritual growth happens, often unexpectedly, throughout children's lives, usually depending on relationships, actions, and images rather than words, particularly for young children. This process may take place within or outside a religious framework. It is neither just internal nor reliant on exotic experiences but dependent on relationships with other people, the wider world, and (for some people) a transcendent Being. Spiritual growth is often manifested and nurtured in everyday actions and through actions and images more than words. Thus, schools and teachers have a vital role in enabling and providing opportunities for this, as part of a holistic approach, where opportunities are created organically across the curriculum, formal and hidden, not only in some subject areas and lessons.

Enabling children's spiritual growth depends more on pedagogy than the written curriculum. Children require time and space to explore and reflect on existential questions, including some of which may be difficult and possibly painful for both children and teachers. Teachers should model behaviors such as curiosity and openness to encourage these in children. Opportunities for children to have experiences of awe and wonder and gain a broader perspective and sense of connectedness with something bigger than themselves is a good start. First-hand experience, notably through the arts and the natural world, provides fertile ground, but such opportunities can arise in any context, often in unexpected ways. Therefore, planning needs to be flexible to allow such opportunities to be created and taken.

For many valid reasons, those on initial teacher education courses may not see children's spiritual growth as a priority and be uncertain how to enable and nurture this, particularly in a system focused on performativity and measurable outcomes. Teacher educators must help them see spirituality not as "tethered" to religion but as a process that overlaps with other aspects of children's development so children can explore issues related to identity, meaning, and purpose rather than just as a set of activities. Moreover, before and after qualification, teachers need to explore such issues themselves and learn to listen and question and not be too definite in providing answers to such questions children.

Since a preservice course is only an early part of a lifelong learning process, one significant aim for teacher educators should be to open up and broaden the thinking of those involved, particularly about those aspects of children's learning that are not measurable. Drawing on the idea of signature pedagogies, teacher educators should model behaviors such as asking open-ended questions, being open to what is hard to understand, and encouraging creative, imaginative, and personal responses.

While this chapter has focussed on challenges and dilemmas, which are considerable, it is appropriate to end on a positive note that exploring and enabling spiritual growth can bring joy and hope not only to young children and their teachers—and teacher educators. Moreover, by challenging some assumptions of current neoliberal approaches to education, considering the issues raised presents the opportunity for a radical rather than a cozy view of what spiritual growth entails. This will also give opportunities to rethink what education is for and how to achieve a more humane and relational approach based more on interdependence and cooperation than on individualism and competitiveness.

REFERENCES

Alexander, R. J. (1995). *Versions of primary education*. Methuen.
Ball, S. J. (2003). The teacher's soul and the terrors of performativity. *Journal of Education Policy, 18*(2), 215–228. https://doi.org/10.1080/0268093022000043065
Berlak, A., & Berlak, H. (1981). *Dilemmas of schooling- teaching and social change*. Methuen.
Berliner, D. C. (2001). Learning about and learning from expert teachers. *International Journal of Educational Research, 35*, 463–482. https://doi.org/10.1016/S0883-0355(02)00004-6
Bregman, L. (2004). Defining spirituality: Multiple uses and murky meanings of an incredibly popular term. *Journal of Pastoral Care & Counseling, 58*(3), 157–167. https://doi.org/10.1177%2F154230500405800301
Corbett, L. (2007). *Psyche and the sacred: Spirituality beyond religion*. Spring Journal Books.
Donaldson, M. (1982). *Children's Minds*. Fontana.
Eaude, T. (2003). Shining lights in unexpected corners: New angles on young children's spiritual development. *International Journal of Children's Spirituality, 8*(2), 151–162. https://doi.org/10.1080/13644360304630
Eaude, T. (2014). Creating hospitable space to nurture children's spirituality: possibilities and dilemmas associated with power. *International Journal of Children's Spirituality, 19*(3–4), 236–248. https://doi.org/10.1080/1364436X.2014.979772

Eaude, T. (2018). *Developing the expertise of primary and elementary classroom teachers: Professional learning for a changing world*. Bloomsbury Academic.
Eaude, T. (2019). The role of culture and traditions in how young children's identities are constructed. *International Journal of Children's Spirituality, 24*(1), 5–19. https://doi.org/10.1080/1364436X.2019.1619534
Eaude, T. (2020). *Identity, culture and belonging: Educating young children for a changing world*. Bloomsbury Academic.
HMSO. (1944). *The 1944 Education Act*.
Hart, T. (2017). Embodying the mind. In J. P. Miller & K. Nigh (Eds.), *Holistic education: Embodied learning* (pp. 299–318). Information Age Publishing.
Hay, D., with Nye, R. (1998). *The spirit of the child*. Fount.
Hull, J. (1996). The ambiguity of spiritual values. In J. M. Halstead & M. J. Taylor (Eds.), *Values in education and education in values* (pp. 33–44). Falmer.
Hull, J. (1998). *Utopian whispers—Moral, religious and spiritual values in schools*. Religious and Moral Education Press.
Hyde, B. (2008). *Children and spirituality: Searching for meaning and connectedness*. Jessica Kingsley.
Kennedy, M. M. (2006). Knowledge and vision in teaching. *Journal of Teacher Education, 57*(3), 205–211. https://doi.org/10.1177%2F0022487105285639
Lieberman, A. (2007). Professional Learning Communities: a reflection. In L. Stoll & K. S. Louis (Eds.), *Professional learning communities: Divergence, depth and dilemmas* (pp. 199–203). Open University Press.
Love, P. G., & Talbot, D. (1999). Defining spiritual development: A missing consideration for student affairs. *NASPA Journal, 46*(4), 614–628. https://doi.org/10.2202/1949-6605.5035
McLaughlin, T. H. (2003). Education, spirituality and the common school. In D. Carr & J. Haldane (Eds.), *Spirituality, philosophy and education* (pp. 185–199). RoutledgeFalmer.
National Curriculum Council (NCC). (1993). *Spiritual and moral development: A discussion paper*.
Nye, R. (2013). *Children's spirituality: What it is and why it matters*. Church House.
Office for Standards in Education (Ofsted). (1994). *Spiritual, moral, social and cultural development*. Ofsted.
Priestley, J. (1996). *Spirituality in the curriculum*. Hockerill Educational Foundation.
Priestley, J. (2000). Moral and spiritual growth. In J. Mills & R. Mills (Eds.), *Childhood studies—A reader in perspectives of childhood* (pp. 113–128). Routledge.
Qualifications and Curriculum Authority (QCA). (1997). *The promotion of pupils' spiritual, moral, social and cultural development*.
School Curriculum and Assessment Authority (SCAA). (1995). *Spiritual and moral development SCAA discussion papers No. 3*.
School Curriculum and Assessment Authority (SCAA) (1996). *Education for adult life: The spiritual and moral development of young people: A summary report SCAA Discussion Papers No. 6*.
Shulman, L. S. (2005). Signature pedagogies in the professions. *Daedalus, 134*(3), 52–59. https://doi.org/10.1162/0011526054622015
Smith, D. (1999). *Making sense of spiritual development*. The Stapleford Centre.

Thomson, P., & Hall, C. (2015). 'Everyone can imagine their own Gellert': The democratic artist and 'inclusion' in primary and nursery classrooms. *Education 3–13, 43*(4), 420–432. https://doi.org/10.1080/03004279.2015.1020660

Westerlund, K. (2016). Spirituality and mental health among children and youth- a Swedish point of view. *International Journal of Children's Spirituality, 21*(3–4), 216–229. https://doi.org/10.1080/1364436X.2016.1258392

CHAPTER 6

"WHO AM I NOW?"

Spirituality in a Faith-Based Teacher Education Program in Canada

Allyson Jule, Carolyn Kristjansson, Yu-Ling Lee, and Kevin Mirchandani
Trinity Western University, Canada

ABSTRACT

In this chapter, we bring forward our interest in understanding the relationship between spirituality, identity formation, and Christian faith-informed teacher education. First, we define Christian spirituality and identity formation as it pertains to the dominant and nondominant discourses in our faith-based teacher education program. Second, we share findings from a qualitative research study we conducted with some of our graduates 10 years after graduation, asking them about their teacher identity formation and who they are today. Finally, we propose what this means for our Christian teacher education program and teacher practice to contribute to the broader discourse concerning spirituality and teacher identity formation.

Keywords: teacher education, professional identity, spirituality and formation, Christian faith

Educators and researchers in teacher preparation programs have long explored how dominant discourses in teacher education impact teacher identity development. Also, the subject of spiritual formation in the profession has been marginalized throughout the 20th century in teacher education as well as in nursing, psychology, medicine, and so forth (Libster, 2018). And yet, according to Elizabeth Tisdell (2008), there has been a "growing discussion about its role" (p. 27). We see spirituality as a critical component of effective teaching and a critical component of teacher education (Zhang & Wu, 2016). This chapter explores spirituality and the formation of teacher identity in a Christian faith-based teacher education program in Western Canada. We ask if and how spirituality impacted teacher identity formation in an explicitly Christian faith-based program.

Developing a teacher identity is often a result of the conformity of practice within the group (Britzman, 2012; Franklin & Van Brummelen, 2006; Jule, 2004; Pudlas, 2009). Certain dominant discourses are often expressed explicitly in program curricula, the methodologies of teacher education courses, and the practicum experiences. It is understood that identity formation leads to the foreclosure of one identity (one of being a student) and the development of another (being a teacher) that emerges during teacher education programs.

In faith-based teacher education, we perceive an emergence of teacher identity alongside spiritual formation. This presents a unique context to explore how much students are aware of how their spiritual formation forms and informs their teacher identity. Spiritual formation in such a context may not be explicitly stated, yet may be present, nonetheless. We wonder: Is spirituality simply encouraged in this teacher education program and/or is the experience more coercive? We explore the views and perceptions of our own students some 10 years after graduation to understand better any spiritual influence they experienced in a faith-based teacher preparation program and how the experience relates to their identities as teachers now.

CHRISTIAN SPIRITUALITY

Durkheim (1898/1975) described religion as a "unified system of beliefs and practices relative to sacred things [...] which unite into one single moral community called a church with all those who adhere to them" (p. 123). In our context, spirituality connects directly with Christianity's symbolic frameworks (such as creedal prayers, reading of scriptures, attending chapel, etc.). Christian spiritual formation is "both informational teaching (teaching that helps ground one in the facts of the Christian story) and formational teaching (teaching that helps one live out the truth of the

Christian gospel)" (Wilhoit, 2008, p. 123). This is a formative, transformative, and holistic educational approach.

Carson (2005) suggests teacher candidates should move beyond instrumentalism and articulate new discourses for teacher development in Canada. Bakhtin (1981) described internally persuasive discourses as those "that are a 'half ours,' and as we struggle to make it our own and as it clashes with other internally persuasive discourses, this discourse is able to reveal ever newer ways to mean[ing]" (p. 42). Other studies suggest that the process of becoming a teacher is embedded in spiritual development and the capacity to reflect (Clandinin, 2019). This reflection is critical in understanding spiritual development. For example, the participants in our study were invited to reflect on their experiences and articulate something they could only understand later. We explore these considerations by reflecting on the original data from a similar study conducted by Jule, Franklin, Etherington, and Pudlas in 2014 on these participants who were teacher-education students. In our study, we return to unearth new insights about the role spirituality continued to play in the teachers our students became.

SOCIOCULTURAL THEORY

A foundational assumption at the root of this research is the theoretical position that all learning is social—and spiritual formation is social as well, connecting spirituality with Vygotsky's sociocultural theory (SCT) (Estep, 2002). SCT does not mention spirituality or spiritual formation, nor has it often been applied to illuminate these topics. However, in recent years that has begun to change, with researchers drawing on SCT to frame and better understand spiritual formation in various populations, including young children (e.g., Goodliff, 2013; Morgenthaler et al., 2014), high school students (Kanakanui, 2017), and students in higher education (Peachey, 2020).

For Vygotsky, the formation of higher mental functions begins in social relations and processes and is thus dependent on an individual's social context and participation in joint activity. From this perspective, learners are viewed as active agents in the process of their growth and development. Furthermore, speech plays a crucial role in mediating social activity and facilitating internalizing external social patterns of behavior. For Vygotsky, language is "a central feature of consciousness with an invisible, but the constant circular relationship between word-thought-word" (Robins, as cited in Peachey, 2020, p. 53). It is a way of acting upon the world, mediating the relationship between self and others. An analysis of an individual's account of their experience can thus bring to light an understanding of their identity in relation to others and the world, along with related shifts that might take place over time. This need not be limited to social understandings but can also encompass insights that shed light on spiritual perspectives (Kristjánsson, 2018).

This framework guides the present study in which we explore the views and perceptions of graduates from a Christian faith-based teacher education program 10 years after graduation. We aim to understand better any spiritual influence they might have experienced during their teacher preparation and how that might relate to how they now view their identities as teachers. We approach this task seeking to answer the following research questions: (1) How do participants understand spirituality and spiritual formation? (2) How did they experience spiritual formation in the Teacher Education program (if at all)? (3) How does spirituality inform their current sense of teacher identity, and how does this connect to their experience in the Teacher Education program (if at all)?

METHODS

Setting

The setting for this study is a Christian-founded institution of higher education in Western Canada. The university offers a five-year undergraduate concentration in education as part of a BA/BEd or BSc/BEd initial teacher preparation led to full teaching certification in the province of British Columbia. It is the only faith-based teacher education program in the province. Christian virtues have framed this "faith-based" approach through what we have called "Virtue Pathways." By this, we mean that we use Christian virtues to articulate behaviors and attitudes that align with teacher attributes and spiritual life, such as patience, compassion, wisdom, and so forth. The Teacher Education program currently enrolls approximately 300 students in the 5-year concurrent program. Ten years ago, there were 40 students in the fourth year of the program (Pudlas et al., 2012). These students were asked, via questionnaires, about their emerging identities as teachers, and 14 responded at that time.

Participants

Participants for the present study were recruited from the same cohort recruited to take part in the first study on emerging teacher identity (Pudlas et al., 2012). Invitations to participate were emailed as well as posted on social media sites associated with the School of Education. Nine alumni from the target group responded to the invitation, including eight who were practicing teachers and one who no longer identified as an educator. While some indicated the kind of school in which they were teaching, others did not. However, longitudinal data on alums from the teacher education program suggest that about 60% of program graduates teach in public institutions and 40% teach in independent schools, the majority of which are Christian schools. We have no reason to believe that the profile of participants in this study was significantly different.

Measures

Given the focus and objectives of the investigation, qualitative measurement was deemed the best fit. Qualitative measures differ from quantitative measurement and procedures which are suited for large participant samples, numerical data gathering, and generalizable outcomes (Creswell & Creswell, 2018). Instead, they are suited to studies that seek a deeper understanding of a phenomenon that is not well known, and fewer participants are needed for rich insights. Such studies will often be based on textual data generated from open-ended data gathering procedures to study and communicate participants' unique perspectives and experiences in their own words, with attention to the meaning they ascribe to their experiences (Creswell & Creswell, 2018). This was the intention of the present study, and data gathering was accomplished utilizing an open-ended online self-report questionnaire. The anonymous questionnaire facilitated maximum transparency and consisted of cohort verification along with 10 open-ended questions with no word limits imposed on responses (see the Appendix). Recruitment and data gathering took place after study procedures and related documents had undergone a research ethics review.

Data Analysis

Whereas quantitative data are processed using mathematically based statistical procedures, qualitative text-based data analysis involves interpretation, meaning, and understanding arrived at through inductive methods (Creswell & Creswell, 2018). In our case, data analysis consisted of an iterative process that began with careful reading and rereading of questionnaire responses by two of the researchers. Participants' language to describe past experiences and present professional realities and identities was examined closely, including for frequency of prominent terms and concepts (Leech & Onwuegbuzie, 2008). This was coupled with a constant comparative approach to identify, code, and classify primary patterns (Merriam, 2002). The second round of coding using NVivo further refined categories and identified related subcategories. Identified themes were validated through an independent review of results and discussion between all researchers.

FINDINGS

How do program alums now working in the field of education understand the connection between their sense of teacher identity and spiritual formation 10 years after graduation? The results of our analysis lead us to insights related to four emergent themes: (1) understandings of spirituality and spiritual formation; (2) convergence of teacher preparation and spirituality; (3) spirituality as a site of tension; and (4) current views of teacher and spiritual identity. We move now to a closer look at each in turn.

Understandings of Spirituality and Spiritual Formation

When asked about their understanding of spirituality, some participants saw spirituality as distinct from religion, while others did not. Eight of nine participants described it in terms of beliefs and faith, with five linking their understanding to a Christian faith perspective with responses such as "Faith in God" (P-B)[1] and "A relationship with God ..." (P-H).

More than half of the respondents mentioned the element of relationship or connection. One participant defined spirituality as "having some connection to something deeper than reality, a faith in something higher" (P-I), while the participant who did not identify as an educator at the time of the study transparently noted the absence of this connection, stating "Spirituality is not something that I'm connected to. I can't quite place it in my life" (P-G).

When asked to describe spiritual formation, eight of nine respondents framed it in terms of growth or development, frequently also as intentional activity. In the words of one participant, spiritual formation is "forming, reframing, exploring and growing into a belief system..." (P-E), while another described it as "building a set of beliefs or way of seeing the world" (P-G). And yet another represented it as having "to do with self-improvement and continual learning" (P-I). Over half of the respondents also linked the understanding of growth or development to perspectives informed by the Christian faith. One person stated that "Spiritual formation is growing closer to God" (P-B), while another described it as "personal and communal and...between God and the person" (P-H). Another participant provided insight into the kind of context conducive to such formative experiences:

> Spiritual formation is being able to explore, discuss and debate difficult/taboo topics without being "cancelled" and in a safe environment. It is about growing with support ... through these crises of faith into a deeper understanding of people and oneself as Christ followers. (P-F)

Taken together, the descriptions of spiritual formation included components of often intentional growth in personal individual knowledge/beliefs and relationships.

These understandings were compared and contrasted with religious belonging. Eight of the nine respondents described this as being part of a church or religious community, as exemplified by the respondent who noted that "religious belonging is about (the) church and that whole community connection" (P-I).

Six participants also commented on the aspect of shared beliefs and practices of such a community, including the respondent who defined religious belonging as "being a part of a group that believes the same things as you" (P-E). Meanwhile, another respondent described it as "how I identify myself with certain groups of people or practices" (P-D). While these comments were primarily neutral or positive in evaluative loading, one respondent observed that "Religious belonging can sometimes feel more rule-based and less personal" (P-A) than spiritual formation.

Convergence of Teacher Preparation and Spirituality

When participants were asked to comment on any connections between their time in the School of Education and their spiritual formation or understanding of spirituality as part of professional identity, all but one respondent saw connections. Overall, the connections they saw pertained to knowledge and skills gained, the influence of faculty, and the related impact on respondents' own spiritual awareness. In the words of one participant, "The culture of care and faith-based lens through which the courses were taught were deeply appreciated and impactful in my own personal understanding and practices" (P-C). Another recalled, "A biblical perspective was woven into all of the classes, which was formative. The professors embodied humility in sharing their personal stories with us as a class, and in this, I was reminded of how we will not 'arrive' in teaching but rather learn from our mistakes and grow in what it means to incorporate faith into this holy profession" (P-E). Yet another noted the sense of relief felt when they realized that professional identity could accommodate spirituality:

> The biggest thing for me was having professors and instructors who weren't trying to teach a "special version of Christian Education." They happened to have a faith but were focused on making sure we were equipped and

trained just as much as anyone from another university. I realized that I can strive for that in my profession and identity—I can do my job well without sacrificing my spirituality. (P-D)

Part of this process included creating a welcoming space for working through as yet unexamined perspectives:

The School of Education was a safe space to explore and unpack views I had growing up that needed to be challenged and enlightened by different perspectives. I felt it was a place that allowed discussion and raw debate while being respectful. Professors didn't railroad my thinking, but mostly allowed dialog[ue]. I see this missing from most non-religious institutions and religious ones. (P-F)

While this was faith-affirming for some, it was not the case for all. One of two respondents at a different place in their journey noted,

The teaching of tolerance and acceptance opened me up beyond my upbringing in a conservative, traditional church. Specifically, the aboriginal studies course has had a major impact in how I understood the world and evolved my empathy which eventually lead (led) me away from a formal church setting. (P-G)

The other respondent also indicated movement away from the Christian faith but did not link it to their experience in the teacher education program. On the other hand, they did credit the program as a noteworthy influence in their appreciation for the importance of spirituality as part of professional identity. For example, P-I stated, "Unfortunately, I can't say I'm very Christian anymore, but I do think having a spiritual aspect to being an educator now gives me a more holistic approach to the process and the people I teach."

Overall, the majority of participants indicated they felt supported and enriched in the understanding of self through opportunities to explore the spiritual dimension of their professional identity. In the words of one, "The School of Education allowed me to explore myself as an educator and the greater impact that calling has. Spirituality is the driving force behind what we do and why we do it. We love God by loving others" (P-H). This participant elaborated further, noting, "The program helped as a lens to see how I can use my gifts and talents to help others and glorify God" (P-H).

Based on the full scope of responses, regardless of participants' self-reported understanding of the spiritual dimension of their identity, their experience in the teacher education program can arguably be summed up in the words of P-I, who had moved away from the Christian faith at the time of the study. P-I commented, "The education program gave me some amazing mentors and examples of ways to walk life. I had good connections and conversations with my professors, for example, over topics of spirituality that I still remember to this day."

Spirituality as a Site of Tension and Ambivalence

Nevertheless, as might be imagined, despite the welcoming environment and safe place described by participants in the comments above, spirituality was not a site without tension with the same educational opportunities experienced differently by students. P-G noted that the program "definitely deconstructed but did not form" their religious faith. Another said they "appreciated the openness and opportunities provided to dive deeper into my own beliefs and to have meaningful dialogues about these beliefs with the instructors and fellow classmates" (P-C). A third of the participants, however, believe the program "helped me move toward a healthy save (safe) positive worldview of the LGBTQ 2+ community as well as the disability community, and gave me the confidence to approach with respect and love, with curiosity … tools to do my job well instead of fear and anxiety" (P-F).

Participants offered mixed responses when asked if they ever felt compelled to be "spiritual" or "religious" in a particular way or context. One respondent was unsure (P-A), three said no, and five said yes. While one of those who responded in the negative simply said "No" (P-B), the other two commented on the diversity encountered "within the umbrella of 'Christian faith'" (P-D). One clarified further, expressing the view that due to the "broad spectrum of faculty and staff as well as students … I didn't feel pressured towards a certain way/context" (P-H).

However, this was not the case for all. Five participants reported experiencing tension to some extent, with two qualifying their remarks to locate this aspect of their experience beyond the School of Education in the broader university context. A third respondent did not specify the location but framed the experience positively, interpreting it as a refreshing, authentic expression of faith: "Yes, to pray and be part of the Christian community. However, this wasn't uncomfortable. It was acceptable and a welcome breath of fresh air at a university. It took shape beautifully as each professor demonstrated their faith uniquely and authentically" (P-F).

For the final two participants who responded in the affirmative, feeling compelled to be spiritual or religious was a shared experience. As one reported, this occurred "all the time at TWU" (P-G) but went on to state that "once I was no longer in that situation, I realized that it wasn't me and I didn't need to put myself in that position" (P-G). The last respondent reported a similar experience, noting that "I felt that at times I was religious the right way during my time in the education program. Whether that was others' faults or just my own, I am still unsure, but it wasn't until I was on my own, post-graduation, that I really started to take my spirituality into my own hands" (P-I).

Current Views of Teacher and Spiritual Identity

How might study participants view their professional identity today? When participants were asked the extent to which spiritual values inform their current practice and if their response was connected in any way to their experience in the School of Education, eight out of nine responded affirmatively regarding the presence of spiritual values. The ninth participant indicated that they were not in the role of educator at present and did not elaborate further (P-G). Of the remaining eight respondents, six explicitly connected their appreciation for, or influence of, spiritual values in their professional practice in some way to their experience in teacher education. Several of these listed specific values they embraced and saw exemplified while in the teacher education program: "values of love, trust, belonging, and acceptance" (P-C). One participant commented on their "willingness to go over and above for my students ... due to my faith values. The School of Education encouraged this excellence and love for students" (P-B). Another participant stated, "I love others because people are precious beyond measure, and they are precious to God. This value for people was demonstrated consistently through every education course during my time without question" (P-F).

In addition, two respondents indicated that they worked at a Christian school, including one who did not make an explicit connection between spiritual values and their teacher education experience. This respondent viewed themselves as "very fortunate that I get to teach openly from a Christian perspective" (P-A), while the other believed that "The School of Education really gave me a head start in understanding how to weave the biblical story into teaching and lesson planning, which I feel prepared me well for what I do" (P-E).

In contrast, another participant wrote about the subconscious influence of underlying spiritual values connected to their teacher education experience but was careful to emphasize, at some length, that this did not come at the expense of professional preparation in the School of Education:

> My spiritual values for sure make up who I am and in turn how I do my job. But rarely do I directly reflect on my spiritual values in order to make decisions or figure out how to do my job. For sure this is connected to my experience at university. I feel like I was trained to do my job and that was always the priority. Of course the school cared about my faith and spiritual

identity, but I appreciate when I'm out doing my job, I have NEVER questioned whether I was lacking any training or experience compared to colleagues from other universities. On the other hand, I often feel like I was more equipped than other colleagues—and I think that was the greatest gift I could have ever gotten from the university. In my opinion, to have explicitly focused more on 'traditional spiritual formation' and less on basic education would have done students a disservice to their spiritual identity in the long run. (P-D)

In short, all study participants who identified as active educators indicated that spiritual values informed how they currently view themselves and their practice. In addition, some explicitly stated that such values were a daily influence and that their beliefs shape who they are and their everyday life.

There was also an understanding that this perspective added something extra, whether these values were implicitly present or more explicitly articulated and acknowledged. As P-I explained,

> I feel like the groundwork of my spirituality was aided by my time in the School of Education, but I think my spiritual values are fully realized throughout my practice of educating. Like I don't indoctrinate, etc, but I can't help but have my values color my decisions and choices when I teach.... I just see who we are as dynamic and holistic. I think as an educator it's so important to teach more than just academics.

The perspective of something more was also underscored by a participant who stated: "My spiritual values impact my practice as an educator daily—in the way I view my students, co-workers, parents, etc. It also gives me a purpose beyond 'education'" (P-H).

In sum, it seems that spiritual values, whether implicit or explicit, form an integral part of the professional identity that study participants claim for themselves and report enacting in their practice. Overall, our graduates encouraged consideration of embedding ongoing discussion about spirituality concerning conscious and unconscious assumptions about what it means to be a part of a Christian learning community.

DISCUSSION

Based on their own accounts, who do study participants say that they are? A decade after their graduation and full-time entry into the teaching profession, alums of the focal teacher education program self-identify as professional educators whose teacher education experience was influenced by spiritual values. This influence informs their understanding of professional teacher identities in public and independent (religious) schools.

The program legitimizes an aspect of human identity excluded from many secular and public education settings. Dillard et al. (2000) have forwarded the view that spirituality has often been equated with religion and therefore dismisses the inclusion of spirituality in public educational contexts. Educators who bring thoughtful, personal identity and come in thinking through at the individual-reflective level seem to embody this in their professional identity. Rather than becoming an area of identity "foreclosure," this in fact leads to a sense of thoughtfully examined holistic awareness on the part of teachers (Friesen & Besley, 2013) as well as awareness and understanding that they have spiritual resources as well as others to draw on when facing the real-world experiences of being an educator.

Understanding of Spirituality and Spiritual Formation

For these participants, spirituality and spiritual formation are intensely personal and informative conceptualizations for their own self-understanding. Many of them turn inward, following a pattern set forth by their Christian religion. Their responses depict spiritual formation as "the Spirit-driven process of forming the inner world of the human self in such a way that it becomes like the inner being of Christ himself" (Willard, 2002, p. 22). We observe a distinction between the religious creedal framework and the broader depiction of spiritual formation. This follows the developing debate between religion and spirituality (Alexander & McLaughlin, 2003; Tisdell, 2008), in which teacher education is no exception. Thus, reflection on an individual's account of their experiences can clarify social understandings and shed light on what it means to belong and be formed by teacher education programs.

Convergence of Teacher Preparation and Spirituality

The participants showcase awareness of spirituality within the teacher education program. This spiritual awareness is understood as part of a Christian spiritual tradition whereby teacher education aligns towards a particular goal of transformation. This kind of spiritual transformation involves:

> The deliberate, systematic, and sustain[s] divine and human effort to share or appropriate the knowledge, values, attitudes, skills, sensitivities, and behaviors as enacted in the teacher education program, resulting in change, renewal, and reformation of persons, groups, and structures ... preeminently in the person of Jesus Christ. (Pazmiño, 2010, p. 360)

While most participants identify the teacher education program as part of the Christian spiritual tradition, at least one participant admits that they do not identify as a Christian. However, that same participant pointed to a "holistic approach" in their educational training that had been formational. This holistic approach prioritizes relationships so that "the sum of the specific human encounters between students and the teacher within a special community is the essence of education" (Braskamp, 2000, p. 21). Lakes (2002) defines four principles of holistic education as the following:

> First, human beings are complex creatures with multiple layers of meaning: biological, psychological, ecological, ideological, socio-cultural, and spiritual. Second, there are stages in a child's development; and transcendence is a long process of unfolding. Third, holistic education is linked to the world of cultural struggle, social justice, democratic action, and sustainable living. Finally, holistic education cannot be reduced to any single technique. It involves cultivation of social relationship through dialogue, connection, and authenticity. (p. 2)

For the participants, their teacher preparation was a time and opportunity to explore complexities in education beyond the traditional framework of the Christian church. Instead, an openness to new educative possibilities was uncovered via informational and formational teaching (Wilhoit, 2008) while in a relationship with one another. In particular, this teacher education program is a space where "the community of truth is practiced" (Palmer, 1997, p. 90) so that these educative possibilities are discovered in connection with one another. Thus, our teacher education program appears to serve as a potentially formative space in which student teachers are invited to explore perspectives on what it means to grow holistically, develop their identity, and clarify their own assumptions in relation to the spiritual expression of others.

Spirituality as a Site of Tension and Ambivalence

In contrast to the previous two themes, several participants suggested that the teacher education program was a site of tension for spiritual discourse and understanding. For example, one participant indicated that the program deconstructed their religious faith but "did not form it." Yet another participant suggested that the classroom learning experience provided a lot of opportunities to connect with professors and peers. While the teacher education program aims to promote a "spirituality that invites us to see the importance of, to acknowledge, and to embrace difference" (Augustine & Zurmehly, 2013, p. 10), there remains ambivalence about the participants' personal experience with their spiritual formation.

Further research is needed to understand the factors that contribute to what we observe as destabilization and re-stabilization that exists when our graduates construct new perspectives that diverge from the personal understanding and outward expression of the spiritualities they bring to their work.

Current Views of Teacher and Spiritual Identity

The responses collectively indicate that as part of the Christian spiritual tradition, a reconstructive paradigm for forming beliefs, knowledge, and values is more consistent with efforts towards training and formation. For example, encouraging reflection and inviting next steps and application to practice echoes the Hebrew word for knowledge, "yada;" we call this particular depth of understanding wisdom, which involves putting one's learning to practice. Willhoit and Howard (2020) posit this wisdom approach, whereas programmatic and efficiency concerns tend "to reduce spiritual formation to a single dimension" (p. 21).

It seems to us that the thoughtful and explicit engagement around spiritual and faith-informed identity in the School of Education program, and values modeled by faculty, in fact, provide an antidote to identity foreclosure in the sense of teacher education students simply "accepting" an ideal and uncritically examined version of professional identity (Friesen & Besley, 2013). However, this does not mean that there are no struggles, including tensions around spiritual values and, for some, a sense of pressure to conform. It also does not preclude the potential for the explorations of unexamined values to be part of a movement away from positions of faith for some, even as for others, it leads to stronger connections and greater intentionality. Nevertheless, based on participants' responses, it would seem that this process is part of an experience that enables teachers to be grounded in an understanding that allows them to bring a holistic sense of self to their work as educators, that enables them to "teach more than academics" and see a purpose in their chosen vocation that is "beyond education." We would recommend further qualitative research on how our graduates specifically operationalize their beliefs in their various workspaces, from the public and independent to international education sites. We also would encourage further exploration into the extent to which our graduates see additional training required as they support their students, who may come from different religious communities and understandings of spiritual formation.

LIMITATIONS

We recognize that our participants did not fully address the complexities of their emerging Christian faith during their undergraduate studies, including potentially negative experiences within the program. Additionally, we are aware that our research is limited to our Canadian postsecondary Christian context, and this focus may not resonate with those in other institutions of teacher education population samples. Our method of data collection has been to understand our graduates solely based on what they can tell us about who they are interpersonally and from the memories of their experiences; thus, self-reporting has limitations. We also observe other limitations derived from population sampling from our small but growing program; we need a larger sample size that reflects the new realities of increased numbers of students enrolled in our program.

FURTHER RESEARCH

In addition to the future research that we have outlined above, replicating this study through more narrative-informed research designs would be profitable as we examine what the stories of our graduates might be able to tell us about what they experience in the teacher education program. Future research could address these limitations by conducting interviews with our graduates and following up in interval stages, 3, 5, and 10 years later, to examine how and what our graduates see their teacher education program impacting who they are. Additional exploration is needed to understand better our graduates' impact on the school and district work environments and partnerships we have regionally. We wonder, how do faith-based teacher education programs facilitate greater public discourse about the role of religion as a part of the human experience? Further investigation of what the districts and schools that employ our grads are saying about our program in terms of our graduates' engagement with spirituality and their understanding of the nature of curriculum and practice is needed. Finally, developing a quantitative instrument and measure to assess the impact of spiritual formation taking place using our program "Virtue Pathways" approach to encourage richer discourse for faculty around what they are observing in our programs is recommended.

CONCLUSION

Is there anything that is distinct about our participants' experience of Christian spirituality as it pertains to teacher education? And if so, what are the implications for the emerging teacher from a faith-based education program? Our participants have experienced a pedagogy rooted in Christian spirituality which has shaped their teaching, learning, and identity formation. Our study found the following: (a) that the teachers in our education program described spirituality and spiritual formation as a process of continually "forming, reframing, exploring, and growing individual beliefs," in contrast to religious belonging, which pertained to identifying with certain group practices and norms; (b) our teacher education program serves as a space to explore perspectives on what it means to grow holistically; (c) spirituality is a site of tension that exhibits a process of destabilization and restabilization when our graduates construct new perspectives that diverge from their spiritualities; and (d) a view towards our teacher education program as a potentially formative space that invites exploration of what it means to grow holistically, encourage professional and personal identity formation, and clarify assumptions in relation to the beliefs held by others for those entering into the teaching profession. While our findings present descriptions that other Christian postsecondary teacher education programs may be able to bring forward and draw parallels from and thus reflect on their own program practice, we would encourage teacher education programs of other religious and nonreligious contexts to explore the dominant and nondominant discourses that are prevalent for them. We would also invite reflection and consideration of how spirituality is integral to the activity of preparing teachers, engaging instruction, and developing programs, given our assessment of its impact on identity formation.

REFERENCES

Alexander, H. & T., McLaughlin. (2003). Education in religion and spirituality. In N. Blake, P. Smeyers, R. Smith, & P. Standish (Eds.), *The Blackwell guide to the philosophy of education* (pp. 356–373). Blackwell.
Augustine, T. A., & Zurmehly, D. J. (2013). Conversations about race. In C. B. Dillard & C. L. E. Okpalaoka (Eds.), *Engaging culture, race and spirituality: New visions* (pp. 10–31). Peter Lang.
Bakhtin, M. (1981). *The dialogic imagination.* University of Texas Press.
Braskamp, L. A. (2000). Toward a more holistic approach to assessing faculty as teachers. In K. Ryan (Ed.), *Evaluating teaching in higher education: A vision for the future* (pp. 19–33). Jossey-Bass.
Britzman, D. (2012). *Practice makes practice: A critical study of learning to teach.* State University of New York Press.
Carson, T. (2005). Beyond instrumentalism: The significance of teacher identity in educational change. *Journal of the Canadian Association for Curriculum Studies, 3*(2), 1–8.

Clandinin, J. (2019). *Journey in narrative inquiry: The selected works for D. Jean Clandinin*. Routledge.
Creswell, J. W., & Creswell J. D. (2018). *Research design: Qualitative, quantitative, and mixed methods approach* (5th ed.). SAGE.
Dillard, C., Abdur-Rashid, D., & Tyson, C. (2000). My soul is a witness: Affirming pedagogies of the spirit. *Qualitative Studies in Education, 13*(5), 447–462.
Durkheim, E. (1975). The elementary forms of the religious life. In W. Pickering (Ed.), *Durkheim on religion: A selection of readings with bibliographies* (pp. 103–166). Routledge & Kegan Paul. (Original work published 1898)
Estep, J. R. (2002). Spiritual formation as social: Toward a Vygotskyan developmental perspective. *Religious Education, 97*(2), 141–164.
Franklin, K., & Van Brummelen, H. (2006). Religious diversity in Western Canadian education: Presumptions, provisions, practices, and possibilities. In F. Selili (Ed.), *Religion in multicultural education* (pp 71–99). Information Age Publishing.
Friesen, M., & Besley, S. (2013). Teacher identity development in the first year of teacher education: A developmental and social psychological perspective. *Teaching and Teacher Education 36*, 23–32.
Goodliff, G. (2013). *Young children's expressions of spirituality: An ethnographic case study* [EdD thesis, The Open University].
Jule, A. (2004). *Gender, silence, and participation in language education: Sh-shushing the girls*. Palgrave Macmillan.
Kanakanui, L. (2017). *Faith development as experienced by Christian high school seniors* [PhD thesis, Liberty University].
Kristjánsson, C. (2018). Church-sponsored English as a second language in western Canada: Grassroots expressions of spiritual and social practice. In M. Shepard Wong & A. Mahboob (Eds.), *Spirituality and English language teaching: Religious explorations of teacher identity, pedagogy and context*. (pp. 172–194). Multilingual Matters.
Lakes, R. D. (2002). Spirituality, work, and education: The holistic approach. *Journal of Vocational Education Research, 25*(2), 199–219.
Leech, N. L., & Onwuegbuzie, A. J. (2008). Qualitative data analysis: A compendium of techniques and a framework for selection for school psychology research and beyond. *School Psychology Quarterly, 23*(4), 587–604. https://doi.org/10.1037/1045-3830.23.4.587
Libster, M. M. (2018). Spiritual formation, secularization, and reform of professional nursing and education in antebellum America. *Journal of Professional Nursing, 34*(1). 47–53.
Merriam, S. (2002). *Qualitative research in practice: Examples for discussion and analysis*. Jossey-Bass.
Morgenthaler, S., Keiser, M., & Larson, M. (2014). Nurturing the infant soul: The importance of community and memories in the spiritual formation of young children. *Christian Education Journal, Series 3, 11*(2), 244–258.
Palmer, P. (1997). *The courage to teach*. Jossey-Bass.
Pazmiño, R. W. (2010). Christian education is more than formation. *Christian Education Journal, 3*(8), 356–365.

Peachey, J. (2020). *Journeying together towards goodness: participant understanding of practices and narratives in a University of the Nations Discipleship Training School* [PhD thesis, Middlesex University]. Oxford Centre for Mission Studies.

Pudlas, K. A. (2009). Leading teachers in professional development for inclusion. In A. L. Edmunds & R.B. Macmillan (Eds.), *Leadership for inclusion: A practical guide* (pp. 117–131). Sense.

Pudlas, K., Franklin, K., Etherington, M., & Jule, A. (2012, May 23–26). *Gender, diversity and freedom: Dominant discourses in a pre-service teacher education program* [Paper presentation]. ICCTE Conference. Azusa Pacific University, Azusa, California.

Tisdell, E. J. (2008). Spirituality and adult learning. *New Directions for Adult and Continuing Education, 119* (Fall), 27–36.

Wilhoit, J. C. (2008). *Spiritual formation as if the church mattered: Growing in Christ through community.* Baker Academic.

Wilhoit, J. C., & Howard, E. B. (2020). The wisdom of Christian spiritual formation. *Journal of Spiritual Formation and Soul Care, 13*(1), 5–21.

Willard, D. (2002). *Renovation of the heart: Putting on the character of Christ.* NavPress.

Yilmaz, K. (2013). Comparison of quantitative and qualitative research traditions: Epistemological, theoretical, and methodological differences. *European Journal of Education, 48*(2), 311–325.

Zhang, K. C., & Wu, I. (2016). Towards a holistic teacher education: Spirituality and special education teacher training. In M. de Souza, J. Watson, & J. Bone (Eds.), *Spirituality across disciplines* (pp. 135–147). Springer.

ENDNOTE

1. As noted in the Methods section, the questionnaire was anonymous. Participants have been identified with a letter, for example, "P-A" represents Participant A, "P-B" represents Participant B, and so forth.

APPENDIX

Questionnaire

1. Please confirm the final year you completed undergrad coursework at [University's] School of Education
2. What is spirituality to you?
3. How would you describe spiritual formation versus religious belonging?
4. How did your years at [University's] School of Education impact your sense of self as an educator? How does "spirituality" fit into that sense of identity?

5. To what extent was your teacher education program instrumental in your spiritual formation? Please explain and provide an example if relevant.
6. To what extent was your teacher education program instrumental in your formation as a person of religious faith? Please explain and provide an example if relevant.
7. Did you ever feel compelled to be "spiritual" or "religious" in a certain way or in a certain context? Yes/No? Please explain and provide examples if relevant.
8. When you reflect back on your experiences at [University's] School of Education, were any practices or relationships that are particularly influential in your spiritual development? Please explain.
9. To what extent do spiritual values inform your current practice as an educator? Would you say this is connected in some way to your experience in the School of Education? Yes/No? Please explain.
10. To what extent would you now say that, spiritually, you seek "connection, healing, and relationships?" What difference does this make to your practice as an educator?
11. What else would you like to tell us about the relationship between spirituality, religious faith, education, and pedagogic practice?

CHAPTER 7

CONNECTING THE HEART AND SOUL OF TEACHING THROUGH SERVICE-LEARNING

Vickie E. Lake
University of Oklahoma

Ithel Jones
Florida State University

Christian Winterbottom
University of North Florida

Miranda Lin
Illinois State University

ABSTRACT

Instead of focusing on testing, content, and accountability, teacher education programs should be helping preservice teachers focus on the heart and soul of teaching. Thus, helping them as they continue their spiritual journey of becoming a teacher. Although there are many ways that teacher educators can support preservice teachers, in this chapter, we argue that service-learning, with its emphasis on social responsibility, is a promising approach.

Keywords: service-learning, spirituality, social responsibility, teacher education

During the past few decades, the academic standards, testing, and accountability education reform movement has dominated teaching and teacher education discourse. Teachers often lament the pressure of high stakes testing and accountability ratings. Yet, faced with demands to improve students' learning, many teachers struggle to navigate between ensuring that students perform well on high-stakes tests and meeting their various needs. That is, they recognize that the heart and soul of teaching are much more than disciplinary content and pedagogical technique.

In and of itself, the act of teaching is a relatively straightforward process, and most individuals would have no difficulty describing what it means to teach. Yet, defining teaching is deceivingly difficult. Because teaching is an activity that can take many forms. Teaching, for example, can be described as instructing or training someone, and, as such, it is an activity that attends to individuals' needs, experiences, and feelings. However, at its core, it is a social activity that involves the uniquely human conditions of caring, sensitivity, kindness, and optimism. As such, we maintain in this chapter that there is a spiritual dimension to teaching and teacher education. As Palmer (2017) noted in his book, *The Courage to Teach*, teaching is a vocation in which intellect, emotion, and spirituality converge. In Palmer's words, "Good teaching cannot be reduced to technique; good teaching comes from the identity and integrity of the teacher" (p. 10).

What, then, is spirituality in education, and why does it matter? Like teaching, spirituality has many varied definitions and has been described as an "elusive" (Palmer, 2003) or "abstract" (Kumar, 2018) concept that is related to religion or morality. Yet, for Jones (2005) and others (e.g., McGreevy & Copley, 1999), spirituality is an inclusive construct that recognizes that all things are interrelated. For Parker Palmer, spirituality refers to a deep connection and a sense of empathy between the student, teacher, and content. For the purposes of this chapter, we adopt Palmer's (2003) definition of spirituality as "the eternal human yearning to be connected to something larger than our own egos" (p. 377). This view of spirituality, according to Jones (2005), refers to a "transcendence and compassion in the classroom" (p. 6) through which the teacher, student, and subject are connected. It follows that when applied, spirituality entails the pursuit of truth, meaning, knowledge, and inner awareness, qualities that are at the heart of what it means to teach. Thus, it is maintained that rather than focusing on testing, content, and accountability, education reform should start with "the transformed heart of the teacher" (McGreevy & Copley, 1999, p. 1). Yet, most teacher education programs in the United States pay scant attention to preservice teachers' (PSTs) spirituality and spiritual awareness.

Typically, teacher education programs in higher education institutions focus on the knowledge base of teaching and pedagogical technique. In this chapter, we maintain that PSTs' spiritual needs should also be supported in ways that can "help them grow larger hearts and souls" (Palmer, 2003, p. 378). Knowing what to do as a teacher can be considered the heart of teaching, whereas the uniquely human conditions of love, kindness, tolerance, compassion, and an ethic of care entail the soul of teaching. Thus, teacher educators should strive to connect not only teaching and learning but also spirituality. While there are many approaches that teacher educators can adopt to address teacher candidates' spiritual needs, service-learning, with its emphasis on social responsibility, is a promising approach. In this chapter, we address what service-learning is and why it is a good approach to attend to PSTs' spiritual needs.

SERVICE-LEARNING

Service-learning is an experiential educational approach that unites meaningful community service with academic learning, personal growth, and civic responsibility (National and Community Service Trust Act, 1990/2009). Previous research has affirmed the benefits of service-learning in teacher education programs. For example, it allows PSTs to apply academic, social, and personal skills to improve or supplement instruction; make decisions that have real, not hypothetical, results; grow as individuals and cooperative groups, gain respect for peers, and increase civic participation; and gain a deeper understanding of themselves, their community, and society (Bringle et al., 2004; Kaye, 2004; Lake & Jones, 2012). As a result, service learning has been embedded in the curriculum and extracurricular or co-curricular activities as a form of citizenship in many teacher education programs across the country to help PSTs engage in the values of the school's mission to promote social action, awareness, and justice.

How Is Service-Learning Practiced?

A service-learning educational model is participatory, democratic, and collaborative in nature. When used in the classroom, it is best practiced by those who are committed and close to the real world of students and their families (Winterbottom & Mazzocco, 2015). This pedagogy is grounded in real-world situations and is carried out by practitioners in collaboration with the community who have a direct and passionate investment in what is occurring inside the classroom; it is a collaboration with people in context (Freire, 1970). Moreover, service-learning is done in the company of peers, construing the domain of education as contingent on interactions and relationships (Pascal & Bertram, 2012). Through action and interaction, the praxeology drives the curriculum revealing underlying assumptions and helping to generate new epistemologies. Conversely, it also shows how teachers can change their approaches to working with learners and their families.

Approaches to Service-Learning

In the classroom, service-learning can be used as an instructional strategy to meet learning goals and/or content standards. The components of effective service-learning include planning, preparation, action, and reflection (Kaye, 2004; Lake & Jones, 2012). Diversity, PST voice, and collaboration should be clearly visible during these components, especially planning and preparation.

Kaye (2004) outlines four approaches to service-learning. The first is direct service. This is where the PST's service directly affects and involves working with partners face to face (Lake & Jones, 2012). For example, PSTs collaborating with a local Parent-Teacher-Association to create and offer activities to engage families at home is an example of direct service. Indirect service is the second approach, and in this type of service-learning, PSTs provide service to the community as a whole. As such, they do not meet or interact with the recipients of the service. For example, canned food drives or book drives are examples of indirect service.

The third is the approach called advocacy. As the name implies, advocacy involves PSTs creating awareness or acting on an issue that is of public educational interest. An example would be when PSTs wrote letters to Oklahoma policymakers concerning the passing of House Bill 1775 (2021) that bans diversity training and teaching examining systemic racism and how race influences American politics, legal systems, and society. No educational organization participated in the creation of HB 1775, and none have supported it. The Tulsa Race Massacre Centennial Commission stated that:

> No matter how poorly written, the intention of the bill clearly aims to limit teaching the racial implications of America's history. The bill serves no purpose than to fuel the racism and denial that afflicts our communities and our nation. It is a sad day and a stain on Oklahoma. (Raache, 2021, p. 18)

Finally, the fourth type of service-learning is research. This approach is where PSTs gather information and report on a topic that is in the public interest. All the above approaches have been successfully used in teacher education programs. However, Lake and Jones (2008) state that PSTs should be engaged in direct service-learning at least once in their teacher education programs to experience the results of their service activity.

Strengths and Limitations of Service-Learning

Service-learning is only one of a myriad of exemplary pedagogical approaches in education and has both strengths and limitations. At its root, service-learning focuses on examining PST-instructor-community practice and exploring what works for teachers and why. This epistemology then informs teaching and learning and provides a framework for shaping future learning. Although to this point, a lot of the evidence that has informed practice has been imposed on the educational field from external sources (Pascal & Bertram, 2012; Winterbottom & Mazzocco, 2015), by using a service-learning approach, teachers can potentially advocate change and reform from within outward.

A key strength of this approach is that those involved in practice can identify ways to improve their teaching methodology, classroom, and school and take responsibility for this action, inspiring and generating collaborative learning and action. Moreover, teachers informing their practice via this paradigm can give a close account of what works, including how and why, ensuring credibility and utility in the real world of practice. Finally, and critically for those who work with PSTs, it has an ethical and values transparent stance (Pascal & Bertram, 2012). As a result, PSTs become engaged with their school community and the wider society.

The limitations for practitioners using this pedagogical approach are also acknowledged. Any theoretical paradigm that does not involve larger-scale interactions necessarily focuses on specific contexts, and smaller numbers and their transferability to teacher training programs are, therefore, influenced by the locality of context (Pascal & Bertram, 2012).

Service-learning is also unable, nor does it set out, to show any cause and effect or to support comparisons or predictions. Moreover, building relationships with the community and collaborators takes time, which involves a deep attachment and ongoing commitment to projects that are not always possible to dedicate to the pursuit of knowledge. Therefore, because of this pedagogical framework, this kind of teaching methodology is sometimes seen to have less credibility and utility in guiding policy decisions due to its lack of perceived rigor in the method (Pascal & Bertram, 2012; Winterbottom & Mazzocco, 2015).

Affective Education

Both spirituality and service-learning draw from theoretical frameworks of scholars who have influenced affective educators for the last four decades (e.g., Goldstein, 1999; Kohlberg 1981; Noddings, 1984). The connection between spirituality and affective education scholars (caring, moral education, virtues) can be found in the pedagogy of service-learning in teacher education programs. Noddings (1984) suggests that one way for students to engage in *caring* behavior is for them to engage in consistent service activities in the school or community. We believe service-learning is an avenue where students can collaborate with the community, including hospitals, community-based organizations, nursing homes, animal shelters, and parks; an expectation of this work would be a true apprenticeship in caring. Noddings's work suggests that teachers should allow children to cooperate with each other to practice caring. Classroom strategies such as group work, cooperative structures, and cooperative learning are among a few that could be useful, and these strategies are what make service-learning successful.

The work of Goldstein (1999) examined previous theories of Noddings's and Vygotsky's. In this work, Goldstein espoused how Vygotsky resisted the separation of cognition and affect, emphasizing the existence of a dynamic system of meaning in which the affective and the intellectual unite. Vygotsky himself saw affect and intellect as interconnected and inseparable.

In much of his work, Kohlberg (1981) attempts to capture and label the logic behind specific actions and virtues and thereby define one's level of moral reasoning. Such virtues as honesty, integrity, fairness, respect, and responsibility can be taught and practiced through service-learning projects. Spiritual characteristics such as character education, particularly moral reasoning, occur as a *hidden curriculum* when students unintentionally practice personal virtues through service-learning projects. The teacher educator's role is to expose the hidden curriculum and engage preservice teachers through discussions and actions.

Extending Kohlberg's work, Gilligan and Wiggins (1988) identified two dimensions of relationships that shape children's awareness of self in relation to others. The first is the dimension of inequality that is reflected when a child becomes aware of being smaller and less capable than adults and older children. As a result, children may feel helpless and powerless as they are dependent on those who are bigger and more powerful. The second dimension focuses on the attachments and the dynamics of the attachment relationship. Attachment relationships "create a different awareness of self— as capable of affecting others, as able to move others and be moved by them" (p. 114). From these two dimensions—inequality and attachment—come two moral visions—one of justice and one of care. These moral visions are connections that preservice teachers make when engaged in service-learning experiences, thus enriching their spiritual growth by having them question *how I treat others fairly* and how *I help others in need*.

Also focusing on the two moral visions, Lickona (1991) believes that teacher educators must engage preservice teachers in the problems facing their community, country, or world before they can be expected to help. He emphasizes the importance of service and explains that preservice teachers must have responsibility and perform caring deeds to strengthen the values of responsibility and caring. "Simply learning about the value of caring may increase students' moral knowledge. But it won't necessarily develop their own commitment to that value, their confidence that they can help, or the skills needed to help effectively" (p. 312).

When addressing holistic education, we cannot overlook Steiner's contribution to the field. Steiner's educational philosophy is based on anthroposophy, a worldview that can be interpreted as combining tenets from the mainstream traditions of Christianity and Vedic knowledge (Pearce, 2019). Steiner proposes that everyone must find the source of awareness within him/herself and must examine everything using his/her own thinking (Rosch, 2017). Pearce's (2019) findings support this stance after observing Waldorf schools in England. Further, "Steiner consistently taught that social improvement and individual inner development must go hand in hand. In the course of his career, he sparked numerous educational, social, and artistic movements that flourish around the world today" (Sunbridge Institute, 2021). Steiner's influence is evident as Steiner argues that the learning process is essentially threefold, engaging the head, heart, and hands—or thinking, feeling, and doing (Steiner, 2000). Simply stated, educators need to nurture and engage children through a curriculum and pedagogy that supports holistic learning-integrates academics, arts (in various forms), and practical skills.

Teacher educators must consider what the optimal expectations are of future teachers. Lickona (1991) states, "Down through history and all over the world, education has had two great goals: to help people become smart and to help them become good" (p. 67). Moreover, in "The Purpose of Education," Martin Luther King Jr. (1947) stated, "Intelligence is not enough. Intelligence plus character, that is the goal of true education." In other words, academic or content learning may allow us to become smart, but the human character is what will enable us to experiment with being good. Thus, integrating service-learning into preservice teacher education programs builds this character and can guide future teachers to fulfill their supporting spiritual growth.

Connections Between Service-Learning and Spirituality

Hoppé (2004) contends that the goal of service-learning "should be an informed and unbiased study of social and civic issues, resulting in a commitment to participation in solving those issues for the benefit of individuals and the good of society as a whole" (p. 148). Service-learning has demonstrated a positive relationship with undergraduates' spiritual growth.

For example, research affirms that commitments to community well-being and social justice can motivate actions and provide an opportunity for personal strength and reflection (Astin et al., 2011; Barrett, 2016; Colby & Damon, 1992; Eyler & Giles, 1999; Lovik, 2011). Service-learning provides the experience by posing students to new situations in the community and engaging students authentically with the world and social concerns (Sokol & Marle, 2019). The most notable and comprehensive study results to date also indicate a powerful impact on the spiritual quest, the ethic of caring, and ecumenical worldview dimensions of spirituality when students participate in service-learning (Astin et al., 2011). Therefore, it is critical to learn how these young adults make decisions and are influenced in their civic and spiritual lives. Recognizing young adults' drive for truth, purpose, and meaning can help us better understand the connection between service-learning and spirituality (Sokol et al., 2017). Moreover, Brandenberger and Bowman (2015) argue that it is imperative to analyze moral, spiritual, and civic responsibility during college since much of the students' moral reasoning is developed while in higher education (Pascarella & Terenzini, 2005).

Meanwhile, Welch and Koth (2013) posit three factors associated with spirituality, (1) the self, (2) the other, and (3) oneness. The components of self, other, and oneness are based on the prominent features of spirituality. The self means one is aware of their values, attitudes, feelings, and feelings that shape their identity and influence how they perceive and react/interact. The other can be a person, group, or idea that is new and outside the realm of the self. As stated by Welch and Koth, there is a transaction between the self and the other: "in the process, the individual self must reflect and make meaning of that experience and interaction with the other that takes place" (p. 623). Otherness means one has to consider the perspective of someone other than one's own perspective. Oneness suggests a complementary and holistic relationship between the self and the other. The self is never "truly complete nor static as it is continually evolving" (p. 624). The findings of Welch and Koth's study suggest that when the service-learning experience is thoughtfully facilitated, students can pursue personal, intellectual, and spiritual learning. This is especially true when students' perceptions of who they are and their perceptions of the world are challenged. Kirsch (2009) states that this contemplative practice can lead to a commitment to social responsibility, being civic-minded, practicing mindfulness, and listening to the voices of self and others. Kirsch further argues that spirituality and contemplation help students become more willing to engage with complex social, cultural, and political issues.

Service-Learning as a Methodology for Teaching Spirituality

Brandenberger and Bowman (2015) contend that higher education student participation in high-impact practices has more substantial prosocial growth. That is to say, high-impact learning experiences such as study abroad, active learning, and service-learning can help students' prosocial development during college. For Brandenberger and Bowman, prosocial is a term that communicates commitment, cognitive or behavioral, to the welfare of others. They posit that "related terms include compassion, caring, altruism and social responsibility" (p. 330).

Palmer et al. (2017) have shown that higher education faces the same problems as the corporate workplace—leadership that shows compromising values, alienation, and the struggle to find one's inner self. However, if teacher educators became more in tune with their spirituality, they could help PSTs grow spiritually. Davalos (2014) contends that universities should be engaged in *servant leadership*, which includes going beyond one's self-interest, as a way to promote spirituality in their faculty and students. We believe that service-learning can be a form of servant leadership and that engaging PSTs in service-learning promotes their spiritual development.

As a methodology, service-learning is a teaching and learning method that connects meaningful community service with academic learning, personal growth, and civic responsibility (Lake & Jones, 2008). Moreover, research reveals that it can enhance and enrich the teaching and learning experiences and positively impact PSTs. Previous research suggests that PSTs engaged in service-learning showed an increase in their compassion and concern for others, their use of multicultural teaching strategies (Portthoff et al., 2000), sensitivity to diversity and issues of tolerance (Beyer, 1997; Boyle-Baise, 1998; Tellex et al., 1995), strengthened their moral development (Beyer, 1997), became more politically aware and active in community service (Donahue, 1999), developed a more significant commitment to teaching and a more profound ethic of care (Freeman & Swick, 2001).

Historically, teacher education programs focus on content knowledge (Buchanan & Hyde (2008). They argue that teacher education programs place

> extensive emphasis on the cognitive dimension of learning, in which the intellect is favoured as the way of knowing above other facets of an individual's ontology, particularly the emotions and intuition, that is, the affective and spiritual dimensions. Resulting in a separation of mind, body and spirit, such an approach is then far from holistic, and may result in a neglect of such non-cognitive dimensions of learning.

Connecting cognitive, affective, and spiritual dimensions of learning is what service-learning does; it connects service/social objectives with learning objectives with the specific intent that the activity changes both the recipients and providers of the service (Jacoby, 2007). Service-learning engages students so that they use what they learn in the classroom to solve real-world problems. Notably, the real value of service-learning is that it connects the university curriculum with the inherent caring and concern PSTs bring with them to the teaching profession (Lake & Jones, 2008). Just as teachers support the development and growth of children's prosocial skills, teacher educators must do the same with their PSTs, and service-learning is one method to do that.

Service-Learning Process

GenerationOn (2021) provides ideas, tools, and resources to engage students in service-learning. They outline six steps: investigation, preparation, action, reflection, demonstration, and evaluation, also known as the IPARDE process. Throughout these six steps, PSTs are spiritually engaged as service-learning also promotes personal and social transformation (Lau et al., 2014).

1. Investigation—engaging PSTs in critical thinking to identify a community need (or needs) or a community partner that extends the course content; identify content and social learning objectives. Talking about potential service-learning projects provides a space for PSTs to discuss their values and beliefs. Knowing why PSTs are interested in these projects provides a space where spirituality is welcome in discussions in higher education. For example, one of our PSTs wanted to research obsessive compulsive disorder (OCD). At first, this seemed like an unusual service-learning project, but she explained that growing up, she had a friend with this diagnosis and described how she struggled in school and how teachers did not know what to do or how to make accommodations. Her vision of herself as a teacher was one who understood what OCD was and had several strategies to implement. While not a common educational issue, she worked with a mental health specialist who stated that educators should have information and plan about OCD as 1 in 100 people have this diagnosis (International OCD Foundation, 2021). This PST could identify kindergarten children in her internship class that demonstrated OCD traits. Researching, then teaching her class about OCD, she was able to help the children in her class move

Connecting the Heart and Soul of Teaching Through Service-Learning 137

from saying that these kids were "weird" to showing tolerance for their behaviors.
2. Preparation—collaborating with the community partner and organizing the project to meet the identified need. Whether PSTs work individually, in small groups, or as a class, they need to meet with their community partner to ensure that the identified need will be met. For example, in the first semester of our program, our PSTs worked with the local homeless coalition. Year after year, they wanted to create a room at the shelter for kids and families that had games, toys, and books; the shelter already had one. Our shelter contact was very patient and was great at guiding them toward their actual needs. Unfortunately, PSTs sometimes enter into service-learning projects with a *fix-it* mindset instead of understanding that it is a true partnership. However, teacher educators and community partners are essential in helping PSTs understand the sociocultural context of the situation or people involved. Namely, teacher educators and community partners can prepare PSTs before they step into the community by learning the context/history of the community and who they would be working with. This way, both PSTs and the homeless shelter could benefit from the partnership. In turn, they could both be transformed.
3. Action—engagement in the service-learning project. This step is where the PSTs implement their plan in collaboration with their community partner. For example, working with the homeless coalition and several churches that were located in an area of town without grocery stores, our PSTs helped the community begin a farmer's market on the weekends that accepted food stamps. Using their plan from Step 2 and guidance from the homeless coalition and church leaders, the PSTs engaged the community members, contacted the farm coop to schedule specific market days, and helped file the required paperwork with the city. For several months they were actively working on their plan.
4. Reflection—PSTs and the community partner communicate their feelings and check in with each other throughout the service-learning experience and at the end of the project. It is imperative for teacher education programs that engage in service-learning to provide time in class to unpack the experiences and scaffold PSTs through sensitive conversations. Our PSTs held conscious and unconscious biases about the homeless that needed to be addressed. Class discussions, readings, and service-learning experiences allowed them to confront these

biases. Thus, strengthening their spiritual development through caring actions.
5. Demonstration—sharing the project and what was learned with others. There are various ways of doing this. For example, our PSTs have shared their projects with their classmates, other teachers in their schools, parents, expanded members of their community partners, and local media.
6. Evaluation-assessing PST learning, the effectiveness of the project from the community partner, and identifying successes and areas for improvement. We usually follow up with the partners via email or by stopping by to acquire their feedback. At the same time, PSTs also share their feedback via guided reflections or reports.

CONCLUSION

Challenges and barriers to teaching spirituality in higher education, specifically teacher education, cannot be underestimated, especially for junior faculty (Zajonc, 2003). The lack of definition, even if one defines it in their manuscript, leaves interpretation open to the readers. Chickering (2003) posits that higher education's focus on truth and knowledge as objective and external de-legitimizes spirituality's open practice and research. Additionally, Raper (2001) states that the study of faith and spirituality is often seen as anti-intellectual. For these reasons, many faculty do not overtly show an active research line in spirituality. We posit that faculty/teacher educators do not have to identify their research and practice as focusing on spirituality if their institutional environment does not lend itself to support it. In this way, the lack of definition can work for those of us in higher education and preservice and in-service teachers.

One can take many roads when teaching spirituality to PSTs, and service-learning is one of them. The reflective experience in service-learning can transform one from "me-ness" to "we-ness" according to Welch and Koth (2009). Welch and Koth believe that this transformation challenges attitudes, values, or beliefs and creates change in perspective and awareness of the other. They further argue that when thoughtfully facilitated service-learning experiences, they can catalyze PSTs to pursue additional personal, intellectual, and spiritual learning. In addition, these experiences often move them further into an intensive exploration of values and personal meaning (Welch & Koth, 2009, 2013).

In addition, aligning with previous research, college students view service-learning as a calling (Dickerson et al., 2017). Many of our PSTs stated that their call emerged from their spirituality and/or religious upbringing that lends itself to the spirituality aspects inherent in service-learning—the ability to make connections and form relationships (Fried, 2001); being able to demonstrate compassion, love, kindness, and peace (Massoudi, 2003); learning how to be a servant leader or servant teacher (Davalos, 2014); and receiving confirmation that their call to teaching would provide meaning to their lives (Fried, 2001; Noddings, 1984, 1986, 2012).

As teacher educators who have worked with PSTs to implement service-learning projects for nearly two decades, we have observed that many of our PSTs who completed their service-learning experiences began better understanding their role and place in the world. As a result, PSTs are more inclined to give of themselves to the betterment of others. Thus, we believe service-learning can better prepare teachers who can intellectually, affectively, and spiritually care for themselves. Namely, service-learning provides a pathway for PSTs to think critically, develop moral reasoning skills and a sense of community and deeper meaning of purpose, and understand spiritual or religious identity. As Welch and Koth (2009) suggest, "spirituality and spiritual formation can be, and perhaps inadvertently has been, incorporated in many disciplines through service-learning within higher education" (p. 2). As we believe, service-learning is a promising approach to educate the whole student.

REFERENCES

Astin, A., Astin, H., & Lindholm, J. (2011). Assessing students' spiritual and religious qualities. *Journal of College Student Development, 52*, 39–61.

Barrett, M. (2016). Dimensions of spirituality fostered through the PULSE program for service learning. *Journal of Catholic Education, 20*(1), 111–135. https://doi.org/10.15365/jovr.2001052016

Beyer, L. (1997). The moral contours of teacher education. *Journal of Teacher Education, 48*(4), 245–254.

Boyle-Baise, M. (1998). Community service-learning for multicultural education: An exploratory study with preservice teachers. *Equity and Excellence in Education, 31*(2), 52–60.

Brandengerger, J., & Bowman, N. (2015). Prosocial growth during college: Results of a national study. *Journal of Moral Education, 44*(3), 328–345 https://doi.org/10.1080/03057240.2015.1048792

Bringle, R. G., Phillips, M. A., & Hudson, M. (2004). *The measure of service learning: Research scales and to assess student experiences*. American Psychological Association.

Buchanan, M. T., & Hyde, B. (2008). Learning beyond the surface: Engaging the cognitive, affective and spiritual dimensions within the curriculum. *International Journal of Children's Spirituality, 13*(4), 309–320.

Chickering, A. W. (2003, Jan./Feb.). "Reclaiming our soul." *Change*, 39–45.

Colby, A., & Damon, W. (1992). *Some do care: Contemporary lives of moral commitment.* Free Press.

Davalos, J. F. (2014). Divided no more: Spirituality in academic leadership. *The Journal of Educational Thought (JET)/Revue de la Pensée* Éducative, *47*(1/2), 7–24.

Dickerson, M. S., Helm-Stevens, R., & Fall, R. (2017). Service-learning in business education: An analysis of spirituality, leadership and motivation. *American Journal of Economics and Business Administration, 9*(1), 1–12. https://doi.org/10.3844/ajebasp.2017.1.12

Donahue, D. (1999). Service-learning for preservice teachers: Ethical dilemmas for practice. *Teaching and Teacher Education, 15,* 685–695.

Eyler, J., & Giles, D. (1999). *Where's the learning in service-learning?* Jossey-Bass.

Freire, P. (1970). *Pedagogy of the oppressed.* Continuum.

Freeman, N. K., & Swick, K. J. (2001). Early childhood teacher education students strengthen their caring and competence through service learning. In J. B. Anderson, K. J. Swick, & J. Yff (Eds.), *Service-learning in teacher education: Enhancing the growth of new teachers, their students, and communities* (pp. 130–140). AACTE.

Fried, J. (2001). Civility and spirituality. In V. M. Miller & M. M. Ryan (Eds.), *Transforming campus life: Reflections on spirituality and religious pluralism.* Peter Lang.

GenerationOn. (2021). *IPARDE process.* https://generationOn.org/

Gilligan, C., & Wiggins, G. (1988). The origins of morality in early childhood relationships. In C. Gilligan, J. V. Ward, J. M. Taylor, & B. Bardige (Eds.), *Mapping the moral domain: A contribution of women's thinking to psychological theory and education* (pp. 111–138). Harvard University Press.

Goldstein, L. S. (1999). The relational zone: The role of caring relationships in the co-construction of mind. *American Educational Research Journal, 36*(3), 647–673.

Hoppe, S. (2004). A synthesis of the theoretical stances. In B. Speck & S. Hoppe (Eds.), *Service learning: History, theory, and issues* (pp. 137–149). Praeger.

International OCD Foundation. (2021). *Who gets OCD?* https://iocdf.org/about-ocd/who-gets/

Jacoby, B. (2007). Service learning in today's higher education. In B. Jacoby (Ed.), *Service learning in higher education* (pp. 3–15). Jossey-Bass.

Jones, L. (2005). What does spirituality in education mean? *Journal of College and Character, 6,* 7.

Kaye, C. B. (2004). *The complete guide to service-learning: Proven, practical ways to engage students in civic responsibility, academic curriculum, and social action.* Free Spirit.

King. M. L. (1947). *The purpose of education.* Morehouse College. https://kinginstitute.stanford.edu/king-papers/documents/purpose-education

Kirsch, G. (2009). From introspection to action: Connecting spirituality and civic engagement. *College Composition and Communication, 60*(4), 827–828.

Kohlberg, L. (1981). *The psychology of moral development.* HarperCollins.

Kumar, S. (2018). A study of perceived workplace spirituality of school teachers. *Psychological Thought, 11*(2), 212–223. https://doi.org/10.5964/psyct.v11i2.298

Lake, V. E., & Jones, I. (2008). Service-learning in early childhood teacher education: Using service to put meaning back into learning. *Teaching and Teacher Education, 24*(8), 2146–2156.

Lake, V. E., & Jones, I. (2012). *Service learning in the PK–3 Classroom. The what, why, and how-to-guide for every teacher.* Free Spirit.

Lau, W. W. F., Hui, H. H., Lau, E. Y. Y., & Cheung, S. (2015). The relationship between spirituality and quality of life among university students: An autoregressive cross-lagged panel analysis. *Higher Education, 69*(6), 977–990.

Lickona, T. (1991). *Educating for character: How our schools can teach respect and responsibility.* Bantam Books.

Lovik, E. (2011). The impact of organizational features and student experiences on spiritual development during the first year of college. *Journal of College and Character, 12*(3), 1–10. https://doi.org/10.2202/1940-1639.1814

Massoudi, M. (2003). "Can scientific writing be creative?" *Journal of Science Education and Technology, 12*(2), 115–128.

McGreevy, A. M., & Copley, S. H. (1999). Spirituality and education: Nurturing connections in schools and classrooms. *Classroom Leadership 2*, 4.

The National and Community Service Act of 1990. (1990/2009). [Amended Through P. L. 111-13, Enacted April 21, 2009]. https://www.congress.gov/bill/103rd-congress/house-bill/2010

The National Service-Learning Clearinghouse. (2009). *The national service-learning clearinghouse.* http://www.servicelearning.org/

Noddings, N. (1984). *Caring: A feminine approach to ethics and moral education.* University of California Press.

Noddings, N. (1986). Fidelity in teaching, teacher education, and research for teaching. *Harvard Educational Review, 56*(4), 496–510.

Noddings, N. (2012). The care relation in teaching. *Oxford Review of Education, 38*(6), 771–781.

OK HB1775, Reg. Sess. (2021). https://legiscan.com/OK/text/HB1775/id/2387002

Palmer, P. J. (2003). Teaching with heart and soul: Reflections on spirituality in teacher education. *Journal of Teacher Education, 54*(5), 376–338. https://doi.org/10.1177/0022487103257359

Palmer, P. J. (2017). *The courage to teach: Exploring the inner landscape of a teacher's life.* Jossey-Bass.

Pascal, C., & Bertram, T. (2012). Praxis, ethics and power: Developing praxeology as a participatory paradigm for early childhood research. *European Early Childhood Education Research Journal, 20*(4), 477–492.

Pascarella, E., & Terenzini, P. (2005). *How college affects students: A third decided of research* (Vol. 2). Jossey-Bass.

Pearce, J. (2019). From anthroposophy to non-confessional preparation for spirituality? Could common schools learn from spiritual education in Steiner schools? *British Journal of Religious Education, 41*(3), 299–314. https://doi.org/10.1080/01416200.2017.1361382

Portthoff, D., Dinsmore, J., Stirtz, G., Walsh, T., Ziebarth, J., & Eifler, K. (2000). Preparing for democracy and diversity: The impact of a community-based field experience on preservice teachers' knowledge, skills, and attitudes. *Action in Teacher Education, 22*(1), 79–92.

Raache, H. (2021, May 8). *Gov. Stitt signs bill that restricts teaching of critical race theory in Oklahoma schools*. https://kfor.com/news/oklahoma-legislature/gov-stitt-signs-bill-that-restricts-teaching-of-critical-race-theory-in-oklahoma-schools/

Raper, J. (2001). "Losing our religion:" Are students struggling in silence? In V. M. Miller, & M. M. Ryan (Eds.), *Transforming campus life: Reflections on spirituality and religious pluralism* (pp. 13–32). Peter Lang.

Rosch, U. (2017). Cosmopolitanism, spirituality and social action: Mahatma Gandhi and Rudolf Steiner. In A. Giri (Eds.), *Beyond cosmopolitanism: Towards planetary transformations* (pp. 131–147). Springer.

Sokol, B., & Marle, P. (2019). Civic and faith life in college: A two-part investigation of university students' political and spiritual engagement. *Journal of Student Affairs Research and Practice, 56*(5), 550–563. https://doi.org/10.1080/19496591.2019.1669454

Sokol, B., Donnelly, K, Vilbig, J., & Monsky, K. (2017). Cultural immersion as a context for promoting global citizenship and personal agency in young adults. In L. M. Padilla-Walker & L. J. Nelson (Eds.), *Flourishing in emerging adulthood: Positive development during the third decade of life* (pp. 285–298). Oxford University Press.

Steiner, R. (2000). *Practice advice to teachers*. Anthroposophic Press.

Sunbridge Institute. (2021). *Rudolf Steiner and anthroposophy*. https://www.sunbridge.edu/about/rudolf-steiner-anthroposophy/

Tellex, K., Hlebowitsh, P., Cohen, M., & Norwood, P. (1995). Social service field experiences and teacher education. In J. Larkin, & C. Sleeter (Eds.), *Developing multicultural teacher education curricula* (pp. 65–78). State University of New York Press.

Zajonc, A. (2003, Winter). Spirituality in higher education: Overcoming the divide. *Liberal Education, 50*–58.

Welch, M., & Koth, K. (2009). Spirituality and service-learning: Parallel Frameworks for understanding students' spiritual development. *Spirituality in Higher Education, 5*(1), 1–9.

Welch, M., & Koth, K. (2013). A metatheory of spiritual formation through service-learning in higher education. *Journal of College Student Development, 54*(6), 612–627. https://doi.org/10.1353/csd.2013.0089

Winterbottom, C., & Mazzocco, P. J. (2015). Empowerment through pedagogy: Positioning service-learning as an early childhood pedagogy for preservice teachers. *Early Child Development and Care, 185*(12), 1912–1927.

CHAPTER 8

HAVENS FOR ACCEPTANCE, FAITH, AND AFFIRMATION

The Spiritual Dimension of Reflection in Teaching for Democracy

Rob Martinelle
Boston University

ABSTRACT

In this interpretive case study, the researcher conceived of an amended conceptual model of reflection, which took into account the more spiritual, coping-based aspects of reflection when teaching in service of ambitious aims. Through this model, the researcher examined the sources upon which four ambitious teachers looked in coping with problems of instructional and existential significance throughout a unit of study. From interview data collected through video-stimulated recall methodology, the study found: (1) Three coping strategies—acceptance, faith, and affirmation—to account for how teachers managed problems and uncertainty. (2) The teachers' *acceptance* of instructional problems was aided by their deep commitment to their moral centers. (3) Faced with profound uncertainty, the teachers employed *faith*, deriving it from their school communities, their sense of responsibility to their students and society, and their understanding of the nature of teaching as demonstrated through metaphors. (4) The teachers found *affirmation* in partial evidence that their students comprehended "big ideas" and in breakthroughs with particular students. This study offers teacher educators at the

---

Rekindling Embers of the Soul:
An Examination of Spirituality Issues Relating to Teacher Education, pp. 143–167
Copyright © 2024 by Information Age Publishing
www.infoagepub.com
All rights of reproduction in any form reserved.

pre-and in-service level conceptual and practical guidance for encouraging reflection in ways that honor the spiritual dimensions of their work.

Keywords: ambitious teaching, coping, reflection, video-stimulated recall, spirituality

(A PERSONAL) INTRODUCTION

Early in my classroom teaching career, I had been hard-pressed to discuss issues of the "soul" and "spirituality" in relation to my practice. Whether its association with religion was an affront to my secular beliefs or it was at odds with the increasingly data-driven school climate in which I found myself (Nagle, 2009), talk of teaching being a spiritual endeavor was neither comfortable nor practical for me. Yet, looking back, there was always a spiritual element to my work. As Palmer (2003) wrote, "Spirituality is the eternal human yearning to be connected with something larger than our own ego ... a connection that [pits teachers], heart and soul, against ego-seducing educational and social conventions of all sorts" (p. 377); as a White history teacher in a high-poverty district, this impulse manifested itself in my resistance to traditional history education norms and in my desire to cultivate the curiosity and hearts of my students. With each passing year, my commitment to this aim and, by extension, democracy deepened and solidified—a spiritual calling indeed.

However, with this aim came an ongoing spiritual crisis of sorts. The more inclusive my curriculum became, the more uneasy I was over the historical narratives that remained excluded. The more agency my assessments afforded students, the less certain I was over how to evaluate them fairly; as my reasons for teaching history became more ambitious and democratic in scope, the harder realizing (and reflecting in service of) they became. Reflection had evolved for me from the activity of solving problems to one of living with and accepting them. I did not know it at the time, but the burden of continually coping with such uncertainty brought me to this study. For ambitious teachers like myself, I began to wonder about the ideas and beliefs that allowed them to continually find meaning, purpose, and comfort in times where resolution and gratification remained elusive. Accordingly, I set out to ask: *What ideas do ambitious teachers look to in coping with problems of instructional and existential significance throughout a unit of study?*

THEORETICAL FRAMEWORK

This study used the concept of reflection as its primary theoretical lens. Traditionally, the reflective process for teachers has been conceptualized as a retrospective (or in-the-moment) act whereby teachers: identify problems, (re)frame and generate possible explanations for them, draw conclusions, hypothesize action plans, and test those plans in practice (Dewey, 1933/1964; Rodgers, 2002; Schön, 1983). However, scholars have noted that, despite this model's utility and the ubiquity of its promotion in teacher education programs (Jones & Jones, 2013), it remains a limiting means of understanding reflection as it actually occurs in practice (Atkinson, 2012; Lampert, 1985). Conventional-rational models of reflection, they argue, falsely presume that all problems of practice can (and should) be solved or that reflection always yields immediate action. More accurately, the complexity and simultaneity of problems routinely under consideration render reflection a balancing act between problem-solving and problem-coping (Roth & Cohen, 1986; Zeichner & Liston, 2014). Because teaching is such emotional and spiritual labor, teachers must learn to cope with problems or *manage* them, as Lampert (1985) uses interchangeably, in order to maintain their capacity to teach and thrive in adverse circumstances (Hammerness et al., 2005).

Such a view of reflection is more akin to the *spiritual-contemplative tradition of reflective practice* (Zeichner & Liston, 2014). Reflection for teachers here, especially those who view their work as a vocation, are often faced with many uncertainties that demand a form of "spiritual discipline" (p. 73) to rediscover meaning in their work. Accordingly, this study conceives of and is informed by an amended conceptual model of reflection that acknowledges this tradition. This model, seen in Figure 8.1, posits three coping strategies crucial to reflection—*acceptance, affirmation, and faith*-based upon concepts discussed in the literature on stress management, teacher attrition, and the sociology of teaching (Burke & Greenglass, 1995; Lortie, 1975; Nolan & Stitzlein, 2011; Roth & Cohen, 1986; Santoro, 2018).

The concept of *acceptance* is loosely derived from the ideas of existential coping (Burke & Greenglass, 1995), avoidance (Roth & Cohen, 1986), and management (Lampert, 1985), referring to how teachers, at times, accept problems they perceive as too complex, uncontrollable, or unworthy of solving. *Faith* constitutes a trusted belief in something important, often in the absence of evidence—an optimistic acceptance of the unknown. As defined here, faith is not a trait, but an imaginative habit employed by teachers to sustain themselves and the belief that problems of significance to them can (and will) one day be resolved. This bears a resemblance to Nolan and Stitzlein's (2011) discussion of pragmatic hope, which they define as "envisioning the best" (p. 4) and "the likelihood of achieving the desired object of one's hope" (p. 3). Finally, I adapt the coping strategy of affirmation from Lortie (1975), who wrote of the intrinsic gratification derived from teachers' evaluations of their work. For teachers whose goals are long-range and not conducive to precise measurement, such

Figure 8.1

Spiritual-Rational Model of Reflection

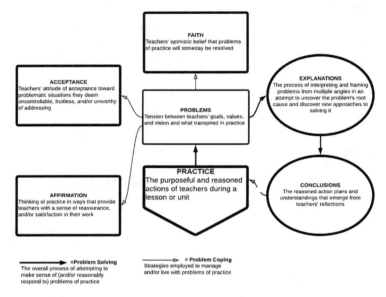

gratification is less than assured, rendering teachers willing and needing to accept "indications of partial effectiveness" (p. 132) to quell lingering uncertainties and affirm their reasons for teaching.

Ambitious Teaching

The construct of ambitious teaching has been utilized over the past 20 years to characterize powerful inquiry-based teaching (Carrol, 2012; Lampert et al., 2011; Smith & Girod, 2003; Stylianides & Stylianides, 2014; Waddell, 2014; Windschitl et al., 2020), often in contexts that encourage otherwise (DiCamillo & Gradwell, 2012; Heafner & Norwood, 2019; Gradwell, 2006; Grant, 2003, 2005; Grant & Gradwell, 2010). Heeding Shulman's (1987) call to document portraits of discipline-specific expertise, cases of ambitious teachers have understandably focused on describing (and explaining) practice in efforts to scaffold for novice teachers ways to cultivate learning environments focused on authentic problem-solving and deep acquisition of subject matter. Such teaching, of course, differs across disciplines. Still, common among teachers profiled in this research is "a spirit of questioning, wondering, and doubting" (Elbow, 1968, p. 191), especially in social studies classrooms where the cultivation of such a spirit among students is integral to the discipline's democratic and justice-oriented mission (Sibbet & Au, 2017; Vinson, 2001). While issues of spirituality and teacher coping are not explicitly mentioned in cases of ambitious teaching, a close examination of their rhetoric and embedded assumptions reveals ambitious teaching to be a spiritual undertaking indeed.

For instance, Grant (2005) aptly notes ambitious teaching to be "more journey than end" (p. 126), in part because ambitious teachers are oriented toward practices that render teaching a more uncertain activity than it already is (Helsing, 2007). They forego traditional practices that would provide them with a (false) sense of control and certainty of their own effectiveness as educators, opting instead to frame their curriculum around meaningful, open-ended questions and assessing students in ways that cannot be objectively measured (DiCamillo & Gradwell, 2012; Grant, 2018). That is because ambitious teachers are deeply committed to outcomes that are unlikely to come to fruition for them in the near future (Martinelle, 2020), outcomes that concern the "deepest needs of the human soul" (Palmer, 2003, p. 379). Coping then is a necessity and natural byproduct of such commitment and pedagogy for teachers, perhaps even more so for those serving students whose spirits have long been (and continue to be) neglected by schools (Love, 2019). At a minimum, it requires teachers to be comfortable with (and affectionate toward) uncertainty, qualities central to the state of spirituality Huebner (1999) deems inseparable from teaching.

Yet despite alluding to the importance of coping for ambitious teachers, there remains a dearth of research that examines what enables them to cope. To a degree, several edited volumes of teacher narratives have incidentally captured this (Grant & Gradwell, 2010; Nieto, 2003, 2014); however, this work is not representative of the coping such teachers do as part of their regular reflective routines throughout and after teaching. If we are to promote ambitious teaching and, by extension, stress the importance of coping as integral to the reflection that must accompany such pedagogy, models, and examples of what makes it possible for ambitious teachers' ability to cope are needed. This study addresses this need and asks: *What ideas do ambitious teachers look to in coping with problems of instructional and existential significance throughout a unit of study?*

METHODS

This study was situated in a high-poverty majority-minority district, the demographics of which, at the time, were: Latinx (41%), Black (36%), White (13%), Asian (8%), and Other/Multiracial (1%). The participants consisted of four experienced secondary history teachers purposefully selected (see Table 8.1) based on two criteria. First, they had a minimum of five years of experience and reputations for teaching through inquiry and with "big ideas," the latter of which is an instantiation of ambitious teaching (Grant & Gradwell, 2010). Teachers with extensive experience can articulate and remain committed to their long-range goals and values in ways novices cannot (Santoro, 2018). Related, the promotion of inquiry necessitates practices neither conducive to control nor precise measurement (Helsing, 2007). These criteria made probable the selection of participants with a favorable disposition toward uncertainty and, therefore, considerable coping skills. Additionally, the teachers' district was where I had taught social studies for six years, a position from which I was on educational leave at the time of the study. I hoped my insider status and the occupational history I shared with participants would engender a rapport between us and allow me to analyze and interpret with extra insight.

Data Collection

I used an interpretive multiple-case design to unearth and study the more spiritual coping-based aspects of teacher reflection (Stake, 2006; Yin, 2009). Data was collected over the course of several months during the 2014–2015 academic year. Five semi-structured reflective interviews were conducted with each teacher, several of which employed video-stimulated recall (VSR) methodology, where video-recorded teaching segments are replayed to teachers to provoke reflection (Ethel & McMeniman, 2000; Reitano, 2006). The first interview focused on their schooling histories, educational purposes, and idealized visions of teaching (Hammerness, 2006). I then observed each teacher three times throughout an inquiry-based unit of their choice. After each observation, the teachers were interviewed and prompted to reflect while watching (and having joint control of the) video of the observed lesson. These interviews were mainly open-ended so not to determine the direction of teachers' reflections and not to undermine their professional agency. The teachers were interviewed a final time at the end of the unit to reflect on its overall success.

Data Analysis

Data analysis began with the generation of formal codes (McMillan & Schumacher, 2010), which were guided by my research questions and theoretical framework. To establish a level of intercoder reliability, hierarchical coding charts were created and discussed with a trusted colleague to decide which codes were most essential and warranted revisiting. From these discussions, I revised, combined, or eliminated various codes and began

Table 8.1

Brief Description of Participants, School Contexts, and Curricular Units

Participant Pseudonym	Background, Education, and Teaching Experience	School Context	Grade and Subject Taught, Question(s) for Observed Unit, Overview of Unit Aims and Activities
Mr. James Brady	White male in early 40s. Earned a BA in history and MEd in special education and was working towards his EdD at the time. Eleven years of teaching experience.	Newbury Academy, a traditional high school of 400 students with no admission requirements and substantially separate classrooms.	9th Grade, U.S. History I Unit Q(s): Whose "more perfect union?" Whole-class discussions; Role-Play Simulation
Ms. Kati Jones	White female in early 30s. Fluent in Haitian-Creole. Earned a BA in International Relations and MEd in Social Studies Ed. through an alternative urban teacher prep. program. Five years of teaching experience.	Arts and Humanities Academy, a Pilot school serving 400 students with a performance audition required for admission and full-inclusion classrooms.	9th Grade, Humanities I Unit Q(s): How important is it to remember slavery? How has your life been informed by the past? Whole-class and small-group discussions; Emphasis on reading and creating poetry and short stories.
Mr. Bill Costa	White male in early 60s. Worked as a public policy lawyer for many years before changing careers and earning an M.Ed. in Social Studies Ed. through an alternative urban teacher prep. program. Nine years of teaching experience.	Hannaford Park High School, a full-inclusion vocational school serving 1,100 students with no admission requirements.	10th Grade, U.S. History II Unit Q(s): Was the New Deal a success or Failure? Formal Debate, Whole-Class Discussions, & Argumentative Writing
Ms. Brianna Rawls	White female in her early 40s. National Board Certified. Earned her BA in literature and history and graduated from the school where she was teaching at the time. Fourteen years of teaching experience.	Greenborough High School, a full-inclusion school serving 1,600 students with admission based on entrance exam scores and grade point average.	9th Grade, U.S. History I Unit Q(s): To what extent do the views of Alexander Hamilton and Thomas Jefferson validate the view of "democracy as becoming rather than being?" Whole-Class and small-group Discussions

(re)indexing all code definitions and grouping them into more prominent themes (Patton, 2002), which were verified with the colleague mentioned above. Empirical assertions were made within each case before probing the data for confirming and disconfirming evidence (Erickson, 1986), after which a cross-case analysis was employed to understand the phenomenon as it appeared across participants (Stake, 2006).

FINDINGS: "HAVENS" FOR ACCEPTANCE, AFFIRMATION, AND FAITH

This study was grounded in the assumption that ambitious teaching, especially when situated in urban social studies classrooms, is regularly accompanied by residual uncertainties with which teachers must learn to cope, a type of reflection that is at odds with more technical short-sighted models (Huebner, 1999; Nagle, 2009). Using a more spiritual-based framework of reflection, the data revealed teachers' coping strategies of *acceptance, faith, and affirmation* to be a natural part of their reflective routines over the course of a unit. As for the ideas that aided their acceptance, acted as sources of affirmation, and nurtured their faith, I refer to them as "havens." The word "havens" implies a place of comfort and refuge, which adequately encapsulated teachers' reasons for seeking out these ideas when faced with problems they deemed uncontrollable or unworthy of consideration.

While reported as distinct, it is essential to note that these havens are interrelated and overlap with one another. For example, teachers' *moral centers* (Santoro, 2018), which proved to help teachers *accept* specific problems, underpin the havens that also affirmed their practices. Likewise, by definition, *faith* necessitates a form of acceptance, albeit usually about problems teachers hope will be resolved. Ultimately, I hope that readers will gain a sense of the interconnectedness among the findings from a careful reading of them in their entirety.

Havens for Acceptance: Teachers' Commitment to Their Moral Centers

While reflecting, the teachers noted a range of problems, some of which they deemed unimportant or dismissive and could accept. Attempting to "solve" them, in their estimation, would compromise their moral centers (Santoro, 2018), which are an amalgam of teachers' most cherished educational ideals, born out of "the values and commitments they bring to and attribute to the work" (p. 49). As such, they are more linked to teachers' long-range goals and, for experienced teachers, catalyze their reflections.

Brianna's moral center hinged upon student agency. It was significant for her that students take responsibility for their learning and understand that learning was predicated on the struggle. This theme coincidentally lay at the heart of her year-long essential question about the fluidity and fragility of democracy. As such, her commitment to her moral center compelled her to accept (and live with) specific problems, one of which pertained to curriculum coverage. For example, throughout her unit, she found it problematic how one section of students was more reluctant to think deeply about her unit question. As a result, they were beginning to lag behind other sections in their progress with the curriculum. "Solving" this issue, however, through speeding up the pace of her class or adopting a pedagogy of coverage would come at the expense of her students' active engagement, thus compromising her moral center. She explained while reflecting on her first lesson:

> That's why it takes me forever to cover anything because ... at the end of the day, maybe we don't get through as much as I want to, but it's a tradeoff because you have to be responsible, especially when I'm scaffolding it for you ... I'm not willing to sacrifice you actively being a learner, 'cause I could stand up there, and I could tell you what they mean and I've modeled for you how to approach a text while I think out loud, so I know that you know what it looks like and I'm not willing to sacrifice it.

Another problem Brianna accepted was the uncertainty regarding her unit's success at its completion. Reflecting, she said:

> There's a way in which it's sort of still ongoing because I won't really know how successful it was until they write their final exam essay where they have to talk about, you know, what they learned this year.... So I guess I won't really know until they ultimately do their essay.... Everything I do I'm very purposefully building towards, and I haven't gotten to the crescendo yet if you will.

Because the success of her unit was in many ways tied to her year-long curricular framework and its accompanying final exam, evaluating the unit by itself was almost impossible for Brianna. Accordingly, she could live with not knowing how successful the unit was because her long-term instructional goals dictated that she must.

Kati's moral center aided her acceptance of similar issues. Given her students' racial and ethnic backgrounds, she was deeply committed to empowering them and engendering a critical view of how (and to whose benefit) historical knowledge is constructed. Her unwavering commitment to this ideal helped her live with lingering uncertainties over whether her unit on the legacy of slavery was effective with her students. Said Kati at the end of the unit: "I feel like just asking these questions: 'Why are some people ashamed to be associated with Africa?' Just asking the question, you're saying, 'This is worthy of dealing with.' And you're unsilencing it, you know?" Here, Kati's ability to live with being uncertain of her effectiveness was enabled by a deepened consciousness of the implicit messages she was sending to students and her belief in the power of those messages. Kati also expressed reservations about the enduring message she feared some of her students of color internalized at the end of her unit. "Is this fostering them into a place of self-pity and inaction?" she wondered aloud.

Nonetheless, for Kati, accepting this uncertainty was a natural consequence of teaching toward such an ambitious goal. She explained, "That's the whole thing, I guess, right? We don't know; we can't control how they make meaning out of it and what they then do with it." Her acceptance of this issue can be traced back to another aspect of her moral center she espoused in our first interview. She said, "Even if they don't get it quite how I want them to, there's a benefit to them discovering it. There's also a benefit to their self-discovery because then it's theirs." For a similar reason, James could accept his Constitutional Convention simulation not going as well as planned because he valued the fact that it would give his students "ownership over the Constitution" when they began studying the actual document in their next unit.

The cultivation of evidence-based argumentative skills and his committed belief in self-discovered learning made up a large part of Bill's moral center. Understandably, that many of his students exhibited argumentative difficulties during an oral debate about the New Deal was a point of contention for him. Yet he accepted this problem, saying: "In a month, I'll have another debate, I don't know on what. Like, we can do: *Should the United States have dropped a bomb on Hiroshima?*" Like Brianna, Bill said a defensive "solution" to this problem, such as assuming his students were incapable of oral debates and abandoning them entirely, would compromise his moral center.

In some ways, there was a reluctant quality to these teachers' acceptance of problems, as they often took little pleasure in the remaining unresolved. Yet, in other ways, acceptance took on a defiant, even courageous, quality. As Sockett (1993) wrote, courage is the "determination to stick to one's principles" (p. 71) in the face of adversity and "in the pursuit of long-term commitments that are morally desirable" (p. 73). Faced with problems to which they could have responded by feeling defeated or lowering their expectations for students, the teachers' attachment to their moral centers rendered those options moot, allowing them not to treat all problems of practice equally and endure the "mental unrest" (Dewey, 1933/1964, p. 13) needed to work in service of ambitious aims.

Havens for Faith

Throughout their reflections, the teachers were faced with or spoke of uncertainty only faith could ease. However, this faith was not religious in nature but more akin to the faith described by Yearwood (2003) in her essay "Teaching as Gardening." She explained:

> I am a year-round gardener.... When I plant my seeds, I believe without a doubt that they will grow. I have no evidence that these particular seeds will grow, but I am firm in my belief that they will. Without that strong conviction, my efforts would be tenuous at best ... I am not a perfect gardener. In spite of all my faith, hope, and love, many of my plants do not thrive and flourish.... However, I keep cultivating. I am aware of my limitations, but my faith is unshaken. (pp. 50–51)

Faith is a necessity for teachers who are routinely faced with questions such as: "How is it that the teaching I love ... brings me to the brink of exhaustion almost on a regular basis?" (Zeichner & Liston, 2014, p. 72); What keeps me going without clear evidence of possible success? Questions like these are likely to be compounded for teachers who, like those featured here, work in very challenging urban school districts (Nieto, 2003, 2014; Simon & Johnson, 2015). The teachers in this study, some more explicitly than others, relied on faith at various points to cope with such issues. The havens they sought refuge in to reaffirm their work and sustain their optimism consisted of their school communities, sense of responsibility toward their students and society, and metaphorical understanding of teaching.

School community. Of all the participants, the theme of faith is most exemplified in the case of Kati, as she explicitly acknowledged its role in her practice and even referred to history teaching as "having a spiritual component to it. Kati was also the only one who generally spoke favorably of her school context. After several years in an unsupportive school district, she described her new school as a "love match." Accordingly, she looked to her school as a haven for faith when faced with deep confusion.

In her final interview, Kati's uncertainty about the effectiveness of her unit on the legacy of slavery gave way to considerable doubt about her self-efficacy as a teacher. These and other unanswerable questions lingered for Kati. In a way, her experiences grappling with "those sort of critical theory-type questions" as a student prepared her for this. Still, the residual uncertainty that accompanied the promotion of such questions was quite burdensome for her. "There's just so many meta-questions for me about the whole thing," remarked Kati. Yet, in thinking of her school and colleagues, all of whom shared a commitment to social justice, some of those doubts were assuaged. She commented:

> My other thing is that these kids are ninth graders, and I have good personal relationships with most of them, so I know that these conversations are not over.... The kind of school we're in, they're gonna continue to be pushed to grapple with so much stuff. Some of my fretting of, "Did they get it?" or "They're too surface level," it'll take care of itself even if it's not in my course.

Though still uncertain about what her students took away from the unit, Kati also said she believed that her collegial relationship with teachers in the school would provide her with insight on the matter. Kati explained, "My colleagues will hopefully be helpful in terms of what they feel their students got and how much can they get." Because Kati saw great alignment between her own aims of education and those of her school, she could believe that, if not immediately, she would one day receive confirmation of her effectiveness. Her reflections confirm that a teacher can maintain faith amongst those who exhibit it (Huebner, 1999).

Responsibility to students and society. Whereas Kati could look to her school as a faith haven, James and Brianna could not and looked elsewhere. In times of deep conflict, they instead turned to their sense of responsibility toward their students and society. During an interview, Brianna found herself overwhelmed by the cognitive-emotional toll the school year had taken on her, so much so that she considered leaving the profession. Brianna said when she reflects, "It happens in a mess." It was clear that juggling the "mess" in her head had become so burdensome that it nearly brought her to the brink of exhaustion. Nevertheless, Brianna's comments directly suggested that there existed a greater reason for this "mess," the explanation for which was profound:

> But then I lived to teach another day, 'cause when I'm thinking about teaching these kids, I just sort of feel like there's a lot at stake.... It's my responsibility to try to help even the playing field and to give you the same advantages that I was given as a student in the [district].... If you're going through the district system compared to people who are in suburban school systems, you're starting, in many ways, behind the line, and so I'm working really hard to bridge that gap, you know? It doesn't matter that I teach history. The value that I see in my work is beyond teaching the kids history.

Whatever issues Brianna was troubled by were trumped by her responsibility toward her students and what she considered her obligation to level the education playing field, a goal unlikely to be realized while she remained a teacher, but she believed it nonetheless.

Likewise, although James did not encounter any moments of existential or professional crisis during our interviews, in our last interview, he admitted such moments do happen, saying:

> It's this empathy for these inner-city kids. So, yeah, I'm constantly thinking about that. That's why I got into the job, and that's why I continue to do it. Every time I think about quitting and doing something else, I think, "Who's going to do this?"

Responsibility is a moral trait that involves thinking about how one's teaching affects students' intellectual and emotional development and the socio-political consequences of one's work (Dewey, 1933/1964; Zeichner & Liston, 2014). In times of crises, James and Brianna especially seemed to resort to their faith in the latter. Because they believed they were contributing, even if only in a small way, to bettering society or the life chances of their students, they could preserve their "potential to keep acting productively day after day, throughout the year" (Lampert, as cited in Hammerness et al., 2005, p. 377).

Metaphors for the nature of teaching. Teachers' final source of faith came from their metaphorical understanding of teaching and teachers. Teachers' metaphors are more evocative and reveal how they conceive their teaching approach and their professional identities' development (Saban, 2006; Zeichner & Liston, 2014). Such metaphors are "somewhat tangled up with metaphors for teachers, metaphors for learners, metaphors for curriculum, and so on" (Badley & Hollabaugh, 2012, p. 54). This assertion is a good description of the metaphors employed by teachers in this study. These metaphors were invoked to comfort and (re)affirm their faith in themselves when faced with unsolvable issues. A summary of these metaphors and what I inferred them to assume about teaching and teachers can be found in Table 8.2.

Like Yearwood (2003), Kati analogized herself to a gardener. Reflecting on one lesson, she said, "When things sort of fall a little flat ... I always sort of console myself with, 'Well, I've planted the seed.'" When faced with doubts about her desired impact on her students, she did exactly that, saying: "As much as I fret about some stuff ... I do feel like I planted some seeds for justice just by focusing on it, you know? Just by being a person of authority ... and being like, 'Yeah, this is worthy of study.'"

Brianna used the metaphor of juggling to describe her work as a teacher. She saw reflection itself as a juggling act, saying in our first interview that she is always "following the moving parts" such as content, students' personal issues, and classroom management while reflecting. In our final

Table 8.2

Metaphors Used by Teachers While Reflecting

	Teaching as	Teacher as	Implied Assumptions About Role of Teachers and/or Teaching
Kati	Planting seeds	Gardener, pastor	Teaching is an act of faith and love; Teachers provoke and heal
James	Juggling, introduction to democracy	Model of democracy, juggler	Teaching is an inherently problematic balancing act that necessitates continuous growth
Bill	Government assistance	Benevolent parent	Teachers create opportunities for students to help themselves
Brianna	Juggling, democracy	Juggler	Teaching is an inherently problematic balancing act that necessitates continuous growth

interview, Brianna said that from reflecting on her work with me, her metaphor was solidified for her, thus engendering a sense of faith in her own abilities as a teacher.

Bill, James, and Brianna all used themes from their curriculum as metaphors at one point. James and Brianna, both of whom were at career crossroads at the time of this study, used their unit themes of democracy as unfinished as tongue-in-cheek metaphors for their future development. For example, reflecting on the teacher he would like to become in his next school, James said, in a clever play on his unit question: *Whose more perfect union?*:

> There is no perfect teacher. So, *whose more perfect teacher* do I want to be? .... I don't idealize a perfect teacher ... you can work towards being this thing that you will never become and be aware that you will never become perfect. And that's the whole point that you are constantly reflecting and changing and allowing for change. The teacher I want to be is the kind of the teacher I am now, constantly reflecting.... It's a journey with no end.

Studies on teachers' metaphors have demonstrated their utility in helping pre-and in-service teachers surface and challenge their beliefs about teaching and how they see themselves as teachers over time (Mahlios et al., 2010; Mellado et al., 2012; Shaw et al., 2008; Stylianou et al., 2013; Thomas & Beauchamp, 2011). Here, we see an added dimension to such metaphors, as they not only appeared "in the natural language of teachers" (Zeichner & Liston, 2014, p. 43) during reflection but were employed as a coping mechanism during times of disillusionment. In looking across their particular metaphors, some common threads emerge to help us understand why. Consider how Kati and Bill employed the metaphors of gardening and government to assess their work, metaphors which suggest rationalized teacher accountability measures are at odds with how teachers see and assess themselves (Cochran-Smith & Lytle, 2009). The metaphors of juggling and democracy carry with them related assumptions, as they both suggest teaching to be "unforgivingly complex" (Cochran-Smith, 2003, p. 4) and teacher learning to be ongoing. All of these metaphors invoke images of teaching in which uncertainty is understood, even embraced, as an ingrained feature of practice. Teachers cannot assure their students will learn any more than a gardener can be sure their plants will flourish. Likewise, neither juggling nor democracy are static in nature; their only assured feature is constant change. Because these metaphors were referenced during times when the teachers' doubts were perceived as unsolvable and too difficult or emotionally taxing to consider, I contend it helped normalize such doubts. From this comforting state of mind, they could, to borrow from Yearwood (2003), accept their limitations and maintain the belief that they could (and should) continue to cultivate their "gardens."

Havens for Affirmation

Reflection necessitates a balance between challenging and affirming one's beliefs and practices (Zeichner & Liston, 2014). Without attention to the latter, "[teachers] would be unable to act or react" (p. 13) and convince themselves they are ineffective or that their goals are unrealistic. As discussed earlier, the attainment of such affirmation is hard to come by for teachers with more ambitious goals, rendering partial evidence of effectiveness the basis for their satisfaction. Such was the case for the teachers here, as they often sought the smallest signs of evidence their goals were being realized as a means of coping. These signs included indications students had comprehended *big ideas* and *breakthroughs*. The former refers to ideas that "go beyond discrete facts or skills to focus on larger concepts" (Wiggins & McTigue, 2005, p. 339) that transcend the subject and academic situations. These ideas are often (but not always) promoted through the essential questions guiding teachers' units and courses. The latter concept resembles Lortie's (1975) view of the "spectacular case" (p. 121), instances of dramatic success with individual students who, prior to that point, had exhibited various cognitive or personal difficulties. Teachers often recognize such cases to "overcome feelings of depression about lack of success with other students" (p. 123).

Comprehension of "Big Ideas." In my first interview with Brianna, we discussed her thought process when designing a curriculum. She emphasized the importance of big ideas and not getting bogged down in the minutiae of content coverage. "I'm always thinking about the big questions.... So as I'm designing my units, I'm thinking about that.... It doesn't matter if I cover everything in the book," she said. What mattered to Brianna was that her students could "see the forest" as well as the trees, or at least understand what she saw as the most important "trees." She explained:

> What we have to do is take ourselves out of this tyranny of coverage.... We need to "pick our trees." Like we need to pick the moments, and we have to use those moments to instill historical thinking skills and things that we value as educators into the students.... So, when I'm planning units, I'm thinking, "What/where am I going to get the most bang for the buck?"

From my analysis of the cases, I found that such thinking naturally extended to how all of the teachers evaluated their effectiveness. While reflecting, they found great reassurance from any hint of evidence that suggested their students saw the "forest." That some students took away from the unit an idea or skill that transcended the unit, or even the course, was a great source of affirmation for teachers.

Although Bill was disappointed in how his New Deal debate went, he latched on to what he saw as a big idea his students gleaned from their class discussion shortly thereafter:

> I was actually happy with the open class discussion ... I also think that it was broadly from life.... They understood the role of government more. I got that sense from them too ... I think they learned that there was a role of government in their life ... I think that became clear to me.... So I was happy about that.

Moments like this were also rewarding for Bill because he felt it helped students connect with history and feel safe talking about their personal lives in class, which was very important to him. Despite his students' struggles to think contextually during their role-play, James took solace in them, distilling from the unit the big idea of how exclusionary the Constitutional Convention was. When asked at the end of the unit about "Whose more perfect union," the Constitution created his students' response in unison of "Rich White people's more perfect union!" was very gratifying to him. Even more reassuring for James was his students' increased interest in history after the unit ended. While this newfound curiosity about the past was not an explicit curricular goal for James, it nevertheless had great utility beyond the unit. For this reason, James described it as the unit's "most important" outcome.

Brianna also cited evidence that some of their students understood the more enduring ideas of her course. For example, she lit up while discussing one student's response to a question raised by her student teacher: "One of the students raised his hand and was like, 'Democracy is a work in progress,' and I was like, 'Yes!' I was like, 'A+ for the year!'"

Finally, while dismayed that her students were not grasping some of her unit's big ideas, Kati found reassurance from some evidence they understood other overarching frames of her course. For example, in recognizing what was successful about her unit, Kati, invoking a different metaphor, first considered the purpose of a history class. "I heard some pastors say that their job is to "comfort the disturbed and disturb the comfortable," you know what I mean? A history classroom is a place of both provocation and healing," she said in our final conversation. To that effect, Kati found affirmation in the unit possibly "disturbing" and "comforting" the students who needed it the most. Consider the reassurance she found from some evidence her unit may have validated her students dealing with internalized racism. Kati explained:

> As a history teacher, I do think that one thing that happened that is positive is that a lot of kids who have silently or privately been struggling with all of these things as members of the Afrikan Diaspora for them to be able to share both in conversation and artistically these things.... Hearing from them, when they share these things they hadn't shared with anyone before about their realities, I feel like there is some healing in that.

Likewise, it was equally rewarding for Kati that she might have disturbed the mindset of her white students:

> And I feel like, for the kids who don't live that, it is powerful for them to hear it. Even if in the short term it breaks them down a little bit, I'm thinking about the white kids now. It makes them feel unsure of themselves, and maybe ... it makes them more thoughtful members of society. Just not to take for granted all the inequality that does exist. In that way, it is a good thing.

For Kati, who saw her practices as linked to making society more just, hints of evidence that her unit provided space for certain students to validate and challenge their beliefs and experiences suggested she was making progress toward this mission, even if only in a small way. Effectively, such evidence helped offset the myriad of other problems she encountered while reflecting. For these teachers, "success" was determined not by their unit's micro-goals but often by their broader macro goals. Like the reflections compiled by Grant and Gradwell (2010), teachers' evidence of these particular gains, even if only partial, indicated that their students had, as

Brianna said, received the most "bang for their buck." For Bill and James, this success was briefly manifested in their students' increased personal and intellectual engagement with history; for Kati and Brianna, it was evident in some of their students grasping an enduring framework through which to view the past, the present, and maybe their own lives. Circling back to an earlier theme, such moments were likely affirming because they nurtured and were an extension of their moral centers.

Breakthroughs. All four teachers derived affirmation from the sense that select students had possibly reached a turning point in their academic or personal development. Bill said of one student's essay, "And Carlos, my Carlos, my pal here. He did a nice job in organizing and putting things together.... I was happy about that. That's a great improvement for him." Even within his oral debate, he saw several personal breakthroughs. He said, "Helena, the woman who spoke with the shawl, quiet as a mouse.... For her to speak in front of the class, huge! To get up in public at a podium, big step for her as a student." James also delighted in his quietest student's increased participation on several occasions, saying at one point, "Even Jaylen here, who is autistic and not very expressive or doesn't really talk much ... he's opening up now."

Kati discussed how one student, struggling throughout the term, positively responded to a song she played for him: "He was provoked by something, he went and researched it ... so that was cool." Finally, Brianna, in a comment that encapsulates the importance of these moments for teachers, said, "when Sunny remembers ... at least he's getting around the idea of mercantilism ... I was like, "Oh, my God, I'm not a complete failure, and my life is not wasted!'"

However, "small" these instances were, how these teachers discussed them suggested the opposite. As for why these moments were such a crucial source of affirmation, two factors stand out. First, they helped offset uneasiness about their sense of self-efficacy and other previously discussed uncertainties they encountered while reflecting. All four teachers expressed doubts on topics ranging from the root of students' confusion to their competency as teachers (see Table 8.3 for examples). Thinking about these breakthroughs effectively generated the "feelings of self-approval" (Lortie, 1975, p. 123) needed in light of these doubts. Second, the teachers knew and cared for their students deeply. As a long line of scholarship on teaching and teacher knowledge makes clear, good teaching is predicated upon understanding students' idiosyncrasies (Grant, 2003, 2005; Grant & Gradwell, 2010; Shulman, 1987). However, this knowledge is usually presented for its utility in planning and implementing instruction, not necessarily for reflecting on (and coping with) its aftermath.

Table 8.3

Examples of Uncertainties Expressed by Teachers

	Focus of Uncertainty	Evidence From Interviews
Kati	Self-efficacy/ student confusion	Did I push the kids whose realities were validated in some way? Did I push them enough beyond that? (Interview, May 19, 2015)
	Effectiveness of unit	Is this fostering them into a place of self-pity and inaction? Is it indulging a sense of a lack of personal efficacy? All of that stuff. I don't know. (Interview, May 19, 2015)
	Self-efficacy/ student confusion	I'm also wondering, for them to have this nuanced understanding.... Is that just what your average ninth grader is capable of grasping, or is it because I did a crappy job? (Interview, May 19, 2015)
James	Student confusion	They were confused about what was going on. I don't know if they were confused by the procedure or didn't want to share, or they were nervous that what they were about to share was wrong. (Interview, March 9, 2015)
Bill	Self-efficacy/ student confusion	I put an outline on the board: topic sentence, thesis, one, two, three.... It was all spelled out for them. I don't know.... That's the most frustrating thing for me. You can devise the best lesson in the world, but if a student won't do it, what is your next step? And then it comes back to, am I not motivating them? And you get that guilt. Is it me? I don't motivate them, what am I doing wrong? (Interview, March 19, 2015)
		What are they doing? They're not following directions....
	Amount of scaffolding	Now, how much of that is my fault? Was I not specific enough, was I not clear enough? I thought I was. But ... how clear do you have to be? That's the million-dollar question. (Interview, March 11, 2015)
		I'm trying to go around and I'm debating in my mind, should I really go in and help them and scaffold? Try to structure this. I want to help them but not help them. (Interview, March 19th, 2015)
Brianna	Self-efficacy	[Discussing her student-teacher] As it is right now, I don't really know how to best support you and I'm doing the best that I can, but I feel like I'm not doing a very good job. (Interview, April 14, 2015)
	Effectiveness of unit	I don't know what the outcome of that is, but you know hopefully like for me it's like pulling these different threads through the narrative like these multiple levels of things that we're trying to learn. (Interview, April 14, 2015)

DISCUSSION

This study reveals that spirituality is not just an inherent dimension of reflection for ambitious teachers but a necessity. In doing so, it builds upon the findings of previous research on ambitious teachers, which referred to the uncertainty with which such teachers must learn to cope but did not explore what enabled them to do so (DiCamillo & Gradwell, 2012; Heafner & Norwood, 2019; Grant, 2005; Grant & Gradwell, 2010). As the cultivation of a reflective stance remains an enduring goal of many, if not all, schools of education (Jones & Jones, 2013), the findings of this study suggest several considerations for teacher educators to be mindful of when promoting reflection among teacher candidates. First, the framework presented in Figure 8.1 can provide teacher educators with the conceptual tools to encourage reflection in ways that equally honor the rational and spiritual dimensions of teaching. In courses and student-teaching seminars, explicit teaching of a comprehensive framework like this could assist preservice teachers in managing and prioritizing the many problems they encounter in practice. Second, the use of this study could also extend to modeling for preservice teachers the type of reflection that accompanies ambitious teaching. There is considerable power in helping teacher candidates understand the tacit uncertainties that like-minded experienced teachers routinely engage with and manage while reflecting (Ethel & McMeniman, 2000). By doing so, beginning teachers might engender a deeper and more realistic understanding of ambitious teaching and take steps toward normalizing the uncertainty they will encounter. This need not be limited to preservice teachers; in-service teachers, who from experience may intuitively understand there to be a more spiritual-coping-based dimension to reflection but lack the conceptual tools to name it, could benefit from engaging with this study as well. They may identify with and find inspiration from how these teachers coped with their uncertainties and other practical shortcomings. Like Brianna did, the stand to develop an increased sense of self-efficacy by being reminded of the many issues they successfully "juggle" while reflecting on.

The importance of the havens sought out by teachers to help them cope cannot be understated as well, their moral centers being the most glaring ones. The teachers' wholehearted commitment to these ideals not only enabled them to discard or accept specific problems but likely underpinned the sense of responsibility that renewed their faith and that which gave them affirmation in their work. Undoubtedly, the teachers' moral centers were born out of years of (reflection on) experience and the democratic inclinations that brought them to their discipline and the populations they served. Still, such ideals can and must be developed and nurtured throughout teachers' careers. The same could be said for teachers' metaphors, the contemplation of which helped them accept their pedagogical limitations at times. School leaders should take from this the importance of understanding teachers' moral centers and how they see their work metaphorically, as these ideas, not the attainment of any daily measurable objective, keep teachers going. From there, school leaders can prioritize time and space for teachers to reflect separately and together on their work in light of them. As Santoro (2018) found, such community can play a vital role in helping teachers remain or rediscover their commitment to their moral centers.

On a cautionary note, this study raises questions about how sustainable it is for teachers, especially those in urban districts marred by high turnover rates (Simon & Johnson, 2015), to solely derive faith, acceptance, and affirmation from evocative imagery and a commitment to their moral centers. Such things helped teachers cope and, at times, were a source of spiritual and professional renewal, but in the absence of a supportive school, such as the one Kati resided in, they may only take teachers so far. Consider James and Brianna, who, after this study, transferred to different schools for this reason. They were not burnt out but demoralized (Santoro, 2018). However inspirational it is to think of teachers coping despite their contexts, school leaders must work to ensure teachers can cope because of their contexts. At a minimum, school leaders must explicitly and frequently acknowledge the spiritual and moral dimensions of teachers' work. From such acknowledgment, teachers may begin to feel that their spirituality is seen and supported or that their moral concerns are heard, conditions which when present, have been found to re-moralize teachers and lower their attrition from the profession (Santoro, 2018). For teachers like those featured in this study, whose spiritual aims necessitate delaying, sometimes indefinitely, the gratification of any success, such support is paramount.

(A PERSONAL) CONCLUSION

In concluding this study, I am compelled to revisit Kati's vision of a history classroom as a place of provocation and healing. The undertaking of this study was, in part, done with a similar goal in mind for teachers like Kati, who, at times, feel as though they are working toward an unreachable endpoint. What I failed to anticipate was how provocative and healing this experience would be for me personally and professionally. From spending time with these teachers and seeing how committed they were to their aims, it was unsettling to realize how, as a classroom teacher, I sometimes allowed my own aims to be compromised. Yet, at the same time, there was some healing in realizing that I was not the only teacher who remained uncertain of when or if their classroom vision would one day become a reality.

Years removed from the study and now a teacher educator, I hope that the findings of this study are as provocative and comforting to other teachers and teacher educators as they have been for me. For prospective teachers who are seduced by the promise of control and certainty, I hope the reflections of these teachers provoke you to be open to alternatives. For teacher educators burdened by the uncertainties and tensions endemic to cultivating ambitious teachers (Berry, 2007), I hope this study strengthens your commitment to that mission. Even though I am fully aware that the seeds I have planted here may never grow, I remain unshaken in my belief that they will rise and bear fruit one day.

REFERENCES

Atkinson, B. M. (2012). Rethinking reflection: Teachers' critiques. *The Teacher Educator, 47*(3), 175–194.

Badley, K., & Hollabaugh, J. (2012). Metaphors for teaching and learning. *Faculty Publications - School of Education, Paper 49*, 52–67.

Berry, A. (2007). *Tensions in teaching about teaching: Understanding practice as a teacher educator* (Vol. 5). Springer Science & Business Media.

Burke, R. J., & Greenglass, E. R. (1995). Job stressors, type A behavior, coping responses, and psychological burnout among teachers. *International Journal of Stress Management, 2*(1), 45–57.

Carroll, D. (2012). Examining the development of dispositions for ambitious teaching: One teacher candidate's journey. *The New Educator, 8*(1), 38–64.

Cochran-Smith, M. (2003). The unforgiving complexity of teaching: Avoiding simplicity in the age of accountability. *Journal of Teacher Education, 54*(3), 3–5.

Cochran-Smith, M., & Lytle, S. L. (2009). *Inquiry as stance: Practitioner research for the next generation*. Teachers College Press.

Dewey, J. (1964). *John Dewey on education* (R. Archambault, Ed.). University of Chicago Press. (Original work published 1933)

DiCamillo, L., & Gradwell, J. M. (2012). Using simulations to teach middle grades US history in an age of accountability. *RMLE Online, 35*(7), 1–16.

Elbow, P. H. (1968). The definition of teaching. *College English, 30*(3), 187–201.

Erickson, F. (1986). Qualitative methods in research on teaching. In M. C. Wittrock (Ed.), *Handbook of research on teaching: a project of the American Educational Research Association* (3rd ed., pp. 119–161). Macmillan.

Ethel, R. G., & McMeniman, M. M. (2000). Unlocking the knowledge in action of an expert practitioner. *Journal of Teacher Education, 51*(2), 87–101.

Gradwell, J. M. (2006). Teaching in spite of rather than because of the test. In S. G. Grant (Ed.), *Measuring History: Cases of State-Level Testing across states* (pp. 157–176). Rowman & Littlefield Education.

Grant, S. (2018). Teaching Practices in History Education. In S. A. Metzger & L. M. Harris (Eds.), *The Wiley International Handbook of History Teaching and Learning* (pp. 419–448). Wiley Blackwell.

Grant, S. G. (2003). *History lessons: Teaching, learning, and testing in US high school classrooms*. Lawrence Erlbaum Associates.
Grant, S. G. (2005). More journey than end: A case study of ambitious teaching. In E. Yeager & O. L. Davis (Eds.), *Wise social studies teaching in an age of high-stakes testing* (pp. 117–130). Information Age Publishing.
Grant, S. G., & Gradwell, J. (Eds.). (2010). *Teaching history with big ideas: Cases of ambitious teachers*. R & L Education.
Hammerness, K. (2006). *Seeing through teachers' eyes: Professional ideals and classroom practices* (Vol. 46). Teachers College Press.
Hammerness, K., Darling-Hammond, L., Bransford, J., Berliner, D., Cochran-Smith, M., McDonald, M., & Zeichner, K. (2005). How teachers learn and develop. In L. Darling-Hammond & J. D. Bransford (Eds.), *Preparing teachers for a changing world: What teachers should learn and be able to do* (pp. 358–359). Jossey-Bass.
Heafner, T. L., & Norwood, J. (2019). An elementary social studies teacher's quest to develop democratic citizens: The boundaries of ambitious teaching. *The Journal of Social Studies Research*, *43*(3), 187–198.
Helsing, D. (2007). Regarding uncertainty in teachers and teaching. *Teaching and Teacher Education*, *23*(8), 1317–1333.
Huebner, D. (1999). *The lure of the transcendent: Collected essays by Dwayne e. Huebner* (V. Hillis, Ed.). Lawrence Erlbaum Associates.
Jones, J. L., & Jones, K. A. (2013). Teaching reflective practice: Implementation in the teacher-education setting. *The Teacher Educator*, *48*(1), 73–85. https://doi.org/10.1080/08878730.2012.740153
Lampert, M. (1985). How do teachers manage to teach? Perspectives on problems in practice. *Harvard Educational Review*, *55*(2), 178–195.
Lampert, M., Boerst, T., & Graziani, F. (2011). Organizational resources in the service of school-wide ambitious teaching practice. *Teachers College Record*, *113*(7), 1361–1400.
Lortie, D. (1975). *Schoolteacher: a sociological study*. University of Chicago Press.
Love, B. L. (2019). *We want to do more than survive: Abolitionist teaching and the pursuit of educational freedom*. Beacon Press.
Mahlios, M., Massengill-Shaw, D., & Barry, A. (2010). Making sense of teaching through metaphors: a review across three studies. *Teachers and Teaching: Theory and practice*, *16*(1), 49–71.
Martinelle, R. (2020). Using video-stimulated recall to understand the reflections of ambitious social studies teachers. *The Journal of Social Studies Research*, *44*(3), 307–322.
McMillan, J. H., & Schumacher, S. (2010). *Research in Education: Evidence-Based Inquiry* (7th ed.). Pearson.
Mellado, L., Bermejo, M. L., & Mellado, V. (2012). Personal metaphors of prospective secondary economics and science teachers. *Asia-Pacific Journal of Teacher Education*, *40*(4), 395–408.
Nagle, J. F. (2009). Becoming a reflective practitioner in the age of accountability. *The Educational Forum*, *73*(1), 76–86.
Nieto, S. (Ed.). (2003). *What keeps teachers going?* Teachers College Press.
Nieto, S. (Ed.). (2014). *Why we teach now?* Teachers College Press.

Nolan, C., & Stitzlein, S. M. (2011). Meaningful hope for teachers in times of high anxiety and low morale. *Democracy and Education, 19*(1), 1–10.

Palmer, P. J. (2003). Teaching with heart and soul: Reflections on spirituality in teacher education. *Journal of Teacher Education, 54*(5), 376–385.

Patton, M. (2002). *Qualitative research and evaluation methods* (3rd ed.). SAGE.

Reitano, P. (2006). *The value of video stimulated recall in reflective teaching practices.* Australian Consortium for Social and Political Research Inc. New South Wales: (ACSPRI) Social Science Methodology Conference.

Rodgers, C. (2002). Defining reflection: Another look at John Dewey and reflective thinking. *Teachers College Record, 104*(4), 842–866.

Roth, S., & Cohen, L. J. (1986). Approach, avoidance, and coping with stress. *American Psychologist, 41*(7), 813–819.

Saban, A. (2006). Functions of metaphor in teaching and teacher education: A review essay. *Teaching Education, 17*(4), 299–315.

Santoro, D. A. (2018). *Demoralized: Why teachers leave the profession they love and how they can stay.* Harvard Education Press.

Schön, D. A. (1983). *The reflective practitioner: How professionals think in action.* Basic Books.

Shaw, D. M., Barry, A., & Mahlios, M. (2008). Preservice teachers' metaphors of teaching in relation to literacy beliefs. *Teachers and Teaching: theory and practice, 14*(1), 35–50.

Shulman, L. (1987). Knowledge and teaching: Foundations of the new reform. *Harvard Educational Review, 57*(1), 1–23.

Sibbett, L., & Au, W. (2017). Critical social studies knowledge and practice: Preparing social justice oriented social studies teachers in the Trump era. In C. C. Martell (Ed.), *Social studies teacher education: Critical issues and current perspectives* (pp. 17–45). Information Age Publishing.

Simon, N. S., & Johnson, S. M. (2015). Teacher turnover in high-poverty schools: What we know and can do. *Teachers College Record, 117*(3), 1–36.

Smith III, J. P., & Girod, M. (2003). John Dewey & psychologizing the subject-matter: Big ideas, ambitious teaching, and teacher education. *Teaching and Teacher Education, 19*(3), 295–307.

Stake, R. E. (2006). *Multiple case study analysis.* Guilford Press.

Stylianides, G. J., & Stylianides, A. J. (2014). The role of instructional engineering in reducing the uncertainties of ambitious teaching. *Cognition and Instruction, 32*(4), 374–415.

Stylianou, M., Kulinna, P. H., Cothran, D., & Kwon, J. Y. (2013). Physical education teachers' metaphors of teaching and learning. *Journal of Teaching in Physical Education, 32*(1), 22–45.

Thomas, L., & Beauchamp, C. (2011). Understanding new teachers' professional identities through metaphor. *Teaching and Teacher Education, 27*(4), 762–769.

Vinson, K. (2001). Oppression, anti-oppression, and citizenship education. In E. W. Ross (Ed.), *The social studies curriculum: Purposes, problems, and possibilities* (pp. 57–85). State University of New York Press.

Waddell, L. R. (2014). Using culturally ambitious teaching practices to support urban mathematics teaching and learning. *Journal of Praxis in Multicultural Education, 8*(2), 2.

Wiggins, G., & McTighe, J. (2005). *Understanding by design* (2nd ed.). Association for Supervision and Curriculum Development.
Windschitl, M., Thompson, J., & Braaten, M. (2020). *Ambitious science teaching*. Harvard Education Press.
Yin, R. K. (2009). *Case study research: Design and methods (applied social research methods)* (4th ed.). SAGE.
Yearwood, J. (2003). Teaching as gardening. In S. Nieto (Ed.), *What keeps teachers going?* (pp. 50–51). Teachers College Press.
Zeichner, K. M., & Liston, D. P. (2014). *Reflective teaching: An introduction* (2nd ed.). Routledge.

CHAPTER 9

SPIRITUAL EXPRESSION IN HISTORICAL NARRATION

Implications for History Teacher Education

Travis L. Seay
Missouri State University

ABSTRACT

The expression of identity through historical narration, particularly among White teachers, has been undertheorized and insufficiently documented. This chapter foregrounds a conceptual framework of *cultural memory* and *cultures of history* that problematizes historical narration from within Whiteness, and it summarizes research on one case of such narration. By investigating enactments of race in history pedagogy, the chapter examines tensions between the quest for holistic, authentic knowledge/narration and the realities of fragmented memory.

Keywords: Cultural memory, historical consciousness, critical whiteness, critical pedagogy, antiracism, teacher education, symbolic violence

INTRODUCTION

In many ways, history is fragmented. This is particularly true of history education in the United States. Differences between academic and K–12 teaching and learning about the past, tensions between local, national, and global histories, and conflicts between marginalized and prioritized narratives in the school curriculum drive much of the dissociation that plagues political discourse (cf. Duara, 2002; Lee, 2006; VanSledright, 2008, 2011; Tyrell, 2002; Wineburg, 1991). As an element of identity (cf. Anderson, 1983; Gellner, 1983), the teaching of national history in schools has long been anchored in content and narratives that flattered the socially advantaged (cf. Baldwin, 1965/1998). For nearly as long, history education has been contested territory for people who have challenged identity wrought by such narration (Brown & Brown, 2010; Brown & Au, 2014; King, 2014a, 2014b, 2015; Shear et al., 2015; Zimmerman, 2002). The cultural backlash against such measures over time has exacerbated historical tensions (Laats, 2015; Zimmerman, 2002) and, I would argue, conditioned diverse and often oppositional expressions of self through historical narration. In particular spaces of teaching and learning, narrations of national history even transcend academic boundaries and become a morality story seemingly ordained by God (cf. Schweber, 2006; VanSledright, 2008). While this sense of identity in relation to historical narration conceptually corresponds to the notion of "spiritually colonized people" (Rotem, 2019, p. 163), it also raises other philosophical concerns about discursive relationships to power and authority that complicate the quest for human wholeness and enables oppressive pedagogies (Orr, 2005; Rotem, 2019).

Undoubtedly, an essential factor in historical sense-making concerns how people relate to race and racism. As factors in the segregation and distortion of history education in American schools, race and racism have received a good deal of academic attention (e.g., Brown & Brown, 2014; King et al., 2012; Vasquez Heilig et al., 2012). However, less attention has been paid to how domination becomes woven into ordinary historical discourse among people interacting in particular spaces (see Chandler & Branscombe, 2015). This chapter focuses on discourses of race in historical and personal narration among White teachers. Based on field research and examined through lenses of critical race theory and critical whiteness studies (e.g., Applebaum, 2010; Bell, 1980a, 1980b; Brown et al., 2017; Delgado & Stefancic, 2017; Ladson-Billings, 1998, 2003, 2013; Leonardo, 2013), it argues that systemic, culturally grounded perceptions of difference sustain many narrations of history. In particular, moral perceptions of racism can shape pedagogical approaches in the history classroom.

The chapter marshals evidence by positing the coexistence of diverse mental maps for history within a particular setting, such as interactions in the school, classroom, and the surrounding community. Drawing from memory scholarship (Brown, 2010; Connerton, 1989, 2009; Lipsitz, 1990; Rüsen, 1989; Terdiman, 1993; Wertsch, 2008), the chapter traces personal and interactive dispositions in the expression of historical meaning.

Spiritual Expression in Historical Narration 171

Conceptualizing historical discourse (cf. Coffin, 2006) as embodied, spoken, and enacted (cf. Butler, 2020; McGuire, 2003), the framework for this chapter envisions schools as spaces of interaction in which historical beings participate in the interpretation of the past (Freire, 1970; Levstik & Thornton, 2018; van Boxtel & van Drie, 2018; Vianna & Stetsenko, 2006). Treating these spaces as sites of identity in which selves become positioned in relation to one another (cf. Buber, 1923/1996; Butler, 2020), the framework makes visible ways in which teachers and students negotiate boundaries of perception about the individual's relation to the whole (Orr, 2005).

In particular, the chapter explores historical narration through glimpses of White identity. As a complex, evolving, diverse, elusive, and often conflicting set of phenomena, whiteness can be challenging to study, particularly from within White positioning. Without grounding it in particular aspects of everyday life (e.g., Jacobson, 1998; Matias, 2016; Painter, 2010; Roediger, 1991; Sleeter, 2015), the study of Whiteness easily becomes mired in mental gymnastics. In this study, I examined narrations of race and history as an enacted/interactive phenomenon within a particular social and cultural context (Clark & Grever, 2018; Lévesque, 2014; Lipsitz, 1990; M'Charek, 2013; Nordgren, 2016). The resulting framework of cultural memory and historical cultures is based on narrative analyses of classroom observations, other instructional data, and teacher interviews. It theorizes social and emotional dynamics of difference and domination in historical narration and treats history as a medium of expression and identity (cf. Freire, 1970/2006; Nordgren, 2016; Rüsen, 2005). While analysis that grounds this framework is ongoing, themes of domination and White supremacy (cf. Leonardo, 2009; Mills, 1997, 1998; Sleeter, 2015) that emerge from the data I have analyzed comport with theoretical, ethnographic, and autoethnographic research on the topic of Whiteness as positionality and authority in educational settings (see, e.g., Applebaum, 2010; Castagno, 2014; Leonardo, 2009, 2013; Leonardo & Porter, 2010; Matias, 2016; Picower, 2009; Rosiek, 2016; Vaught, 2011).

To examine history education in this way acknowledges that discussions of history and race are segregated largely by place (cf. Rosiek, 2016), including spaces that reach well beyond traditional locations of education. Spaces people share and do not share condition stories that become narrated and occluded. They influence how cultural meaning attaches to the past (cf. Chau, 2019; Connerton, 1989, 2009; Nordgren, 2016). In mapping ways that various people make sense of the past, we can say that the diversity of *historical cultures*—spaces and processes in which people use history for various purposes (cf. Nordgren, 2016)—is evident. Nordgren (2016) defined historical culture as "all references to the past that are available in a given context, such as artifacts, rituals, customs, and narratives"

(p. 481). I pluralize *culture* to emphasize locality, presence, and interaction within and across diverse contexts, and I place schools at the center of cultural investigation.

I examine processes of historical sense-making that condition narration and counternarration within and between historical cultures. In pilot studies, I explored the idea that these processes intersect moral narration in ways that go largely unnoticed in the academic literature (cf. Sidat, 2019). For the current study, I investigated a pedagogical stance taken by a White history teacher and examined it as one of nonviolence (cf. Wang, 2013) that was grounded in elements of historical culture. The following paragraphs represent a way to understand her sense-making paths—her ways of connecting past to present, her instructional choices, and some of her interpersonal and intrapersonal deliberations about race. The chapter argues that narration of the past and present along these paths became a means of exercising moral narrative authority (cf. Barton & Levstik, 2004; King & Chandler, 2016) while avoiding critical confrontations of race.

Although the research summarized in this chapter focuses on problems of teaching and learning history from stances of whiteness, there is no intention or desire to essentialize race or to ascribe particular intellectual traits to all White people. Nor is there an equation of "whiteness" with specific characteristics of spiritual belief. Instead, the research represented in this chapter focuses on the narration of history, while the framework that guides it problematizes narrative authority in cultures of history. In raising the question of authority in cultures of history education (cf. Bourdieu & Passeron, 2000; Nordgren, 2016), the framework points to largely concealed notions and aspirations that guide historical narration. The ultimate purpose of this research is not to reinforce or replace existing conceptual frameworks that position race and historical consciousness in relation to cultural authority; its purpose is to help theorize, synthesize, and test frameworks that have the potential to address these matters effectively.

POSITIONALITY

As a scholar, I study race as a social and cultural element of identity and a feature of history pedagogy (see King & Chandler, 2016; Lee, 2006). As a White man and veteran classroom history teacher, and like numerous social studies educators, I have had problematic encounters with race and racism in the curriculum and the communities where I taught. As a result, I began to face some of my own deeply entrenched fears, habits, and beliefs about topics of oppression and exclusion, the role of history in addressing such complex issues, and my role as a student and teacher of history.

As a researcher in education and the social sciences, my spiritual sense is grounded in the pragmatic, tangible, and experiential relations to life. It is also attentive to rhythms, patterns, and rituals that commemorate, conceal, and deny particular memories. Such systems' interpersonal and cultural parameters are fascinating to me. As a White male academic from a working-class background, father of a White son, and a person recovering both racist and antiracist elements in my own life, my identity does not make me an objective observer. Nevertheless, it provides a field of view in which I can imagine, contextualize, and compare the contours of oppression and domination in teaching and learning.

REVIEW OF LITERATURE

History curricula in the United States often marginalize historically underrepresented social experiences and tend to reinforce ideologies of whiteness (cf. Shear et al., 2015). Scholars recognize the reinforcement of historical knowledge and the systemic reproduction of cultural and social dynamics—particularly in schools (Bourdieu, 1970; Leonardo, 2009, 2013)—as a function, in part, of historically perpetuated master scripts. Master scripts can be understood as discursive terrains that legitimize pervasive and uncritical conceptions of race (cf. Leonardo & Porter, 2010; Leonardo & Manning, 2017). They permit paradigms for defining normality and for imposing a concept of universal experience (A. Brown & K. Brown, 2010; K. Brown & A. Brown, 2010; Brown & Brown, 2014; King, 2014b; Ladson-Billings, 2003; Mills, 1997, 1998). The exclusion of minoritized perspectives from the curriculum over time in history education (see Journell, 2008, 2009; Shear et al., 2015; Vasquez et al., 2012) has replicated much of the "intellectual conformity" of the past and allowed long-term and systematic effects of racism to go largely unchallenged in schools and the curriculum (Brown & Brown, 2014; Zimmerman, 2002).

Although scholars have problematized dominant representations of historical experiences and argued for a more equitable history curriculum (Busey & Walker, 2017; King, 2014b; Ladson-Billings, 2003), the deployment and negotiation of master scripts in classrooms have not been studied adequately. To be sure, studies have addressed teacher and student positionalities about race and have brought insight to teaching methods in different settings (Chandler & Branscombe, 2015; Hawley, 2010; King, 2016; King & Swartz, 2014; Picower, 2009; Salinas & Alarcón, 2016; Salinas et al. 2012; Washington & Humphries, 2011). Still, situational barriers to more equitable history education—including cultural dynamics that influence White teachers' stances toward critical approaches—are poorly understood. Self-studies by White educators (e.g., Martell, 2015; Sleeter,

2015) have exemplified critical White self-examination, although some of the insights that result from such examination can be limited by too much introspection from within whiteness (Seay, 2020).

Other studies of White social studies teachers (e.g., Crowley & Smith, 2015; Smith & Crowley, 2015; Garrett & Segall, 2013) provide helpful dispositional findings about novice educators. These findings include discomfort and defensiveness toward critical conceptions of race and a lack of knowledge about such conceptions. Garrett and Segall (2013) problematized the terms "resistance" and "ignorance" in studies of White teacher candidates and argued for more nuanced interpretations of findings in the literature. They suggested investigations of contextual and psychosocial factors that influence phenomena of resistance and ignorance, and they recommended further inquiries into the structures of these phenomena.

The use of critical lenses to study pedagogical approaches among White in-service secondary-level history teachers is also fairly rare (e.g., Chandler & Branscombe, 2015; Martell & Stevens, 2017). One consequence of this gap in the research is that interactional, enacted, embodied, and contested aspects of historical sense-making (Hahn, 2003; Yancy, 2017) in many educational spaces go largely undocumented. Especially in spaces where narrative authority comports with the habits and preferences—political, racial, ideological, and so forth—of the majority or the powerful (Bonilla-Silva, 2014; Castagno, 2014), the need to identify and address the deployment of master narratives and counternarratives has become more urgent. The ability to notice, document, prepare for, and trouble, rather than reify, social relationships that reinforce master scripts (Hook, 2011) has become increasingly important in teacher education.

Finally, moral and spiritual dimensions of narration have received too little attention in the context of history education, particularly in the United States. While research locates everyday people who seek personal or moral authenticity in tracing the past into the present (Barton & McCully, 2005; Epstein, 2000; Wertsch, 2008; Woodson, 2015, 2016), entanglements of spiritual and historical sense-making are all but invisible in the scholarly literature on history education. Scholarly support for this heuristic nexus, so to speak, does exist. However, it exists mainly in theoretical deliberation among scholars in historical consciousness studies (see Nordgren, 2016; den Heyer, 2004).

For example, Jörn Rüsen's argument for "cognitive coherence" and "narrative competence" (den Heyer, 2004, p. 203) contrasted with what he viewed as a sort of default moral imperative in historical narration outside of academia. In other words, Rüsen theorized that moral interpretation of the past and present drives much historical narration. I understand him to mean that this manifestation of moral consciousness (Rüsen, 2004) is historically contingent. Theoretically, in Rüsen's conception of "historical consciousness," cognitive coherence (the sense-making part) and narrative competence (the construction and deployment of narratives) affect consciousness (cf. Freire, 1970/2006) in such a way that moral deliberation is possible through the medium of history (cf. den Heyer, 2004). In this way, the moral imperative becomes the topic, rather than simply a premise, for historical deliberation. As it stands, history education in the United States is a selective, largely segregated, and fragmented collection of institutions and cultures of history (cf. Kammen, 2008; Loewen, 1995/2018; VanSledright, 2008). As a result, it does not fully support truth-seeking initiatives, authentic and coherent narration, and epistemological wholeness that we might associate with spiritual education—or for that matter, historical consciousness.

The case-study research represented in this chapter addresses situational barriers to critical approaches in the history classroom. Examining a local culture of history (Nordgren, 2016), this study attends to historical, social, and structural elements of narration in relation to the perspective of a White Christian woman in the southeastern United States. It considers tensions in her moral and historical narration. It provides a framework for tracing some of her meaning-making processes as a history teacher.

CONCEPTUAL FRAMEWORK: CULTURAL MEMORY AND CULTURES OF HISTORY

In examining historical sense-making, it is necessary to observe spaces and references in which different people appear to make sense of and use the past. Drawing from Rüsen (1987, 2005), Nordgren (2016) described historical culture as inclusive of "the networks through which these references are distributed, such as schools, cultural institutions, and the media" (p. 481). When historical meaning becomes expressed, such as communicated through speech and action from within culture, history becomes a medium of expression (Nordgren, 2016). It is important to note that history may be used in many ways, and its uses may also be limited—and amplified—via cultural preferences and dispositions (cf. Bonilla-Silva, 2014). It is also important to emphasize that historical cultures are complex and contain many moving parts.

The framework of cultural *memory* and cultures of *history* accounts for perception, expression, and deployment of discourses, artifacts, texts, and so forth, in sociocultural contexts (cf. Bonilla-Silva, 2014; cf. Lipsitz, 1990), particularly in circumstances in which narratives and discourses may conflict. Anthony Brown (2010) discussed the concept of countermemory (cf. Lipsitz, 1990) in connection to cultural memory in order to investigate historical approaches to curriculum writing that challenged racial narratives about African Americans. Brown defined cultural memory as "discourses, texts, and artifacts that inform how students and teachers can imagine a group's historical experience" (Brown, 2010, p. 55). From this perspective, countermemory is a lens for challenging the cultural domination that memory can impose.

Tensions between countermemories and dominant memories are essential to historical culture (Nordgren, 2016). In Terdiman's (1993) concept of history as a system of remembering *and forgetting*, one can view such tensions as intrinsic to the historical culture. However, how this system operates in the daily lives of individuals remains a largely unexplored topic in education studies. Nora (1989) and Terdiman (1993) examine history as a complex system of mnemonic regulation whose operation relies partly on individual agents. On the other hand, as a system of forgetting (Connerton, 2009; Terdiman, 1993), history also has an autonomous and anonymous function (cf. Rosiek, 2016). Put another way, forgetting is not simply a circumstance of accidental omission or individual lapse of memory; it is built—historically—into particular aspects of cultural interaction and expression, including ways in which many use the past for political and other ends (cf. Nordgren, 2016).

Particularly in U.S. history, heuristic processes that guide generational perceptions of power and social difference have been bifurcated from the outset (cf. Kendi, 2016; Omi & Winant, 1994). Scholars have proposed that the origins of modern racial ideologies and division lie within Europeans' pre-modern and early modern attempts to reconcile "Christian metaphysics" with global realities of human difference (cf. Gutierrez, 1991; Kendi, 2016; Omi & Winant, 1994). Indentured servitude and enslavement in the Americas predated policies and cultures of difference and separation that have sustained ideological and social differences (Harris, 1993; Painter, 2010; Roediger, 1991). Political and social embodiments of such ideologies continue to separate people.

Over time, these social formations enabled some people to exercise their freedom to cast others—narratively, verbally, and physically—into categories of nonhuman and anticitizen (Busey & Dowie-Chin, 2021; Coulthard, 2014; cf. Roediger, 1991). Moreover, long-standing racial segregation in education, de jure and de facto, in the past and present (cf. Rosiek, 2016), has helped to reproduce segregation in cultural memory (cf. Bourdieu & Passeron, 2000; Brown, 2010; Lipsitz, 1990). In this sense, many cultures of history, including schools and especially in the United States, have developed mainly as racial formations (cf. Omi & Winant, 1994). Although there are diverse formations, many share interests in preserving particular linear narratives of progress and freedom (VanSledright, 2008) and protecting or concealing sources of cultural authority (Bourdieu, 1986).

The diversity of ways in which whiteness presents is attributable in part to discursive intersections between the social/ideological prerogative of being "White" and historical discourses of being "independent" and "free," particularly among poor and working-class people who became "white" (cf. Jacobson, 1998; Painter, 2011; Roediger, 1991). It is also attributable to idiosyncratic and historical processes by which White policymakers and voters have leveraged their freedom. Legal scholar Cheryl Harris (1993) argued that a historical process of judicial and legislative decisions concerning status and property rendered whiteness "the characteristic, the attribute, the property of free human beings" (p. 1721). The entitlement of whiteness as "status property" has adapted over time, continually reinforcing enactments of whiteness that claim and preserve the benefits of being White (Harris, 1993, p. 1734; cf. Painter, 2010; cf. Sleeter, 2015). Social enactments of race over time (Omi & Winant, 1994)—including racial violence and segregation policies—have largely isolated whiteness from a critical sense of its own being (cf. Rosiek, 2016; Seay, 2020). Put another way, the idiosyncrasies of whiteness betray important points of unity and disunity: the freedom to forget (cf. Streich, 2002) shapes some historical cultures while the absence of such freedom shapes other historical cultures. Over time, emergent cultural differences—in terms of historical and spiritual sense-making—can become dialogically incompatible.

Historical Racism, Violence, and Nonviolence

While the study of history bears out connections between racism and violence (e.g., Coulthard, 2014; Trouillot, 1995; Wilder, 2004), memory can distort these connections in such a way that it leaves historical wounds untended. Yet we encounter these wounds in spaces of conversation about race, which can flummox and emotionally strain discussants (cf. Bonilla-Silva, 2014; Mitchell, 2020). Intuitively, behind the specter of race lurks the specter of violence (Brown, 2010; Chandler & Branscombe, 2015; hooks, 1992; Seay, 2020) and the discomfort and stress it brings. For many, avoiding such spaces can appear safer than approaching them in good faith (Leonardo & Porter, 2010; Leonardo & Zembylas, 2017). Deconstructing these spaces as aspects of historical culture can reveal unexamined links between self and past, allowing the investigator to map spiritual sense-making as an element of historical narration.

In the United States, an averred historical exceptionalism provides cover for those who wish to avoid historical realities of class and racial conflict or deny the existence of historically expansive architectures and infrastructures of segregation and oppression. One can imagine using freedom from entanglement in racial dialogue to declare one's independence from history or perhaps from "politics" (cf. VanSledright, 2008). One can imagine this exercise of freedom expanding the idea of historical exceptionalism into personal realms of belief, identity, and memory. These hypothetical complications of what Joyce King (1991) called "dysconscious racism" might preclude meaningful dialogue between many people who use very different means of connecting past and present.

Although sense-making and experiential paths that link present to past can become dialogically incompatible, these differences are not always *discursively* incompatible. Judith Butler's (2020) description of *violence* and *nonviolence* helps with this distinction. While Butler treats these terms as socially and politically contested, "ethics of non-violence" addresses a critical difference between individual and collective identity:

> There is a sense in which violence done to another is at once a violence done to the self, but only if the relation between them defines them both quite fundamentally.... For if the one who practices non-violence is related to the one against whom violence is contemplated, then there appears to be a prior social relation between them; they are part of one another, or one self is implicated in another self. Non-violence would, then, be a way of acknowledging that social relation, however fraught it may be, and of affirming the normative aspirations that follow from that prior social relatedness. As a result, an ethics of non-violence cannot be predicated on individualism, and it must take the lead in waging a critique of individualism as the basis of ethics and politics alike. (p. 9)

I am arguing that the relational construction that Butler proposes for a critical rendering of nonviolence proceeds based on historical consciousness—that is, rendering the past and present as implicated in one another, just as "one self is implicated in another self" (Butler, 2020, p. 9). Yet affective dimensions of "individualism" in the construction of self, race, and memory remain largely out of view in the study of history education (see Garrett & Segall, 2013).

In part by affective separation of the "I" from the "we" (Matias, 2016) and in part through historical self-positioning against the relative disadvantages and perceived characteristics of the "other," especially people of color (cf. Busey & Dowie-Chin, 2021; Painter, 2010; Roediger, 1991), uncritical expressions of whiteness privilege spaces in which private constructions of race and racism might go unchallenged. However, in the absence of historical consciousness or cultural memory that accounts for "prior social relatedness" (Butler, 2020, p. 9), the violence of the past reverberates in social spaces that people occupy together (hooks, 1992).

Cultural Authority and Remote Solidarities

As an aspect of cultural authority in official curricula and classrooms, the narration of history from uncritical stances of whiteness can be problematic (e.g., Chandler & Branscombe, 2015; King & Chandler, 2016). Problems that arise are not only issues of factual/historical omission in teaching. They also include conceptual and affective gaps in interpretation and processes of narrating the past, including entanglements of experience, interpretation, emotion, and expression in teaching and learning difficult history (see Garrett & Segall, 2012; Leonardo & Zembylas, 2013; Zembylas, 2017).

The concept of *remote solidarities* grew from data analysis for the current study, which addresses part of the theoretical gap described above. As a personal construction of ideas pertaining to people and events in the past, the remote solidarity operates as a narrative anchor, so to speak, by marking a point and direction for narration. The anchor sits outside one's direct field of experience (e.g., in a different time/place), and it attaches to the realm of direct experience (in the present) via a "warp" or tether. While this tether may be invisible to the outside world, it remains within the narrator's affective cognition and purpose for narrating. The narrator is not always aware of how the tether appears to other people and may conceal aspects of it from others. The warp's dimensions and makeup may be obscure even to the narrator. However, its presence is evidenced in tensions along the line between the remote past and live memory and experience. Layers of obscurity and concealment necessitate examination of metaphorical threads in the cord (or links in the chain) of the "warp" to trace and describe the relationship between narrator and narrative purpose.

Narrative preferences that aid the selection of remote solidarities follow moral and cultural inclinations (cf. Chandler & Branscombe, 2015). Another way to say this is that remote solidarities are symbolic of moral identity and can reflect transcendent, affective sensibilities that guide historical narration (see Garrett & Segall, 2012; VanSledright, 2008). These moral anchors are highly diverse and consist of narratives left behind by people, reformulated over time, and deployed in the present—through teaching, policy making, and uses of cultural memory (see Nordgren, 2016; VanSledright, 2011). They anchor official histories in moral definitions provided in founding documents (see VanSledright, 2008), shape spaces of counternarration when they appear, for example, in narratives of enlightened leaders (cf. Alridge, 2006; Woodson, 2016), and may represent oppressive elements of history, even inspiring physical violence. In short, they anchor "cognitive and epistemological operations," the personal heuristics that aid social and narrative reproduction (Terdiman, 1993, p. 16). In addition to referencing elements of emotional/affective positioning (cf. Anderson, 2016; Matias,

2016; Zembylas, 2017) the remote solidarity may respond to interpretations of power and authority in settings where historical narration occurs (Popen, 2002; VanSledright, 2008). For example, the use of authority in the present means, in part, leveraging the memory of historical authority to narrate the past. This use of authority can range from considered narration of historiographical literature on a given topic to reliance on discourses of singular greatness—what Alridge (2006) referred to as a Judeo-Christian "messianic" worldview (cf. Schweber, 2006; cf. Woodson, 2016).

The remote solidarities identified in this study relate what Bourdieu (1980/1990, 1986) called *cultural arbitrary*, as they helped justify particular historical narrations. I use the concept of cultural arbitrary in referring to the hiddenness, or concealment, of the source of cultural authority in a school, classroom, or culture of history (Bourdieu, 1980/1990; Bourdieu & Passeron, 2000; Nordgren, 2016). I subsume under this category moral narration, or the moral imperative in narrating history (den Heyer, 2004). Operating as personal connections to the past in negotiating cultural authority, remote solidarities aid moral narration. However, as anchors for particular narrative threads, they also conceal aspects of cultural authority that support their historical narration.

Concealment and Disclosure

The study of cultures that sustain official history can reveal aspects of authority that become enacted through narrative and interpersonal means. For this study, it was instructive to consider historical narratives prescribed (by the state) to a habitus of narration (cf. Bourdieu, 1980/1990, 1986; Bonilla-Silva, 2014) and compare these narratives to those collected from within the habitus. The examination of interactions between self and narrative, self and other, and one's perceptions of the other in relation to the narrative, help to disclose discourses of humanity and nonhumanity, citizen and anticitizen, "nature" and its counterparts (Busey & Dowie Chin, 2021; Mills, 1997, 1998). Examining official history in diverse teaching and learning settings becomes a way of interrogating and refiguring processes that conceal these discourses. "Hegemonic forms of narrative production," reproduction, "and interpretation" become more visible (Popen, 2002, p. 386) in light of a framework of concealment and disclosure.

These "forms of narrative production" often arrive with a veneer of objectivity, which can make the application of such a framework challenging. Still, especially where stances of moral narration become the starting point, foundation, and cultural authority—rather than a point of deliberation—for historical narration (den Heyer, 2004), one can infer and indeed demonstrate narrative bias (Journell, 2008, 2009; Shear et al., 2015; VanSledright, 2008), including racial bias. Significantly, where racial bias distorts historical context and omits content that is culturally relevant to students' lived experiences, the resulting historical narration becomes arbitrarily exclusive.

These patterns of exclusion exemplify what Bourdieu (1980/1990) called *symbolic violence*. He meant the concealment of conditions and processes that replicate power and authority. Also known as symbolic *domination* (cf. Leonardo, 2009; Schubert, 2013), the concept refers to culturally and socially embedded processes. *Concealment* and *hiddenness* thus refer to systems that do not necessarily operate according to individuals' intentions or beliefs (cf. Garrett & Segall, 2013; Rosiek, 2016). One feature of this impairment is that everyday people become constrained by enormous mnemonic gaps (cf. Wertsch, 2008).

In schools and out in the world, symbolic violence takes various forms. In history education, it appears as master narratives in textbooks, decontextualized war monuments, omissions in the written curriculum, and as elements of instructional decision-making (cf. King, 1991; King & Chandler, 2016). In terms of *interpersonal* spaces, it extends to ways in which a teacher might address a student, students' conceptions of self and others, and how people learn to address one another. Moreover, domination and violence are also a matter of *intrapersonal* experience and adaptation. Finally, the internal mechanisms of forgetting are implicated in broader social contexts.

Often what becomes concealed in these forms of interaction and narration is a response to terror (Chandler & Branscombe, 2015; hooks, 1992) that links past and present. While they remain out of view, the concealment, the response, and the terror shape the cognitive and social landscapes in which people encounter one another and the past. As a stance about concealment, disclosure warrants the interrogation of processes that protect arbitrary moral precepts and fears of engaging in humanizing discourse.

METHODOLOGY

The qualitative case study summarized in this chapter examined heuristic systems in which a White teacher narrated the past and made sense of her teaching in relation to the teaching and learning context. While the broader target of this study is White narrations of violence in cultures of history, I treated this case as a particular aspect of the target. The case operated as a socially and culturally embedded, "bounded" and "integrated" system (Merriam, 1998; Nordgren, 2016; Stake, 1995) of narration.

The process used in this study was largely inductive and comparative (Merriam & Tisdell, 2016). Namely, the research findings evolved from an iterative process, meaning that data collection and analysis occurred through repeated steps of data examination, coding units of data, combining codes, developing new criteria for coding, and documenting the emergence of broader data categories.

I examined teaching materials, classroom artifacts, transcripts from a combined 480 minutes of semi-structured teacher interviews (on topics of race, state instructional standards, and teaching history in the local community), and notes from 300 minutes of classroom observations. During the interview, I used elicitation techniques (cf. Barton, 2015; Boucher, 2018a, 2018b) to draw out responses to mostly violent historical racial enactments captured on film. As I collected data, I compared them to the research literature. Finally, I analyzed them through emergent themes in the conceptual framework: concealment/disclosure, forgetting and symbolic violence, and relationships to the past, including remote solidarities, countermemory, and "prior social relatedness" (Butler, 2020, p. 9).

In designing this study, I considered its pilot studies and previous research on some of the difficulties many White people encounter when attempting to discuss race (Bonilla-Silva, 2014; DiAngelo, 2011), particularly as a historical topic (cf. Chandler & Branscombe, 2015; King, 2016; King & Chandler, 2016). As described above, research reveals a default stance of emotional distance from the topic, and this stance can become defensive. Ms. M, the participant in this study, was selected partly for her willingness to discuss her teaching of history in relation to race.

A veteran White high school U.S. history teacher in the southeastern United States, Ms. M taught in a small town called Emerson.[1] According to the U.S. Census Bureau, Emerson's 2017 population (at just under 1,000) was 47.7% African American and 48.8% White (U.S. Census, 2017), and the students at Emerson High School (EHS) reflected this ratio. Emerson is a high-poverty community, with about 29% of the population living below the poverty line (U.S. Census, 2017). For children under the age of 18, the poverty rate was higher. EHS had been designated a low-performing school by the state; it had been under threat of closure for nearly a decade.

A liberal White Christian teaching in a diverse though still predominantly White, conservative environment, Ms. M described and demonstrated a history pedagogy of nonviolence and nonracism that contrasted with conceptions of critical nonviolence and antiracism in the literature (cf. Butler, 2020; Chandler & Branscombe, 2015; King & Chandler, 2016). Having earned a bachelor's degree in history and a master's degree in education at the local university, Ms. M has taught for two decades in high-poverty, ethnically diverse schools in and around Emerson. Ms. M explained that she had been working out elements of cultural competence in her teaching and cultural relevance in the curriculum for a long time. She grew up in a middle-class White family. Her father was a scientist and university professor, and her mother was a homemaker. Embarrassed by her mother's occasional displays of racism, she made efforts to educate herself about social inequalities by studying the past.

The research questions that guided this study were:

1. How does a White history teacher position her pedagogical and curricular decision-making in relation to historical racism and racial violence?
2. How does her positioning relate to the moral and/or psychosocial aspects of narration, especially in deploying master and counternarratives?
3. What implications do her narrative choices—particularly their ways of framing relationships between the individual and (the whole) society—have for history teacher education?

These questions reflect rhythms and patterns that move from the particular to the general and back again in the investigation of a case (Merriam, 1998). In conjunction with the conceptual framework, they enabled me to conceptualize racial enactments, narratives of self and society (the individual and the collective), and historical narration within the integrated, bounded system represented in this case.

FINDINGS

My first impression was that Ms. M tried to convey a culturally relevant curriculum (cf. Martell, 2015). The classroom walls displayed large images of Mohandas Gandhi, Nelson Mandela, and Rosa Parks. Black and White students sat close to each other in long columns of desks below these posters, chatting and getting ready for class. At the beginning of one class period, Ms. M asked students to journal about Italian and German nationalism (as part of a lesson on fascist aggression during World War II). To outward appearances, this was a safe environment in which students might grapple with difficult and potentially sensitive topics. Still, this summary of findings shows significant challenges to achieving antiracist teaching (cf. King & Chandler, 2016) in the classroom. These challenges arose largely from boundaries imposed by the official instructional curriculum and the local historical culture.

Universalizing Narrative

In her teaching, Ms. M sought narratives that elevated examples of moral rectitude, individual initiative, and racial equality. However, in hewing narratives that matched these purposes, she also excluded narratives depicting morally reprehensible behavior, collective initiatives, and enduring racial inequalities (cf. Chandler & Branscombe, 2015). These purposes comport with curricular and pedagogical patterns of "universal values" (Fitchett et al., 2015; cf. King & Swartz, 2014) and narrations of "universal experience" (Lipsitz, 1990).

Part of the explanation for this approach lies in the state instructional standards. During our interviews, Ms. M discussed her approaches to meeting the standards that addressed minoritized groups. The instructional standards resemble standards in other states that do not explicitly require discussions of race, systemic racism, or racial violence. Vasquez Heilig et al. (2012) have referred to this type of curricular whitewashing (cf. Bachelier, 2017; Epstein, 2000; VanSledright, 2008) as an "illusion of inclusion." Additionally, Ms. M taught in a state whose education law requires the teaching of U.S. history "according to the universal principles stated in the Declaration of Independence." Indeed, the narratives about race at the center of Ms. M's pedagogical stance on universal morality sometimes appeared inclusive. Still, they consisted of selections (Kammen, 2008; Loewen, 1995/2018) meant to avoid tensions between master and counternarration in the classroom (cf. Chandler & Branscombe, 2015).

Another factor in this avoidance was tension in the local historical culture (cf. Nordgren, 2016). This tension was marked by Ms. M's decision to "pull back" on narratives of racial violence a decade before I met her. She had once occasionally taught about the regional history of lynching, using examples from communities outside Emerson to punctuate the proximity of historical events. However, in 2010, an encounter with an angry White parent shook her emotionally and made her rethink her approach to teaching history in Emerson.

She had organized a Black history fair in 2010, and the fair had prompted the visit by the angry father of one of her students. The student, a White girl, had plagiarized and failed an assignment on Black history that was meant to be part of the display at the fair. Sitting in the conference room with the principal, an African American woman, and Ms. M, the man had berated the "liberal" curriculum, saying that teaching Black history was "wrong." He had then casually mentioned his gun collection. Later, according to Ms. M, he attempted to organize a public demonstration against the school. The Black History fair did not occur again at EHS after this incident, and Ms. M's encounter with the parent had left her unsteady. Her demeanor changed when the topic came up. She became animated and expressed fear, anger, and disgust toward the White parent who had aggressively opposed the teaching of Black history.[2] In effect, the written curriculum and the local culture (cf. Martell & Stevens, 2017) merged as the basis of narrative authority in Ms. M's class.

Ms. M positioned messianic voices (cf. Woodson, 2016) of racial equality as carriers of universal principles. Her history pedagogy drew heavily on language and principles provided by Civil Rights-era figures, such as primary sources selected in step with the state's instructional standards. For example, early in the interview, she verbalized her definition of racism by paraphrasing a portion of Martin Luther King, Jr.'s "I Have a Dream" speech. She understood it was essential not to discriminate against people "because of the color of their skin" but to form opinions about people based on the "content of their character." Such phrase-craft punctuated our discussion of her purposes for teaching about race in history. These bits of primary sources were the raw material for a moral narrative about the universal principle of equality. These factors enabled a story of a finished ideal grounded in the language of freedom (cf. VanSledright, 2008).

Civil Rights Movement as Remote Solidarity

For Ms. M, the American Civil Rights Movement was an anchor that enabled her to narrate the past from a stance of moral authority. The state instructional standards included provisions for teaching about the Civil Rights Movement, mainly as the Movement unfolded in the state. In Ms. M's teaching, what preceded Civil Rights—murder, discrimination, Jim Crow, and early 20th century authors and activists—was the movement's prologue. However, such topics were largely in the background; the violent aspects of pre-Civil Rights history had fallen away from her teaching. Indeed, it became apparent during the course of this study that although Ms. M raised issues of segregation, oppression, and struggles for equality in U.S. history, race and racism were not central to the history curriculum (cf. Chandler & Branscombe, 2015; Martell, 2018). Moreover, anchoring moral narration of the past in the Civil Rights Movement may have enabled her to avoid difficult discussions about racism and its long-lasting effects on history.

When I asked whether it made sense to exclude narratives about heinous race crimes, given the centrality of such violence to the rise of the modern movement—especially in the state where she taught—Ms. M told me that she was not interested in showcasing this kind of immorality. The discomfort she experienced around the topic of racialized violence was her most frequently cited reason for avoiding discussions about racism. "Violence is unnatural," she told me when I inquired further about her discomfort. I asked her whether or not she thought about the angry White parent when these emotions came up, and she told me "sometimes," and that she tried to keep that experience locked away from her conscious thoughts.

Attempting to unravel her rationale, I asked her to think aloud (Barton, 2015; Boucher, 2018a; Wineburg, 2001) while viewing a series of images, including an open casket photo of Emmett Till taken in 1955 and a 1930 photograph showing the lifeless bodies of Thomas Shipp and Abram Smith in Marion, Indiana. Most of her commentary about the photos occurred as she viewed the image from the Marion lynching, and most of it referred to the group of White people assembled around the bodies of Shipp and Smith. She explained:

> It kind of strikes a chord of how can human beings—how is this possible, you know what I mean? You just kind of fundamentally on an emotional level don't understand. That's ... hard to put into words.

One insight that stands out from this response is Ms. M's self-distancing from the White people in the photo (cf. Case & Hemmings, 2005; Picower, 2009; Segall & Garrett, 2013). Her use of *you* instead of *I* may also indicate a degree of emotional distancing from the topic as well as a means of expressing a universal moral imperative of nonviolence.

This moral positioning (cf. Rüsen, 2006) was more visible in other parts of the interviews. Referring again to the Marion photo, Ms. M explained,

> I come from a point a point of view, spiritually speaking—and I have to use that word—that all humans are equal. All of them. So this [violence] is really far away from that particular belief. And I think it lessens everyone in this photograph. It's harmful to all of them to hold that point of view.

Her expression of "universal values" (cf. Fitchett et al., 2015) stood out as a companion to the lessons she drew from the Civil Rights Movement. Equality was a value to be celebrated and showcased instead of problematized and carefully examined.

Despite her pedagogical focus on universal equality, Ms. M had difficulty relating to White people whom she believed to be racists. When she suggested that the White people in the image were "not living their true humanity," I asked whether or not this description would apply to the angry White parent. "Oh," she said, "probably.... Mostly, I feel sorry for [the parent and his family]," who were "poor and uneducated." There was an inexplicable inequality of perspectives that separated her from these people. She felt a way about them that was hard to put into words.

Ms. M's use of the Civil Rights Movement (cf. Nordgren, 2016) as a moral anchor allowed her to take a spiritual stance in her narration of history and in leveraging the official curriculum. In short, her stance in opposition to anti-Black racism converged with a universalizing narrative of equality and nonviolence. However, her conception of universal values was incomplete, as it sometimes conflicted with expressions of counter-memory among African American students in her class (Seay, 2019). It was incomplete also because it excluded an explanation for the nonbelievers, as it were—White racists who angered, flummoxed, and confounded her. Perhaps because she could not understand them, they remained outside her bounds of moral narration.

Ms. M reported that the backlash against the Black History fair had strained her relationships with a few White school employees. Office staff, whom she believed to be friends, stopped talking to her. In the wake of this disruption—the "trouble" she felt she had caused—she reflected on some of the resulting shifts in her personal perspective. Foremost among these shifts was the shock of recognizing a habitus (Bonilla-Silva, 2014) that became at once familiar and foreign. It was a disorienting experience for her, and her description of it resembled the dissonance that White educators might experience during interpersonal encounters with race (see Bonilla-Silva, 2014).

Following the Black history fair, Ms. M's narrative choices retained an additive approach (Banks, 1994) to Black history while focusing on a Civil Rights trajectory of equality and progress. Standing in opposition to the "white power structure" of the past, her pedagogy of nonviolence supplanted narratives about white supremacy, which reaches across boundaries of time and space into the present.

Among the most salient findings in this study was Ms. M's othering of White racists. If teaching about the Civil Rights Movement became a way of expressing solidarity with principles of equality and diversity, it was also a means to shut out narratives of violence and inhumanity. In short, Ms. M. used the movement as a buffer. It became central to a pedagogy of nonviolence—one expressing morality and unity—while it excluded a great deal of historical context and human suffering. Narrative authority was nonracist, and it fulfilled a moral ideal that the teacher wanted to be true.

DISCUSSION

The findings in this study nuance Robin DiAngelo's (2011) claim that "white moral objection to racism increases white resistance to acknowledging complicity with it" (p. 64). "Whites who position themselves as liberal," writes DiAngelo, "often opt to protect what they perceive as their moral reputations, rather than recognize or change their participation in systems of inequity and domination" (p. 64). In Ms. M's case, White racists were positioned as moral foils, while she maintained her own individual status as "good" (Applebaum, 2010).

Her adherence to the letter of the standards and her fear of reprisals from the community in the wake of the Black history fair represent a convergence of interests (cf. Delgado & Stefancic, 2017) in favor of a universal narrative that omitted racial conflict and thus avoided social tensions associated with the airing of such conflict. This combination of interests conditioned a decidedly nonracist approach to U.S. history instead of an antiracist approach (cf. King & Chandler, 2016).

Fear of White terror (Chandler & Branscombe, 2015; hooks, 1992) in her own community accounted for many of Ms. M's narrative choices, including the abstract condemnation of violence. I view these choices as an aspect of her moral positioning (cf. DiAngelo, 2011; den Heyer, 2004; Rüsen, 2006). This positioning was also reflected in the protection of her "moral reputation," as she gestured against White racists and against the fear of being thought of as racist by her students. Moral narrative authority thus rested in the concept of universal values, a premise of personal goodness, and discomfort with implications of historical violence. Yet, this authority remained largely hidden from students, as Ms. M did not broach the incident with the angry parent, did not confront racial tensions as an enduring aspect of American history and did little to contrast historical violence with her conception of nonviolence. Nor did she attempt to address tensions in the meaning of "universal values."

While she recognized official curricular limitations on the topic of race, Ms. M consciously chose to "pull back" on her teaching of the topic instead of addressing curricular gaps, as she once had attempted to do. Instead of being an objective of critical instruction, the disruption of local conservative norms became a boundary not to be crossed. Maintaining a public stance of neutrality, nonracism, and nonviolence (Delgado & Stefancic, 2017; Gounari, 2008; King & Chandler, 2016), Ms. M censored herself. These were the parameters that limited her ability to engage in counternarration.

Ms. M's treatment of the Civil Rights Movement conjured a memory of racial reconciliation that had dismantled the most problematic White power structures and left more extreme elements of anti-Black racism (cf. Busey & Dowie Chin, 2021) as outliers in a landscape taking shape in a history of progress (Loewen, 1995/2018; VanSledright, 2008, 2011). While she consistently referred to the unhealthy "spiritual" condition of racists, she showed no desire to historicize this condition or to treat it as an aspect of white supremacy (cf. Chandler & Branscombe, 2015; Leonardo & Zembylas, 2013).

In avoiding patterns of racial violence as a link *between past and present*, Ms. M also narratively distanced herself from other reminders of White racism. As a topic of historical narration, the persistence of racism became less important than its pastness. The extraction of White anger and inhumanity (cf. Anderson, 2016) from history cast oppressive actions as aberrant and exceptional when they are not (Delgado & Stefancic, 2017). Violence was "unnatural," and one of her purposes in teaching history was to illuminate the true "nature of humanity." However, her approach to "humanity" as a socially experienced phenomenon operated as an uncontested term. Inhumanity—and the language that accompanies it—dropped into occasionally useful though distant memory.

In standing against White *racists*, Ms. M overlooked the symbolic violence of narrating history from within the fear of terror. Instead, she prioritized personal freedom from discomfort and projected this freedom onto all students. Her fear of upsetting the wrong people or "causing trouble" guided her instructional decision-making at a fundamental level. These decisions rendered an uncritical form of "nonviolence" as the moral purpose behind historical narration, while they left silent the violent interactions that preceded this moral imperative. The result was a pedagogy of history that flattered (cf. Baldwin, 1965/1998) and protected a culture that prioritized White emotionality (Bonilla-Silva, 2014; Leonardo & Porter, 2010; Leonardo & Zembylas, 2013).

CONCLUSION

In recognizing elements of social context that operate as narrative boundaries or barriers, teacher educators can help their students express and hone their purposes for teaching history, particularly in settings where official narratives may dominate teachers' engagement with the curriculum. To aid the process of recognition, it can be helpful to assign preservice teachers critical literature as part of an extended practicum experience (cf. King, 2016). Centering historically marginalized voices in course readings, developing frameworks for noticing instances of symbolic violence, and requiring observational and interactive activities with diverse students and teachers in classrooms could help to mitigate some of the epistemological and pedagogical blind spots that accompany novice teachers.

Even with such practices in place, it is easy for teachers to slip into the comfort of conventional narration and actively avoid the risk of causing "trouble." Particularly for people who grew up accepting the freedom narratives of U.S. history (VanSledright, 2008), familiar currents of culture and place can impede authentic connections to countermemory. These currents tend to wash away much of the ruthlessness that has historically masqueraded as freedom. They may treat countermemory as an accompaniment to history rather than an integral aspect of historical culture. For these reasons, it is crucial to emphasize rituals and conditions of forgetting with preservice teachers—how they manifest in social spaces and in the narratives we privilege and discard.

Finally, teacher educators must recognize and problematize common moral imperatives that frame historical narration. In particular, it is helpful to document and study uses of history (Nordgren, 2016) that sustain private, unconscious, or otherwise abstract perceptions of race and whiteness. Learning from such observation and study would be especially useful for White preservice teachers, whose links to the past and humanity are often dysconscious (King, 1991) and tenuous.

REFERENCES

Alridge, D. P. (2006). The limits of master narratives in history textbooks: An analysis of representations of Martin Luther King, Jr. *Teachers College Record, 108*(4), 662–686. https://doi.org/10.1111/j.1467-9620.2006.00664.x

Anderson, B. (1983) *Imagined communities: Reflections on the origin and spread of nationalism*. Verso.

Anderson, C. (2016). *White rage: The unspoken truth of our racial divide*. Bloomsbury.

Applebaum, B. (2010). *Being white, being good: White complicity, white moral responsibility, and social justice pedagogy*. Lexington Books.

Bachelier, S. (2017). Hidden history: The whitewashing of the 1917 East St. Louis Riot. *Confluence*, (2150–2633), 16–25.

Baldwin, J. (1965/1998). White man's guilt. In D. Roediger (Ed.), *Black on white: Black writers on what it means to be white* (pp. 320–325). Schocken.

Banks, J. A. (1994). Transforming the mainstream curriculum. *Educational leadership, 51*, 4–8.

Barton, K. (2015). Elicitation techniques: Getting people to talk about ideas they don't usually talk about. *Theory & Research in Social Education, 43*(2), 179–205. https://doi.org/10.1080/00933104.2015.1034392.

Barton, K. & Levstik, L. (2004). *Teaching history for the common good*. Lawrence Erlbaum & Associates.

Barton, K., & McCully, A. W. (2005). History, identity, and the school curriculum in Northern Ireland: An empirical study of secondary students' ideas and perspectives. *Journal of Curriculum Studies, 37*(1), 85–116. https://doi.org/10.1080/0022027032000266070

Bell, D. (1980a). Brown v. Board of Education and the interest-convergence dilemma. *Harvard Law Review, 93*(3), 518–533.

Bell, D. (1980b). Racism: A symptom of the narcissistic personality. *Journal of the National Medical Association, 72*(7), 661.

Bonilla-Silva, E. (2014). *Racism without racists: Color-blind racism and the persistence of racial inequality in the United States*. Rowman & Littlefield.

Boucher, M. (2018a) Interrogating whiteness: Using photo-elicitation to empower teachers to talk about race. In M. Boucher (Ed.), *Participant empowerment through photo-elicitation in ethnographic education research: New perspectives and approaches* (pp. 201–225). Springer.

Boucher, M. (2018b). Conclusion: Troubling Empowerment. In M. Boucher (Ed.) *Participant empowerment through photo-elicitation in ethnographic education research: New perspectives and approaches* (pp. 201–225). Springer.

Bourdieu, P. (1970). *Reproduction and education.* SAGE.

Bourdieu, P. (1980/1990). *The Logic of Practice.* Stanford University Press.

Bourdieu, P. (1986). The forms of capital. In J. G. Richardson (Ed.), *Handbook of Theory and Research for the Sociology of Capital* (pp. 241–258). Greenwood Press.

Bourdieu, P. & Passeron, J-C (2000). *Reproduction in education, society and culture.* SAGE.

Brown, A. (2010). Counter-memory and race: An examination of African American scholars' challenges to early twentieth century K–12 historical discourses. *Journal of Negro Education, 79*(1), 54–65.

Brown, A., & Au, W. (2014). Race, memory, and master narratives: A critical essay on U.S. curriculum history. *Curriculum Inquiry, 44*(3), 358–389.

Brown, A., & Brown, K. D. (2010). Strange fruit indeed: Interrogating contemporary textbook representations of racial violence toward African Americans. *Teachers College Record, 112,* 31–67.

Brown, A., & Brown, K. D. (2014), The more things change, the more they stay the same: Excavating race and the enduring racisms in U.S. curriculum. *National Society for the Study of Education, 114*(2), 103–130. https://doi.org/10.1177/016146811511701405

Brown, K. D., & Brown, A. (2010). Silenced memories: An examination of the sociocultural knowledge on race and racial violence in official school curriculum. *Equity & Excellence in Education, 43*(2), 139–154. https://doi.org/10.1080/10665681003719590

Brown, A. L., Brown, K. D., & Ward, A. (2017). Critical race theory meets culturally relevant pedagogy: Advancing a critical sociohistorical consciousness for teaching and curriculum. *Social Education, 81*(1), 23–27.

Buber, M. (1996). *I and thou* (W. Kaufmann, Trans., 1st Touchstone ed.). Touchstone. (Original work published 1923)

Busey, C., & Dowie-Chin, T. (2021). The making of global Black anti-citizen/citizenship: Situating BlackCrit in global citizenship research and theory. *Theory & Research in Social Education 49*(2), 153–175. https://doi.org/10.1080/00933104.2020.1869632

Busey, C. & Walker, I. (2017). A dream and a bus: Black critical patriotism in elementary social studies standards. *Theory and Research in Social Education, 45*(4), 456–488.

Butler, J. (2020). *The force of nonviolence: An ethico-political bind.* Verso.

Case, K. A. & Hemmings, A. (2005). Distancing strategies: White women preservice teachers and antiracist curriculum. *Urban Education, 40*(6), 606–626.

Castagno, A. (2014). *Educated in whiteness: Good intentions and diversity in schools.* University of Minnesota Pres.

Chandler, P., & Branscombe, A. (2015). White social studies: Protecting the white racial code. In P. Chandler (Ed.), *Doing race in social studies: Critical perspectives* (pp. 61-88). Information Age Publishing.

Chau, C. (2019). Very superstitious: Reclaiming Chinese spiritualities to transgress. In N. Wayne, R. A. Torres, & D. Nyaga (Eds.), *Transversing and translocating spiritualities: Epistemological and pedagogical conversations* (pp. 99–122). Nsemia Publishers.

Clark, A. & Grever, M. (2018). Historical consciousness: Conceptualizations and educational applications. In S. A. Metzger & L. M. Harris (Eds.), *The Wiley international handbook of history teaching and learning* (pp. 177–202). Wiley-Blackwell.

Coffin, C. (2006). *Historical discourse: The language of time, cause, and evaluation*. Continuum. The New Press.

Connerton, P. (1989). *How societies remember*. Cambridge University Press.

Connerton, P. (2009). *How modernity forgets*. Cambridge University Press.

Coulthard, G.S. (2014). *Red skin, white masks: Rejecting the colonial politics of recognition*. University of Minnesota Press.

Crowley, R. M. & Smith, W. (2015). Whiteness and social studies teachereducation: tensions in the pedagogical task. *Teaching Education, 26*(6), 160–178.

Delgado, R., & Stefancic, J. (2017). *Critical race theory: An introduction*. NYU Press.

DiAngelo, R. (2011). White fragility. *International Journal of Critical Pedagogy, 3*(3), 54–70.

Duara, P. (2002). Transnationalism and the challenge to national histories. In T. Bender (Ed.), *Rethinking American history in a global age* (pp. 25–46). University of California Press.

Epstein, T. (2000). Adolescents' perspectives on racial diversity in U.S. history: Case studies from an urban classroom. *American Educational Research Journal, 37*, 185–214.

Fitchett, P. G., Merriweather, L., & Coffey, H. (2015). "It's not a pretty picture": How pre-service teachers make meaning of America's racialized past through lynching imagery. *The History Teacher, 48*(2), 245–269.

Freire, P. (2006). *Pedagogy of the oppressed*. Continuum. (Original work published 1970)

Garrett, H., & Segall, A. (2013). (Re) considerations of ignorance and resistance in teacher education. *Journal of Teacher Education, 64*(4), 294–304.

Gellner, E. (1983). *Nations and nationalism*. Cornell University Press.

Glaser, B. G., & Strauss, A. L. (2012). *The discovery of grounded theory: Strategies for qualitative research*. Aldine Transaction. (Original work published 1967)

Gutierrez, R. (1991). *When Jesus came the corn mothers went away: Marriage, sexuality, and power in New Mexico, 1500–1846*. Stanford University Press.

Hahn, S. (2003). *A nation under our feet: Black political struggles in the rural South from slavery to the Great Migration*. Harvard University Press.

Harris, C. (1993). Whiteness as property. *Harvard Law Review, 106*(8), 1707–1791.

Hawley, T. (2010). Purpose into practice: The problems and possibilities of rationale-based practice in social studies. *Theory and Research in Social Education, 38*(1), 131–162.

Hook, D. (2011). Retrieving Biko: A black consciousness critique of whiteness. *African identities, 9*(1), 19–32. https://doi.org/ 10.1080/14725843.2011.530442

hooks, b. (1992). Representing whiteness in the Black imagination. In L. Grossberg, C. Nelson, & P. Treichler (Eds.), *Cultural studies* (pp. 338–346). Routledge.

Jacobson, M. F. (1998). *Whiteness of a different color: European immigrants and the alchemy of race*. Harvard University Press.

Journell, W. (2008). When oppression and liberation are the only choices: The representation of African Americans within state social studies standards. *Journal of Social Studies Research, 32*(1), 40–50.

Journell, W. (2009). An incomplete history: Representation of American Indians in state social studies standards. *Journal of American Indian Education, 48*(2), 18-32.

Kammen, M. (2008). The American past politicized: Uses and misuses of history author(s). *Annals of the American Academy of Political and Social Science, 617*, 42–57.

Kendi, I. X. (2016). *Stamped from the beginning: The definitive history of racist ideas in America*. Bold Type Books.

King, J. E. (1991). Dysconscious racism: Ideology, identity, and the miseducation of teachers. *Journal of Negro Education, 60*(2), 133–146.

King, L. (2014a). More than slaves: Black founders, Benjamin Banneker, and critical intellectual agency. *Social Studies Research and Practice, 9*(3), 88–105.

King, L. (2014b). When lions write history: Black history textbooks, African American educators, and the alternative Black curriculum in social studies education, 1890-1940. *Multicultural Education, 22*(1), 2–11.

King, L. (2015). "A narrative to the colored children in America": Lelia Amos Pendleton, African American history textbooks, and challenging personhood. *The Journal of Negro Education, 84*(4), 519–533.

King, L. (2016) Teaching black history as a racial literacy project, *Race Ethnicity and Education, 19*(6), 1303–1318. https://doi.org/10.1080/13613324.2016.1150822

King, L., & Chandler, P. (2016). From non-racism to anti-racism in social studies teacher education: Social studies and racial pedagogical content knowledge. In A.R. Crowe & A. Cuenca (Eds.), *Rethinking social studies teacher education in the twenty-first century* (pp. 3–21). Springer.

King, L., Davis, C., & Brown, A. (2012). African American history, race and textbooks: An examination of the works of Harold O. Rugg and Carter G. Woodson. *Journal of Social Studies Research, 36*(4), 359–386.

King, J. E., & Swartz, E. E. (2014). *"Re-membering" history in student and teacher learning: An Afrocentric culturally informed praxis*. Routledge.

Laats, A. (2015). *The other school reformers: Conservative activism in American education*. Harvard University Press.

Ladson-Billings, G. (1998). Just what is critical race theory and what's it doing in a nice field like education? *International Journal of Qualitative Studies in Education, 11*(1), 7–24. https://doi.org/10.1080/095183998236863

Ladson-Billings, G. (2003). Lies my teacher still tells: Developing a Critical Race perspective toward the social studies. In G. Ladson-Billings (Eds.), *Critical race theory perspectives on the social studies* (pp. 1–14). Information Age Publishing.

Ladson-Billings, G. (2013). Critical race theory—What it is not! In M. Lynn & D. Dixson (Eds.), *Handbook of critical race theory in education* (pp. 34–47). Routledge.

Lee, P. (2006). Understanding history. In P. Seixas (Ed.), *Theorizing historical consciousness* (pp. 129–163). University of Toronto Press.

Leonardo, Z. (2009). *Race, whiteness, and education*. Routledge.

Leonardo, Z. (2013). The story of schooling: Critical race theory and the educational racial contract. *Discourse: Studies in the Cultural Politics of Education, 34*(4), 599–610. https://doi.org/10.1080/01596306.2013.822624

Leonardo, Z., & Manning, L. (2017). White historical activity theory: toward a critical understanding of white zones of proximal development. *Race Ethnicity and Education, 2*(1), 15–29.

Leonardo, Z., & Porter, R. K. (2010). Pedagogy of fear: Toward a Fanonian theory of 'safety' in race dialogue, *Race Ethnicity and Education, 13*(2), 139–157. https://doi.org/10.1080/13613324.2010.482898

Leonardo, Z., & Zembylas, M. (2013) Whiteness as technology of affect: Implications for educational praxis. *Equity & Excellence in Education, 46*(1), 150–165. https://doi.org/10.1080/10665684.2013.750539

Lévesque, S. (2014, October 2). Between memory recall and historical consciousness: Implications for education. *Public History Weekly* [Web blog journal post]. https://public-history-weekly.degruyter.com/2-2014-33/memory-recall-historical-consciousness-implications-education/

Levstik, L., & Thornton, S. (2018). Reconceptualizing history for early childhood through early adolescence. In S. A. Metzger & L. M. Harris (Eds.), *The Wiley international handbook of history teaching and learning* (pp. 473–502). Wiley-Blackwell.

Lipsitz, G. (1990). *Time passages: Collective memory and American popular culture*. University of Minnesota.

Loewen, J. W. (2018). *Lies my teacher told me: Everything your American history textbook got wrong*. Touchstone. (Original work published 1995)

Martell, C. (2015). Learning to teach culturally relevant social studies: A white teacher's retrospective self-study. In P. Chandler (Ed.), *Doing race in social studies: Critical perspectives* (pp. 41–60). Information Age Publishing.

Martell, C. (2018). Teaching race in U.S. history: Examining culturally relevant pedagogy in a multicultural urban high school. *Journal of Education, 198*(1), 63–77. https://doi.org/10.1177/0022057418800938

Martell, C., & Stevens, K. M. (2017). Equity- and tolerance-oriented teachers: Approaches to teaching race in the social studies classroom. *Theory & Research in Social Education, 45*(4), 489–516.

Matias, C. (2016). *Feeling white: Whiteness, emotionality, and education*. Sense.

McGuire, M. B. (2003). Why bodies matter: A sociological reflection on spirituality and materiality. *Spiritus: A Journal of Christian Spirituality 3*(1), 1–18.

M'Charek, A. (2013). Beyond fact or fiction: On the materiality of race in practice. *Cultural Anthropology, 28*(3), 420–442. https://doi.org/10.1111/cuan.12012

Merriam, S. B. (1998). *Qualitative research and case study applications in education.* Jossey-Bass.
Merriam, S. B., & Tisdell, E. J. (2016). *Qualitative research: A guide to design and implementation.* Jossey-Bass.
Mills, C. W. (1997). *The racial contract.* Cornell University Press.
Mills, C. W. (1998). *Blackness visible: Essays on philosophy and race.* Cornell University Press.
Mitchell, T. (2020). Working to unsettle settler colonialism: (While) tripping over my whiteness. In A. Hawkman & S. Shear (Eds.), *Marking the invisible: Articulating whiteness in social studies education* (pp. 685–710). Information Age Publishing.
Nora, P. (1989). Between memory and history: *Les Lieux de Mémoire Representations, 26,* Special Issue: Memory and Counter-Memory, 7–24.
Nordgren, K. (2016). How to do things with history: Use of history as a link between historical consciousness and historical culture. *Theory & Research in Social Education, 44*(4), 479–504. https://doi.org/10.1080/00933104.2016.1211046
Omi, M., & Winant, H. (1994). *Racial formation in the United States: From the 1960s to the 1990s.* Routledge.
Orr, D. (2005). Minding the soul in education: Conceptualizing and teaching the whole person. In J.P. Miller, S. Karsten, D. Denton, D. Orr, & I. Colalillo Kates (Eds.), *Holistic learning and spirituality in education.* State University of New York Press.
Painter, N.I. (2010). *The history of white people.* Norton.
Picower, B. (2009). The unexamined whiteness of teaching: How white teachers maintain and enact dominant racial ideologies. *Race Ethnicity and Education, 12,* 197–215. https://doi.org/10.1080/13613320902995475
Popen, S. (2002). Democratic pedagogy and the discourse of containment. *Anthropology & Education Quarterly, 33*(3), 383–394.
Roediger, D. (1991). *The wages of whiteness: Race and the making of the American working class.* Verso.
Rosiek, J. (2016) Critical race theory, agential realism, and the evidence of experience: A methodological and theoretical preface. In J. Rosiek & K. Kinslow (2016). *Resegregation as curriculum: The meaning of the new segregation in U.S. public schools* (pp. xiii–xxvii). Routledge.
Rotem, R. (2019). Dilemmas in decolonizing spirituality: Thoughts for educators. In N. Wayne, R. A. Torres, & D. Nyaga (Eds.), *Transversing and translocating spiritualities: Epistemological and pedagogical conversations* (pp. 161–180). Nsemia Publishers.
Rüsen, J. (1987). Historical narration: Foundation, types, reason. *History and Theory, 26,* 87–97.
Rüsen, J. (1989). The development of narrative competence in historical learning—An ontogenetic hypothesis concerning moral consciousness. *History and Memory, 1,* 35–59.
Rüsen, J. (2005). *History: Narration, interpretation, orientation.* Berghahn Books.
Rüsen, J. (2006). Historical consciousness: Narrative structure, moral function, and ontogenetic development. In P. Seixas (Ed.), *Theorizing historical consciousness* (pp. 63–85). University of Toronto Press.

Salinas, C., & Alarcón, J. (2016). Exploring the civic identities of Latina/o high school students: Reframing the historical narrative. *International Journal of Multicultural Education, 18*(1), 68–87.

Salinas, C., & Sullivan, C. (2007). Latina/o teachers and historical positionality: Challenging the construction of the official school knowledge. *Journal of Curriculum and Pedagogy, 4*(1), 178–199.

Schubert, D. (2013). Suffering/Symbolic violence. In M. Grenfell (Ed.), *Pierre Bourdieu*. Routledge.

Schweber, S. (2006). Fundamentally 9/11: The fashioning of collective memory in a Christian school. *American Journal of Education, 112*, 392–417.

Seay, T. (2019). *"I don't want to cause trouble": A White history teacher's negotiation of racial boundaries in a diverse rural school* [Unpublished doctoral dissertation]. University of Florida.

Seay, T. (2020). What does whiteness have to do with teaching history? Toward racial historical consciousness in history teacher education. In A. Hawkman & S. Shear (Eds.) *Marking the invisible: Articulating whiteness in social studies education* (pp. 603–634). Information Age Publishing.

Segall, A., & Garrett, J. (2013). White teachers talking race. *Teaching Education, 24*(3), 265–291. https://doi.org/10.1080/10476210.2012.704509

Shear, S. B., Knowles, R. T, Soden, G. J., & Castro, A. J. (2015). Manifesting destiny: Re/presentations of Indigenous peoples in K–12 U.S. history standards. *Theory and Research in Social Education, 43*(1), 68–101. http://dx.doi.org/10.1080/00933104.2014.999849

Sidat, H. (2019). Putting to sleep the wailing ghosts of the past: Exploring historical trauma and spirituality. In N. Wayne, R. A. Torres, & D. Nyaga (Eds.), *Transversing and translocating spiritualities: Epistemological and pedagogical conversations* (pp. 29–44). Nsemia Publishers.

Simon, R., Rüsen, J., & others (2006). A dialogue on narrative and historical consciousness. In P. Seixas (Ed.), *Theorizing historical consciousness* (pp. 202–215). University of Toronto Press.

Sleeter, C. (2015). Multicultural curriculum and critical family history. *Multicultural Education Review, 7*(1–2), 1–11. https://doi.org/10.1080/2005615X.2015.1048607

Smith, W. L., & Crowley, R. M. (2015). Pushback and possibility: Using a threshold concept of race in social studies teacher education. *The Journal of Social Studies Research, 39*, 17–28.

Stake, R. E. (1995). *The art of case study research*. SAGE.

Streich, G. W. (2002). Is there a right to forget? Historical injustices, race, memory, and identity. *New Political Science 24*(4), 525–542. https://doi.org/10.1080/0739314022000025363

Terdiman, R. (1993). *Present past: Modernity and the memory crisis*. Cornell University Press.

Trouillot, M.-R. (1995). *Silencing the past: Power and the production of history*. Beacon Press.

Tyrell, I. (2002). Beyond the view from Euro-America: Environment, settler societies, and the internationalization of American history. In T. Bender (Ed.), *Rethinking American history in a global age* (pp. 168–190). University of California Press.

U.S. Census Bureau. (2017). *American community survey*. Retrieved from https://factfinder.census.gov/faces/nav/jsf/pages/index.xhtml

van Boxtel, C., & van Drie, J. (2018). Historical reasoning: Conceptualizations and educational applications. In S. A. Metzger & L. M. Harris (Eds.), *The Wiley international handbook of history teaching and learning* (pp. 149–176). Wiley-Blackwell.

VanSledright, B. (2008). Narratives of nation-state, historical knowledge, and school history education. *Review of Research in Education, 32*, 109–146. https://doi.org/10.3102/0091732X07311065

VanSledright, B. (2011). *The challenge of rethinking history education: On practices, theories, and policy*. Routledge.

Vasquez Heilig, J., Brown, K. D., & Brown, A. L. (2012). The illusion of inclusion: A critical race theory textual analysis of race and standards. *Harvard Educational Review, 82*(3), 403–439.

Vaught, S. (2011). *Racism, public schooling, and the entrenchment of white supremacy*. SUNY Press.

Vianna, E., & Stetsenko, A. (2006). Embracing history through transforming it: Contrasting Piagetian versus Vygotskian (activity) theories of learning and development to expand constructivism within a dialectical view of history. *Theory & Psychology, 16*(1), 81–108. https://doi.org/10.1177/0959354306060108

Wang, H. (2013). A nonviolent approach to social justice education. *Educational Studies, 49*(6), 485–503. https://doi.org/10.1080/00131946.2013.844147

Washington, E. Y., & Humphries, E. K. (2011). A social studies teacher's sense making of controversial issues discussions of race in a predominantly white, rural high school classroom. *Theory & Research in Social Education, 39*(1), 92–114. https://doi.org/10.1080/00933104.2011.10473448

Wertsch, J. (2008). Blank spots in collective memory: A case study of Russia. *The Annals of the American Academy of Political and Social Science, 617*(1), 58–71. https://doi.org/10.1177/0002716207312870

Wilder, G. (2004). Race, reason, impasse: Cesaire, Fanon, and the legacy of emancipation. *Radical History Review* (90), 31–61. https://doi.org/10.1215/01636545-2004-90-31

Wineburg, S. (1991). On the reading of historical texts: Notes on the breach between school and academy. *American Educational Research Journal, 28*(3), 495–519.

Wineburg, S. (2001). *Historical thinking and other unnatural acts: Charting the future of teaching the past*. Temple University Press.

Woodson, A. N. (2015). "There Ain't No White People Here": Master narratives of the Civil Rights Movement in the stories of urban youth. *Urban Education, 52*(3), 316–342. https://doi.org/10.1177/0042085915602543

Woodson, A. N. (2016). We're just ordinary people: Messianic master narratives and Black youths' civic agency. *Theory and Research in Social Education, 44*(2), 184–211. https://doi.org/10.1080/00933104.2016.1170645

Yancy, G. (2017). *Black bodies, white gazes: The continuing significance of race in America*. Rowman & Littlefield.
Zembylas, M. (2017). Teacher resistance to engage with 'alternative' perspectives of difficult histories: The limits and prospects of affective disruption. *Discourse: Studies in the Cultural Politics of Education, 38*(5), 659–675. https://doi.org/10.1080/01596306.2015.1132680
Zimmerman, J. (2002). *Whose America? Culture wars in the public schools*. Harvard University Press.

ENDNOTES

1. All names associated with these findings are pseudonyms.
2. I am using the terms *Black* and *African American* interchangeably in this study, as this was the way the participant and I used the terms in conversations on teaching U.S. history in Emerson.

CHAPTER 10

SPIRITUAL UNDERPINNINGS OF A TEACHER EDUCATION PROGRAM

Ann Mary Roberts
Radford University

Thomas Lucey
Illinois State University

ABSTRACT

This chapter examines one teacher educator's efforts to cultivate a spiritual sense of connectedness/relationships, faith, forgiveness, and love/compassion/caring to support teacher candidates in a teacher education program and how she introduced these topics. These spiritual attributes are fundamental qualities helpful for teacher candidates to cultivate as they engage in student teaching. At the core of this process lies the relationship between the concepts of spirituality and character education. While scholarship frequently aligns spirituality with a social organization such as religion and citizenship, the processes described in this chapter instill a spiritual sense of belonging based on the development of self and community.

Keywords: teacher education program, faith, forgiveness, connectedness, spirituality

INTRODUCTION

Facilitating safe learning spaces that value the wellness of all members necessitates an appreciation for the spiritual elements of their identities. Through exploring spirituality, young children experience the potential to make meaning of their lives and thereby develop an openness to possibilities for future development (Kessler & Fink, 2008).

This chapter describes the first author's experience working with teacher candidates to develop their sense of spirituality. It begins by considering the nature of spirituality and its relationship to character education. Next, it draws from this relationship to explain how understanding notions of spirituality can provide a basis for supporting preservice teachers in their professional development. A discussion of the traits that receive program emphasis is then described before presenting a case study that conveys the importance of emphasizing compassion.

UNDERSTANDING SPIRITUALITY AND ITS RELATIONSHIP TO CHARACTER EDUCATION

The abstract and elusive nature of spirituality provides a challenge for those who seek to describe it. Cottingham (2003/2013) points out that spirituality includes elements of both science and abstractness, and Crossan (2015) characterizes it as that which gives life to a body. Regarding education research, it should not be surprising that similar difficulties exist with attempts to define Spirituality and situate it in education research (Wright, 2002). McLaughlin (2003/2013) observed that spirituality holds both independent and integrated relationships to religion.

Scholarship has adopted a view of spirituality that is rooted in human nature. Watson (2003) observed that scholarship in *The International Journal of Children's Spirituality* provided an evolving interpretation from one associated with religion to one associated with citizenship., This connection to citizenship was a view affirmed by Estanek (2006). Thus, scholars seem to interpret spirituality as related to social relationships and loyalties. This view is confirmed by Helminiak (2015), who considers Spirituality as the nature of spontaneous impulses that guide a person's decision-making. Hay (2007) observed that:

> Spiritual awareness is commonly the context out of which religion grows. But Spirituality is not religion. Like Hardy, I believe it is prior to religion and is a built-in, biologically structured dimension of the lives of all members of the human species. Therefore there are secular as well as religious expressions of Spirituality. (pp. 48–49)

Hay concluded that humans are wired for spirituality as a species. His observations supported a program in which preservice teachers ground themselves in their spiritual sense of self to strive to understand the universe and their place in it.

The connection of spirituality to character education may be found in Peterson and Seligman (2004). Peterson and Seligman were a part of the positive psychology movement and developed the Values in Action (VIA) Classifications of Strength. They identified qualities associated with "strength of character" and helped create an individual's well-being. Peterson and Seligman identified 24 characteristics, including spiritual attributes, kindness, forgiveness, and a separate category of transcendence "strengths that forge connections to the larger universe and provide meaning" (p. 30). Under the category of transcendence, the attributes of hope, gratitude, humor, and religiousness are included. Consequently, Peterson and Seligman viewed spirituality as having traits similar to character education components. Peterson and Seligman also noted that spirituality "describe(d) both the private, intimate relationship between humans and the divine and the range of virtues that result from that relationship. These virtues are believed to manifest in the pursuit of principled life and a life of goodness" (pp. 602–603).

Yet research also experienced a convergence of moral/education socioemotional learning such that:

> Certain behaviors are needed to assert one's values when the mainstream is not in agreement. In other instances, lack of skills in affective awareness or problem solving may lead to an inability to see or take advantage of opportunities for moral action that may exist in one's environment. (Elias et al., 2008, p. 264)

Developing students who possess these traits and skills requires a community of acceptance, compassion, discipline, and trust (Kessler & Fink, 2008; Watson, 2008).

The embedding of spirituality in Ann's teacher education program invited students to consider how they connect to the greater world. The purpose was to look at elements of spirituality that would equip teacher educators to develop the necessary skills, dispositions, and attributes needed to help them endure the standards-driven education field. The process of determining what aspects of spirituality to emphasize contemplated how spirituality differed from aspects of character education. The characteristics of character education seemed similar to the development of qualities to become a productive, effective citizen (Bialik et al., 2015). So, naturally, the characteristics reflected the values of time (Watts, 2011).

WHO ARE ANN'S STUDENT TEACHERS, AND HOW DOES TALKING ABOUT SPIRITUALITY HELP THEM?

Ann perceives that every student who enters teaching wants to make a difference. He or she may have been helped by a teacher or have felt the power of helping a student learn new content. The traditionally aged students continue to be risk-takers who are influenced by their peers and who try to define who their identities place in the universe. In some ways, they exhibit residual behaviors similar to the students they are preparing to teach. This intervention seeks to support students who are still transitioning from their adolescent development and starting the journey of introspection in such a way that they recognize when they are bringing in their own pasts or operating out of what Jung (2006) calls their shadow side, reflecting their imperfections.

Her Students Are "Here to Be Seen"

Ann realizes that her charges want to be seen and understood as they navigate their last hurdles of adolescent development. They thirst for connection, empathy, and space to figure out who they are and who they are not, all the while preparing to become teachers. As her students develop the knowledge, dispositions, and skills necessary to become teachers, Ann wants to ensure they are exceptionally skilled in developing resiliency and self-awareness. Teaching is a challenging career, and her students will need resiliency in order to thrive in this complex system. For example, in a longitudinal study conducted on middle school students, Kor et al. (2019) demonstrated how spiritual attributes supported well-being and "pro-sociality."

Helen Fox (2012) described millennials as students who are deeply committed to "serve humanity" and deeply rooted in social justice and peace. However, Fox also found that these students are emotionally fragile and prone to stress and anxiety. They have been enveloped in a protective cocoon created by parents who push and support them. She suggested the importance of finding ways to support their "spiritual stamina" (p. 5). Nash and Swaby (2011) make an even stronger statement regarding millennials and spiritualty, stating "spirituality matters a great deal in American students today" (p. 118).

Spirituality needs to be addressed in the college curriculum. Ann's students want to entertain ideas of how they fit in the world and who they are in relation to their fellow beings. This is why Ann embeds spiritual attributes in her classes. Her objective is to help students develop the necessary resiliency for teaching. Being a teacher in a classroom is like being in a huge swirling cauldron of human interaction—the best and worst of a teacher are mirrored in that classroom. Biases, prejudices, and failures also have the potential to serve as strengths, successes, and love. She encourages them to develop the capability to see themselves and others as they are in the present moment and have them respond with compassion, love, and faith. When her students struggle, she coaches them to embrace their failures and that of their students, framing the failures as ways to get stronger, wiser, and more compassionate while showering themselves and their charges with forgiveness and compassion as necessary.

ATTRIBUTES THAT WE FOCUS ON

Spiritual concepts that relate to compassion and acceptance contrast with the state regulations mandates topics that regulate classroom management, lesson planning, and assessments. While both sets of qualities are essential for a balanced teacher preparation program, the intervention employs the qualities of connectedness/relationships, forgiveness, faith, and love/compassion/caring as beneficial attributes for the teacher candidates to foster. Scholarship indicates these as essential for building a compassionate community (Kessler & Fink, 2008).

Connection/Relationships

"Sawubona "Sikhona" (Zulu greeting)
"I See You—I Am Here to Be Seen"

Why connection? How is that spiritual? First, the connection seems to be at the core of all that exists on earth and is the essence of being human. Lynn Margulis and Dorian Sagan (1998) suggested a new way of perceiving evolution from a symbiotic perspective. Rather than "survival of the fittest," evolution was a by-product of organisms working together, as they are interconnected. Margulis and Sagan supported the concept of Gaia, claiming everything was interrelated as a way to keep the earth functioning. McGonigal (2015) wrote about how, as a species, humans are hard-wired for relationships. She pointed out that the hormone oxytocin is a part of the internal arsenal to deal with stress. Oxytocin's primary function is "to strengthen social connection" (p. 53). When under stress, the human body sends signals via oxytocin to seek out others for support or to support them. Similarly, Johann Hari (2016) said, "the opposite of addiction is connection" (p. 299), meaning that when humans have a connection to others, there is no need to obsess with substances to fill the void of lack of connection.

The importance of these relationships extends to the classroom, where cooperative learning processes may offer hope for resistance to addiction to screen technology (Lucey & Lin, 2020). Connection with others provides resiliency. Shoshani and Slone (2016) looked at middle school students in areas of war and conflict. They found that students in crisis who reached out to others and had strong connections with people assisted in counteracting the effects of post-traumatic stress disorder. In addition, the adolescents were more resilient when they had people in their lives to whom they could talk to. In their book, *The Secrets of the Bullet Proof Spirit*, Khamisa and Quinn (2018) also spoke about how relationships with others provide people with the resiliency and ability to better cope with life's situations.

Ann views the connection as an authentic relationship where there is space for acceptance and the deepening of experiences. Buber (1970) distinguished between the I-Thou relationship and the I-It relationship. The I-Thou viewed relationships as reciprocal and interconnected, where the recipients find meaning from interactions. The I-It relationship makes the "other" in the relationship more like an object. These two distinctions will be important when discussing how we approach our students.

Part of an authentic relationship is willing to be vulnerable and open to sharing your imperfections. Chödrön (2019) perceived that to be fully human; one needs to recognize his/her imperfections and embrace them to grow in wisdom and enlightenment. She used the analogy of the lotus and the mud. The beauty of the lotus is grown from the nutrients of the mud underneath the pond's waters. Likewise, we grow when we connect with each other and are transparent regarding our human flaws. Our natural inclination is to hide them for fear of rejection, humiliation, and judgment; however, if we are courageous enough to share our imperfections, often the result is self-compassion, awareness, and empathy. Being vulnerable with sharing our whole self deepens the relationship with others. Connection is the spiritual journey to understand who we are.

Ann finds that her students are often at a loss to develop the type of connection that Buber (1972) and Chödrön (2019) describe. When sharing with her students that part of life is about loving and being loved, there is a palpable energy of longing and a desire for that type of connection. Yet, some of her students are able to articulate that it is not achievable in this day and time. It seems the students struggle with the aspects of authenticity and acceptance in relationships with others. They find as much difficulty accepting their own magnificence and imperfections as they do when they bump up against others' humanness, whether it is their classmates, students, mentors, or professors. Chödrön sees being honest, courageous, compassionate, and authentic in relationships as a cornerstone of spiritual practice. It is hard for them to be so open because admitting to flaws is like admitting to failure, leading back to forgiveness. All these spiritual attributes interact with each other.

To find that space, Ann challenges her students to take emotional risks in connecting with one another. For example, students are constantly pushed to resist using their cell phones as a safety net and sit with the discomfort of being in the room with others and the awkward silence that often is present before class starts or during breaks. Ann asks her students to view relationships as a way of working on themselves. Everyone is their teacher. "People with super spiritual resiliency consciously reframe their connections with other people as perfect vehicles for spiritual and personal growth, and this helps them to handle the heartbreaking hits and inevitable challenges that accompany all human interactions" (Khamisa & Quinn, 2018, p. 46). Their relationships and connections with their prospective students will experience some of their greatest teachers, mirroring their magnificence and imperfections.

To connect to others is to find a place of belonging, a tribe, a home base. Teachers are often very isolated either because they are physically contained in their classroom, lack meaningful support from colleagues, or feel overwhelmed by school demands (Ostovar-Namehi & Sheirhahmadi, 2016). For teachers to thrive, they must develop their support group of friends and colleagues where they can be themselves. "Spiritually bulletproof people are willing to receive and are resourceful in finding the support and assistance they need" (Khamisa & Quinn, 2018, p. 72). When teachers connect to each other and share all that unfolds in their lives as educators, it deepens the network of support, reinforces they are not alone and gives them the resiliency to show up as their authentic selves every day. James et al. (2010) talk similarly of the spirituality of communion where genuine collegiality is the necessary ingredient if we believe that all of humanity is connected and that for the "one body" to thrive, it depends on how well the parts communicate and function together. This stance is also supported in the Bhagavad Gita, where Lord Krishna instructs Arjuna that living entities are part and parcel of the supreme. Thus, living entities are connected (Prabhupada, 2006).

So how does the connection of living entities relate to the teacher education program? Authentic, spiritual connection is vital to student teachers' relationships with themselves, peers, mentors, and students. The goal is a quality of relationship that transcends the superficiality society has grown to accept (Nash & Swaby, 2011) and creates a deeper, more spiritual connection with others which entails courage in looking at themselves and what they bring to the relationship. This process requires that they continually work on themselves and bring their authentic selves at that moment into the relationship (Agne, 1999).

Ann asks her students to be present with others and not project their past issues, conflicts, and limitations onto others. Namely, Ann's students need to be fearless at looking at their past, their flaws, their biases, and all the while, they must learn to be kind to themselves and not judge what they find but make courageous decisions to see where this newfound awareness takes them (Chödrön, 2019). These expectations may prove a challenge for teacher candidates who are still trying to figure out their identities as they transition from adolescence and move into adulthood.

Connection and relationships are at the spiritual core of teaching. When teachers are not equipped to understand how to proceed in relationships at a more spiritual level, they become resentful and burned out when dealing with their daily interactions (Atmaca et al., 2020). Teachers get pulled around by their lack of ability to navigate the delicate dance of relationships. Their feelings get hurt by students or parents, or peers. They personalize the transgressions of others' imperfections when they are merely bit players in a much bigger drama (Palmer, 2007). As Alexander (2001) suggests, when we do not look at ourselves, we deny ourselves the opportunity to grow and change. The solution is to approach these relationships and connections at a deeper level. To be successful in this type of connection, teacher candidates need to work on other spiritual qualities, including compassion, forgiveness, and faith.

Making A Case for the Spiritual Path of Forgiveness

John was a student who was very difficult and uncommunicative. The other teachers struggled with his defiance and disinterest in school. Yet Ann perceived the good in him. He would often censure bullies in the halls, lend subtle support to new students, and disregard what other students felt as he stood up to what he thought was wrong. John had a moral compass that included justice and equity. Ann would say hello every day as John came into class, and he would grunt back in the typical middle school boy language she knew so well. Nevertheless, he understood her humor and would put effort into her history class, partly because he liked history and partly because he liked her.

One day John did something in class, which prompted Ann to ask him to step out into the hall. She knew this would strain their relationship, and when she described his behavior and suggested consequences, he was flippant and disrespectful. The next day when she saw him, she was sunny and said, "Hello." However, he made no eye contact and moved into the classroom. She asked him to step outside. Instead, John blew up and stormed out the door. "John," Ann said, "do you think that I don't like you anymore because you made a mistake yesterday?" His response was down-turned eyes and a slight shrug. "John, YOU are supposed to make a million mistakes.... That is how you figure out who you are, and I am to forgive you a million times. I think the world of you, and you can't do anything to change that." He shrugged again and made no eye contact, but she knew he would watch out for her and knew that she had his best interests at heart. Forgiveness changed him.

Forgiveness is inherent to most world religions and can be seen as a spiritual practice (Bush, 2013). Koç et al., (2016) observed that "Forgiveness usually refers to releasing resentment toward an offender ... or restoring relationships and healing inner emotional wounds" (p. 202). Forgiveness impacts connections with others because transgressions can muddy any relationship's nature without forgiveness (Chödrön, 2019). While forgiving others and forgiving oneself can be difficult, spiritual paths are integral for these student teachers to develop resiliency.

Lehrer (2010) describes how people interpret and deal with mistakes. When framing mistakes or failures as data points to make changes and improve, people wire our brains to be more intuitive and creative when learning. Unfortunately, Ann's students are so scared of failure and view mistakes as a character flaw that sometimes paralyzes them from pushing forth into uncharted waters. In the era of high-stakes testing, children are afraid of failure, which can mean not attempting new avenues of learning (Hilppö & Reed, 2020). Ann's students went through primary and secondary schooling during this era and displayed the effects of these conditions.

The biggest consequence of fear of failure and absence of forgiveness is the students' lack of courage to attempt new teaching strategies or ways of dealing with classroom behavior. In addition, these emotional imprints potentially affect the students' future classroom practice. Lucey and Lorsbach (2021a) observed relationships between the nature of preservice teachers' developmental experiences and their perspectives on facilitating classroom community. In practice, preservice teachers can sometimes interpret their students as extensions of their success or failure; as a result, there can be resentment when their students fail. In general, when people do not forgive themselves, they feel depressed and anxious, resulting in self-punishment (Maltby et al., 2001).

Ann also observes that student teachers find it difficult to forgive themselves; they can be equally challenging to their students, which is a problem in schools. Teachers can hold anger toward children when they misbehave in the classroom (Sutton et al., 2009). Ann's observations of student teachers' discussions note such anger at the student teachers' students, which appears to imply that the transgression was of a personal nature. In a compassionate environment, the teacher is merely a placeholder for them to work out issues with another person (Mayes, 2005). These mistakes would be approached as a teachable moment, including forgiveness for the act.

For the children's sake, the adults' responsibility is to forgive them and self-reflect for preserving their self-esteem and sense of self-worth (Purvis et al., 2013).

The spiritual path of forgiveness is essential to a teacher education program because it can strengthen teacher resiliency. Unfortunately, few teacher education programs address forgiveness, which is unfortunate since addressing forgiveness increases teacher self-efficacy (Sezgin & Erdogan, 2018). Furthermore, forgiveness can also strengthen the relationships between students and teachers. Therefore, forgiveness is an integral part of being a teacher.

Faith

After experiencing the educational process for most of their years, Ann's students develop a picture of their ideal teacher (McLean, 1999). They use that ideal as a yardstick, comparing it to their mentors, judging who they will and will not be. Finally, when they are in their last semester, Ann's students will experience a full load of teaching, responsible for the whole classroom from attendance to teaching to parent conferences. The comparisons of their ideal and their actual performance continues. Inevitably, they will encounter students who will resist their help and continue on a destructive path no matter how much attention, care, and support they may receive. Some student teachers might be depressed when they do not reach that student; some might be resentful and angry that their help is rejected. What is the antidote when a student teacher does everything possible to help a student emotionally, educationally, and personally only to have the student fail, try, or be destructive? How do they resist collapsing into thinking they failed that student? What will give them the resiliency they need to learn from the experience and continue? It is faith, according to Phillips (2021).

Faith represents a sense of trust. Faith might be based on religion, their concept of humanity, or the history of life. Faith represents a more appropriate term than hope because we perceive faith as being in the present and accepting that whatever happens is supposed to happen. Hope is in the future, and one is more likely to put a picture of what that future might be like. The spiritual part is that we have to trust and have faith in the unknown future and not know the consequences.

Teachers need to have faith that the outcome is supposed to happen after giving their best to help, educate, and mentor students. Even if students do not achieve a particular goal, faith trusts that they received what they needed, although the teacher may not have known at the time what it was. For example, Ann believes that if she did her part to be the best teacher she could be, providing knowledge, compassion, love, forgiveness, and presence, the students would receive what they needed.

Faith is necessary to counteract students' hopelessness when they hear about tragic stories and feel helpless to impact the situation. Faith is especially critical to be present with students who were so beaten down by the educational system that they refuse to try. Faith is the antidote to giving up on a student who is resistant to all their attempts at helping them.

If students are not afraid of unpacking who they are and learning about themselves, if they work hard to learn the craft of delivering lessons and mastering content, then they must have faith in the process that they are making the proper decisions.

LOVE, COMPASSION, AND CARING

Love and aspects of love seem to be fundamental spiritual traits (Miller, 2008). Love is so complex, with many types and variations. The ancient Greeks used words to recognize the nuances of love, including Philia-friendship, Storge-familial, Agape-universal, Eros-sexual, and Philautia-self-love (Burton, 2016). In his book, *Four Loves*, C. S. Lewis (1960) describes some Greek terms slightly differently—Storge-affection, Agape-charity, and Eros-romantic. Carl Rogers and colleagues (2014) believed a fundamental building block to teaching is empathy and compassion, developing the concept of unconditional positive regard, which he thought was necessary for any child to flourish in the classroom. Paulo Freire said education is an act of love (Douglas & Nganga, 2015). Agne (1999) researched Teachers of the Year and found that deep caring was a typical trait and was quintessential to becoming a master teacher.

Conversations about love, compassion, and caring should ensure that students see the spiritual depth of love's applications in the classroom. Ann observes that students often articulate that they become teachers because of their love for children. They believe if they love that struggling defiant student enough, the students will be transformed into loving schools and doing well. Yet, she also perceives that their limited appreciation for love's depth challenges their ability to realize its presence in practice.

Darder (2009) speaks to a stronger type of love, which Ann feels is more useful for her students.

> I want to speak to the experience of love as I came to understand it through my work and friendship with Freire. I wanted to write about a political and radicalized form of love that is never about absolute consensus, or unconditional acceptance, or unceasing words of sweetness, or endless streams of hugs and kisses. Instead, it is a love that I experienced as unconstructed, rooted in a committed willingness to struggle persistently with purpose in

our life and to intimately connect that purpose with what he called "our true vocation"—to be human. (p. 180)

In learning to be a teacher, we need self-love, which is difficult for all of us (Borich, 1999). Self-love involves a sense of acceptance of the personal challenges that we experience, such that we can be open to the challenges with which our students wrestle. Ann's students struggle with looking at their strengths and claiming them. Parker Palmer (2007) viewed dealing with oneself as vital to being a good teacher:

> As she teaches, she projects the condition of her soul onto her students, her subject, and the way of being together. The entanglements she experiences in the classroom are often no more or less than the convolutions of her inner life. Viewed from this angle, teaching holds a mirror to the soul. If she is willing to look in that mirror, and not run from what she sees, she has a chance to gain self-knowledge—and knowing herself is as crucial to good teaching as knowing her students and her subject. (p. 1)

Palmer articulates that universal limitation we have at not fully being in the present, seeing things for what they are. We cannot help but bring our past into the present. Chödrön (2019) uses the Buddhist term *shenpah* which means "hook." Some situations will inevitably pull us into painful past events where people then get stuck. We are no longer in the present. It takes self-compassion and love to help disentangle from placing past events onto current situations.

Through processes of mindfulness, it is possible to engage in developing the skills of disentanglement that empower one to live in the present. When one undertakes the necessary inner work, he/she needs courage which takes compassion and self-love. The encounter of dark places and imperfections that require one to forgive him or herself necessitates he or she possess tools of compassion and self-love to examine their meanings. Therefore, the presence of love and compassion are essential for students to journey on the spiritual path of awareness.

How might teacher candidates be taught to realize the manifestations of love in the classroom? This question presents a complex answer because love manifests in many ways. Many preservice teachers may possess distorted understandings of love (Lucey & Lorsbach, 2021b). Keeping boundaries, negotiating struggles, and accepting differences and imperfections are all aspects of this discipline. When Ann talks to teacher candidates about caring and love, they immediately think about affection. They love their students in an affectionate, caring way. However, they do not always have the experience of a parent to understand that part of love is "taking that child on" and providing the needed structure they need in order to succeed academically.

Ann has often used Cesar Millan's (2006) work in her Classroom Management course. Millan (2006) says that dogs need three things, exercise, boundaries/rules/limitations, and affection. So, part of loving a child is to be consistent with rules and boundaries. When a child out of boredom puts his or her head down on the desk for the 10th time, that is not a time to give up. Ann's middle school students had often said the part they loved the most about her was that she did not give up on them even when they continued to be their worst. Students do not want to be ignored. They act out for many reasons, and one way to love and care about students is to recognize that their behavior is born out of needs and potential fears. Once a teacher realizes that, instead of bearing resentment for that student, the teacher can respond with compassion and care (Agne, 1999).

Finally, acceptance is integral to love, compassion, and caring. Every child deserves a valued place in the classroom. Caring and compassionate teachers better engage students in the learning while fostering their sense of self-worth (Noddings, 2005). Experiencing a child or having anger and resentments towards a child affords the perfect place to unpack what is happening with them.

Love and compassion are more than just affection. C. S. Lewis (1960) said, "to love at all is to be vulnerable" (p. 121). Love means loving oneself enough to bestow forgiveness and acceptance on oneself. Likewise, being a compassionate teacher means viewing students for who they are and not projecting their imperfections onto them or getting weighed down by bias. Love, compassion, and caring are at the core of spiritual paths and reside at education's heart.

TEACHING THE PROCESS

When looking at connectedness, forgiveness, faith and love, compassion and caring, how do we even approach those topics in a teacher education program? How do we create an environment where student teachers become fearless in looking at themselves and recognizing when they are reacting instead of responding? How do we help them reframe forgiveness and faith? Ann uses stories, groups, and supervision while doing her best to model what Ann is asking her students. The context of her work is working with middle school and secondary teacher candidates.

Christ taught through parables. The desert fathers shared their stories in the Jewish tradition. Native Americans were taught through oral tradition. And Sukadeva Goswami instructed Pariksit Maharaja on the meaning of life through historical stories in seven days and nights (Prabhupada, 1972). A part of most religious traditions is the telling of wisdom stories. Moore (1991) talks about narrative theology and education, and she suggests, "this is the idea that story is a form of indirect communication that conveys truths that cannot be communicated directly" (p. 141). Sometimes stories help look at complex concepts and are potent vehicles for looking at self. Kurtz and Ketcham (1993) equated our humanity to stories when they said, "Listening to stories and telling them helped our ancestors to live humanly—to be human" (p. 8).

Ann uses stories a lot for many reasons. First, stories can be a safe medium as Ann asks students to look at preconceptions and experiences that shape their identity. Second, Ann tells many stories to help fortify their construct of faith. For example, Ann tells them success stories of students who came back decades later to say what Ann did matter even though Ann did not see it at the time. Third, her student teachers are too young to have their reservoir of stories to pull from, but Ann tells them to start collecting anecdotes as soon as they begin their field experiences. Fourth, stories can provide a buffer from intense emotions regarding a topic. Instead of directly addressing a topic that might be fraught with feelings and values, a story can give a bit of distance and perspective.

Ann's favorite story involves a humble, shy six-foot-five ex-football player who was a student teaching in a middle school. He came to her discouraged because a student was being horrible to him. The more he tried to develop a relationship with her, the meaner she got. Ann observed this dynamic and realized this girl had a crush on her student teacher, which he immediately dismissed. That week they had a parent conference to deal with the disrespectful student. When the student teacher introduced himself, the parent laughed. "Oh, YOU'RE the famous Mr. Smith! There is not a free space in any area in her house that does not have "I LOVE MR. SMITH written on it!" He was shocked, but it was a great lesson for him to learn that students misbehave for reasons one may never know. Ann has shared that story with subsequent classes, one of many to illustrate how teachers are sometimes actors in a play that they have no idea what it is about. All these stories and processes help students develop faith, learn about the power of forgiveness, discover faith, learn about the power of forgiveness, and find the different ways love manifests in the classroom.

Part of Ann's students' experience is participating in a social-emotional education group that focuses on the self-regulation of emotions, including stress management, conflict, self-care, feedback, and mindfulness. The groups meet weekly and are facilitated by master's students in the counselor education program. The facilitators are supervised by faculty, and it is totally confidential. Students are encouraged to process aspects of their field experience where they might have had intense feelings regarding an incident. The goal is to support students to build resiliency and the skills necessary to deal with some of the emotional aspects of teaching. Ann supplements the group by introducing additional topics like Marshall

Rosenberg's (2015) nonviolent communication and reflective listening skills, which support relationships and connection.

When Ann supervises her students, she looks beyond their lesson plans, content, and classroom management. Ann explores more profound concepts by asking them about their experiences in relationship to the spiritual aspects of teaching. Ann and the student teachers talk about how their student teaching experience might have been reminiscent of their own high school experiences. Inevitably, *shenpah,* that hook to the past, arises as Ann hears stories of how certain students who cause them problems are just like the students they struggled with in high school. This strategy helps them release their past experiences. Ann helps remind her student teachers to reframe the experiences of their defiant students by using compassion and forgiveness. Ann shores their courage to engage challenging students, reminding them that it means being willing to confront difficult/challenging issues if they love their students. Overall, Ann uses supervision as an opportunity for one-on-one coaching to develop these spiritual qualities in education.

Ann also teaches through modeling. She demonstrates the process of unpacking life lessons by sharing stories of when things went badly during her early teaching years. Ann practices vulnerability when talking about her own unconscious bias and imperfections. Ann attempts to model (I am human too) how to use a painful life lesson as a source of wisdom and compassion, not as a weapon to inflict pain and keep one feeling small. Ann continues her practice by utilizing mindfulness practices and reading spiritual materials. To fully embrace the spiritual path of teaching, Ann has to live it and share the mistakes and successes of this journey.

CONCLUSION: THE SPIRAL DANCE

The dance of spirituality and education has existed for some time. Framing teaching as a spiritual practice allows educators to recognize deeper meaning in the education process, especially in terms of relationships with students and the disciplines. While literature untethers spirituality from religion and associates it with citizenship, schools primarily teach about citizenship as a process of loyalty and leadership within an established system (Watson, 2003: Westheimer, 2015). Preston (2017) describes how contracting a disease represents a process in defining the story of a human body. When considered in that sense, spirituality represents a sense of understanding oneself in a broader context that realizes one's relationship with the more general environment.

The importance of Ann's work with her student teachers lies in its conceptualizing spirituality as different from an abstract loyalty to a specific cultural ideal. Instead, it represents a psychological condition that allows a dimensioned acceptance of the individual for the story that he or she brings to a community. It involves an experience of faith and discipline that engages a system of love to nurture the students through a process of patience and endurance such that they can engage in a dimensioned acceptance of their students and create a sense of community-based on their collective spirituality.

This chapter has described the relationship of spirituality to character education and how efforts at one institution of higher learning to teach student teachers to experience self-love and compassion afforded a potential for self-discipline in practice. Student teachers who are just beginning their professional journey can utilize the spiritual qualities of connectedness, faith, forgiveness, love, and compassion to develop loving classroom communities. However, as teacher candidates persevere in nurturing the depths of their inner selves, they will be more adept at serving their students with humility.

We encourage the research and development of professional environments to mentor the spiritual growth of student teachers. This process requires an intimate familiarity with areas of mindfulness, spirituality, and love to provide them with the openness to guide their charge's spiritual development. Nevertheless, teacher educators need to remember that individual learning differences extend to the paces and paths of spiritual growth and that everything occurs on its own time.

It is a lifelong, deepening process of negotiating the world of deception and manipulation. However, engagement with patience, kindness, and acceptance may illuminate a sense of self-love in our student teachers that prompt the development of self-loving classroom communities. We would invite teacher education programs across the globe to consider this as a daily practice. So let's let the dance begin.

REFERENCES

Agne, K. (1999). Caring: The way of the master teacher. In R. P. Lipka & T. M. Brinthaupt (Eds.), *The role of self in teacher development*, (pp. 165–188). State University New York Press.

Alexander, H. A. (2001). *Reclaiming goodness. Education and the spiritual quest*. University of Notre Dame Press.

Atmaca, C., Rizaoğlu, F., Türkdoğan, T., & Yayh, D. (2020). An emotion focused approach in predicting teacher burnout and job satisfaction. *Teaching and Teacher Education*, *90*, https://doi.org/10.1016/j.tate.2020.103025

Bialik, M., Bogan, M., Fadel, C., & Horvathova, M. (2015). *Character education for the 21st century: What should students learn?* Center for Curriculum Redesign. http://curriculumredesign.org/wp-content/uploads/CCR-CharacterEducation_FINAL_27Feb2015-1.pdf

Borich, G. (1999) Dimension of self that influences teaching. In R. P. Lipka & T. M. Brinthaupt, (Eds.), *The role of self in teacher development* (pp. 92–119). State University New York Press.

Buber, M. (1970). *I and thou*. Touchstone.

Burton, (2016). *There are seven types of love ... and how we can ignore the most available and potentially fulfilling types*. https://www.psychologytoday.com/us/blog/hide-and-seek/201606/these-are-the-7-types-love

Bush, P. L. (2013). *The human and the divine—Factors that mitigate forgiveness through sacred relationships* [Paper presentation]. The annual meeting of the Adult Education Research Conference, St. Louis, MO.

Chödrön, P. (2019). *Welcoming the unwelcome: Whole hearted living in a brokenhearted world*. Shambhala.

Cottingham, J. (2013). Spirituality, science, and morality. In. D. Carr & J. Haldane (Eds.), *Spirituality, philosophy, and education* (pp. 37–52). Routledge. (Original work published 2003)

Crossan, J. D. (2015). *How to read the Bible and still be a Christian: Is God violent? An exploration from Genesis to Revelation*. HarperOne.

Darder, A. (2003). Teaching as an act of love: Reflections on Paolo Freire and his contributions to our lives and our work. In A. Darder, M. Baltodano, & R. D. Torres (Eds.), *The critical pedagogy reader* (2nd ed., pp. 567–578). Routledge.

Douglas, T.-R., & Nganga, C. (2015). What's radical love got to do with it: Navigating identity, pedagogy, and positionality in pre-service education. *International Journal of Critical Pedagogy, 6*(1), 58–82.

Elias, M. J., Parker, S. J., Kash, M., Weissberg, R. P., & O'Brien, M. U. (2008). Social and emotional learning, moral education, and character education: A comparative analysis and a view toward convergence. In L. P. Nucci & D. Narvaez (Eds.), *Handbook of moral and character education* (pp. 248–266). Routledge.

Estanek, S. M. (2006). Redefining spirituality: A new discourse. *College Student Journal, 40*, 270–281.

Fox, H. (2012). *Their highest vocation: Social justice and the millennial generation*. Peter Lang.

Hari, J. (2016). *Chasing the scream. The first and last days of the war on drugs*. Bloomsbury.

Hay, D. (2007). *Something there. The biology of the human spirit*. Templeton Foundation.

Helminiak, D. A. (2015). *Brain, consciousness, and God: A Lonerganian approach*. State University of New York.

Hilppö, J., & Reed, S. (2019). "Failure is just another try": Re-framing failure in school through the FUSE studio approach. *International Journal of Educational Research, 99*. https://doi.org/10.1016/j.ijer.2019.10.004

James, M., Masters, T., & Uelmen, A. (2010). *Education's highest aim. Teaching and learning through a spirituality of communion*. New City Press.

Jung, C.G. (2006). *The undiscovered self: The dilemma of the individual in modern society*. Berkely.

Kessler, R., & Fink, C. (2008). Education for integrity: Connection, compassion, and character. In L. P. Nucci & D. Narvaez (Eds.), *Handbook of moral and character education* (pp. 431–456). Routledge.

Khamisa, A., & Quinn, J. (2018). *The secrets of the bulletproof spirit: How to bounce back from life's hardest hits*. Waterside Press.

Koç, M., Çolak, T. S., İskender, M., & Düşüncelı, B. (2016). Investigation of the effect of intolerance of uncertainty and the effect of anger control on the relationship between forgiveness and psychological well-being through structural equation modeling. *Sakarya University Journal of Education, 6*(3), 201–209.

Kor, A., Pirutinsky, S., Mikulincer, M., Shoshani, A., & Miller, L. (2019). A longitudinal study of spirituality, character strengths, subjective well-being, and prosociality in middle school adolescents. *Frontiers in Psychology, 10*. https://doi.org/10.3389/fpsyg.2019.00377

Kurtz, E., & Katcham, K. (1993). *The spirituality of imperfection. Storytelling and the search for meaning*. Bantam.

Lehrer, J. (2010). *How we decide*. Houghton Mifflin.

Lewis, C. S. (1960). *The four loves*. HarperCollins.

Lucey, T. A., & Lorsbach, A. W. (2021a). Formative assessment: The developmental shaping of future teachers. *Critical Issues in Teacher Education, 28*, 22–28.

Lucey, T. A., & Lorsbach, A. W. (2021b). The doors they choose: Solutions to "The Lady or the Tiger." *Citizenship, Social, and Economics Education, 20*(3), 145–158. https://doi.org/10.1177/20471734211038328

Lucey, T. A., & Lin, M. (2020). Ghosts in the machine: Understanding digital citizenship as the struggle for students' souls within classroom technology. *International Journal of Children's Spirituality, 25*(2), 91–108. https://doi.org/10.1080/1364436X.2020.1797641

Maltby, J., Macaskill, A., & Day, L. (2001). Failure to forgive self and others: A replication and extension of the relationship between forgiveness, personality, social desirability, and general health. *Personality and Individual Differences, 30*(5), 881–885. https://doi.org/10.1016/S0191-8869(00)00080-5.

Margulis, L., & Sagan, D. (1998). *Microcosmos: Four billion years of microbial evolution*. University of California Press.

Mayes, C. (2005). *Teaching mysteries. Foundations of spiritual pedagogy*. University Press of America.

McLean, S. V. (1999). Becoming a teacher: The person in the process. In R. P. Lipka & T. M. Brinthaupt (Eds.), *The role of self in teacher development* (pp. 55–91). State University New York Press.

McGonigal, K. (2015). *The upside of stress: Why stress Is good for you and how do you get \good at it*. Avery

McLaughlin, T. H. (2013/2003). Education, spirituality, and the common school. In D. Carr & J. Haldane (Eds.), *Spirituality, philosophy, and education* (pp. 185–194). Routledge.

Millan, C. (2006). *Cesar's way: The natural: Everyday guide to understanding and correcting common dog problems*. Three Rivers Press.

Miller, J. (2008). *Educating for wisdom and compassion*. Corwin Press.

Moore, M. E. (1991). *Teaching from the heart. Theology and educational method*. Trinity Press International.

Nash, R. J., & Swaby, M. (2011). Helping college students discover meaning through spirituality. In H. Chang & D. Boyd (Eds.), *Spirituality in higher education: Autoethnographies* (pp. 111–125). Left Coast Press.
Noddings, N. (2005). *The challenge to care in schools. An alternative approach to education* (2nd ed.). Teachers College Press.
Ostovar-Nameghi, S. A., & Sheikhahmadi, M. (2016). From teacher isolation to teacher collaboration: Theoretical perspectives and empirical findings. *English Language Teaching, 9*(5), 197–205.
Palmer, P. (2007). *The courage to teach: Exploring the inner landscape of a teacher's life.* Jossey-Bass.
Peterson, C., & Seligman, M. E. P. (2004). *Character strengths and virtues: A handbook and classification.* Oxford University Press.
Phillips, R. (2021). Teachers' faith, identity processes, and resilience: A qualitative approach. *British Journal of Religious Education, 43*(3), 310–319. https://doi.org/10.1080/01416200.2021.1891860.
Prabhupada, S. B. (1972). *Srimad Bhagavatam.* Bhaktivedanta Book Trust.
Prabhupada, S. B. (2006). *Bhagavad Gita as it is.* Intermex.
Preston, D. (2017). *Lost kingdom of the monkey god.* Grand Central.
Purvis, K. B., Cross, D. R., Dansereau, D. F., & Parris, S. R. (2013). Trust-based relational intervention (TBRI): A systemic approach to complex developmental trauma. *Child & Youth Services, 34*(4), 360–386. https://doi.org/10.1080/0145935X.2013.859906.
Rogers, C. R., Tausch, R., & Lyon H. C., Jr. (2014). *On becoming an effective teacher: Person-centered teaching, psychology, philosophy, and dialogues with Carl R. Rogers and Harold Lyon.* Routledge.
Rosenberg, M. B. (2015). *Nonviolent communication: A language of life* (3rd ed.). Puddledancer Press.
Sezgin, F., & Erdoğan, O. (2018). Humility and forgiveness as predictors of teacher self-efficacy. *Educational research and reviews, 13*(4), 120–128. https://doi.org/10.5897/ERR2017.3449.
Shoshani, A., & Slone, M. (2016). The resilience function of character strengths in the face of war and protracted conflict. *Frontiers in Psychology, 6.* https://doi.org/10.3389/fpsyg.2015.02006
Sutton, R. E., Mudray-Camino, R., & Knight, C. C. (2009). Teachers' emotion regulation and classroom management. *Theory into Practice, 48*(2), 130–137. https://www.jstor.org/stable/40344603
Watson, J. (2003). Preparing spirituality for citizenship. *International Journal of Children's Spirituality, 8*(1), 9–1. https://doi.org/10.1080/13644360304641
Watson, M. (2008). Developmental discipline and moral education. In L. P. Nucci & D. Narvaez (Eds.), *Handbook of moral and character education* (pp. 175–203). Routledge.
Watts, M. (2011). A historical analysis of character education. *Journal of Inquiry and Action in Education, 4*(2). https://digitalcommons.buffalostate.edu/jiae/vol4/iss2/3
Westheimer, J. (2015). *What kind of citizen? Educating our children for the common good.* Teachers College Press.
Wright, A. (2002). *Spirituality and education.* Routledge.

ABOUT THE AUTHORS

Susan Browne is an associate professor in Language, Literacy and Sociocultural Education at Rowan University. She teaches undergraduate and graduate reading courses, advises master's and EdD candidates, and teaches in the Language and Literacy PhD Program. Her research focuses on critical literacy, reader response, and diverse literature for children and adolescents.

Tony Eaude was, for nine years, headteacher of the first school in Oxford, U.K. Since completing his doctorate in 2003, he has worked independently and published widely in areas related to children's spirituality, identity and culture, and moral education and pedagogy when teaching young children. More details are on www.edperspectives.org.uk

Ithel Jones is a professor of early childhood education and Associate Director of the School of Teacher Education at Florida State University. Prior to pursuing academic work, Dr. Jones was a teacher and primary school principal in Wales. He is engaged in a program of research examining the influence of peer relationships and social networks on early education and development, science teaching in early childhood, service learning in early childhood education, and early childhood teacher education.

Allyson Jule, PhD, is a Professor of Education and Dean of the Faculty of Education, Community and Human Development at the University of the Fraser Valley in Abbotsford, BC, Canada. She has taught in Teacher Education for many years and has written extensively on the topic of gender, language, and religion.

ABOUT the AUTHORS

Carolyn Kristjánsson, PhD, is an Associate Professor of Applied Linguistics, School of Education and School of Graduate Studies, Trinity Western University, Canada. She has been a cross-cultural educator for over 30 years; her research and publications include work on theological influences and Christian faith in English language teaching and learning.

Vickie E. Lake is a Professor in the Department of Instructional Leadership and Academic Curriculum and the Associate Dean for the Jeanine Rainbolt College of Education-Tulsa at The University of Oklahoma. Her primary areas of research interest are translation app use with dual language learners, service-learning, and issues in teacher education.

Yu-Ling Lee, PhD, is Director of Education Graduate Programs and Assistant Professor at Trinity Western University. His research interests include education, media and technology, and spirituality.

Eilidh Lamb is an associate tutor at the School of Education at the University of Glasgow. Eilidh has worked in the community development field in Scotland and taught English overseas.

Shannon Leddy (Métis) is a Vancouver-based teacher and writer. Her PhD research at Simon Fraser University focused on contemporary Indigenous art as a dialogic prompt for decolonizing. She is an Associate Professor of Teaching at UBC and Cochair of the Institute for Environmental Learning.

Miranda Lin is a professor of early childhood educationat Illinois State University. Before becoming a faculty in higher education, she taught children of various ages and in multiple countries. Her research interests include anti-bias education, service-learning, global education, home-school partnerships, and teacher preparation. Miranda is the coeditor of *Critical Issues in Early Childhood Teacher Education* (2020).

Thomas Lucey is a professor of elementary education at Illinois State University. His research focuses on financial literacy, social justice issues, and moral education. His current project involves the professional development of elementary teachers in women's studies.

Rob Martinelle is a former Boston Public School history teacher and current lecturer at Boston University's Wheelock College of Education and Human Development. He teaches foundations of education and several social studies education courses. His research focuses on the self-study of teacher education practices (S-STEP) and justice-based social studies teaching.

About the Authors

Kevin Mirchandani, PhD Student in Educational Studies at Biola University, is an Adjunct Professor of Education, School of Education at Trinity Western University and the K–12 Director of Instruction at Langley Christian School. He studies the intersection of Christian faith-informed leadership, spirituality in learning communities, and educational change.

Yvette Onofre is a doctoral student in Urban Education at Rowan University. Yvette received her MSW from Stony Brook University and MS in Exercise Science and Health Promotion from the California University of Pennsylvania. At Rowan University, Yvette is an Adjunct for the Department of Health and Exercise Science.

Ann Mary Roberts has been a professor in Middle Level Education at Radford University since 2005. Dr. Roberts began her educational career as a student assistant counselor in Hampton, Virginia. After receiving her master's in Secondary Education, Dr. Roberts taught social studies at an alternative school and a middle school for eight years. Dr. Roberts is also heavily involved in the Peace Studies Program at Radford University, including acting as program coordinator for several years.

Travis L. Seay is an assistant professor in the Department of History at Missouri State University. He researches cultural aspects of history education in American schools, including racialized dimensions of curriculum and instruction.

Mary Shanahan is Director of Religious Education at St Angela's College, Sligo. Mary completed her undergraduate studies—BEd (Religious Education and English)—at Mater Dei Institute (MDI). She completed postgraduate studies—MA and PhD—in philosophy at University College Dublin. Mary is the editor of *Does Religious Education Matter?* (Routledge, 2017), *An Ethics of/for the Future?* (Cambridge Scholars Press, 2014), and coeditor of *The Taylor Effect* (Cambridge Scholars Press, 2010).

Christian Winterbottom is an Associate Professor and Department Chair at the University of North Florida. For four years, he taught preschool and elementary students in Japan, and when he moved to Florida, he worked extensively with preschools and Head Start programs. He currently teaches undergraduate and graduate courses in early childhood education. His research primarily focuses on working with marginalized populations and reconceptualizing early childhood pedagogy through praxeological learning methodologies.

Printed in the USA
CPSIA information can be obtained
at www.ICGtesting.com
LVHW080846100124
767999LV00001B/2